THE RISE
1958- 1988

ALEX HAHN

LAURA TIEBERT

Mad Cat Press

Boston   New London   New York   Chanhassen

IN MEMORY OF NICOLE HAHN RAFTER
1938-2016

ALSO IN MEMORY OF PRINCE ROGERS NELSON
1958-2016

CONTENTS

FOREWORD

How many bands around the world played "Purple Rain" or another Prince song on or near April 21, 2016, in settings ranging from arenas to dive bars? Chances are it was thousands.

On April 23, Bruce Springsteen performed a passionate and faithful version of "Purple Rain." Pearl Jam followed suit. Then, Jimmy Buffett. At the Coachella music festival on April 23, the idiosyncratic folk artist Sufjan Stevens performed yet another "Purple Rain." The same night at the festival, perhaps doing Prince the greatest justice, the techno outfit LCD Soundsystem ripped through a pained, pulsating rendition of "Controversy."

Every musician in the world, it seemed, wanted to say goodbye.

I learned of Prince's death at about 1:30 p.m. while writing in a coffee shop in Cambridge, Massachusetts. It was my 50th birthday. The artist who had most defined my adult life was gone. The term "living legacy," long applicable to Prince's work, was now legacy only.

But what a legacy it was.

Prince's death, and the worldwide outpouring of emotion that followed, underscored the enormity of his accomplishments as a songwriter, instrumentalist, performer, and cultural figure. Perhaps not since the death of John Lennon had we lost a musician of such influence and impact.

How to choose the domain where Prince's footprint was the largest? As a performer in the concert setting, where his skills, commitment, and energy never flagged across a nearly 40-year career? As the creator of an album and rock film, *Purple Rain,* whose impact rivals any such effort in music history? As a multi-instrumentalist who riffed with equal mastery on guitar, synthesizer, piano, drums, and bass? As the composer of innumerable pop hits that have not only stood the test of time, but long ago became timeless?

As fans and observers, we all have our own answer. And they are all correct.

The Beatles forever redefined the use of melody in pop and rock. Jimi Hendrix's inimitable guitar work redefined the instrument. But just as importantly, Prince created a hybrid style that began to redefine pop music immediately upon its arrival. He blended multiple constituent elements – the funk of James Brown, the synths and drum machines of New Wave, the melody of Top 40 pop, the energy of hard rock, and even the angst of punk – in a manner no pop artist had remotely conceived of. By no more than 90 seconds into "Controversy" – perhaps the first definitive expression of Prince's vision – a new direction for popular music had been set.

The influence of that sound would reverberate through the subsequent decades and beyond, permeating countless subgenres of music. That Prince altered the trajectory of music in the late 20th century is not in doubt. But well into the 21st, not just a portion, but rather a preponderance of contemporary artists continue to owe him a direct debt.

That any of this occurred was hardly preordained. Michael Jackson, by contrast, had a pedigree and inherited apparatus that promised a shot at stardom. The Beatles were bestowed with such melodic ability that their impact seemed divinely prefigured. Prince's path was different, and never remotely as obvious. Nothing was ever guaranteed to a shy black kid from Minneapolis, a skinny motherfucker with a high voice and a huge Afro.[1] He succeeded because his talent, as bountiful as it was, was exceeded by his work ethic and ceaseless energy.

But if no one had ever achieved superstardom in the same manner, Prince left a roadmap that seemingly anyone could follow. Get a multi-track machine and start laying down ideas; form a band that includes girls and boys, blacks and whites,

---

[1]Prince, in the incarnation of his alter ego "Bob George," referred to himself as a "skinny motherfucker with a high voice."

straights and gays. Have the men dress like women, and vice versa. Welcome everyone, and allow anything.

But Prince also taught us this: when making musical recordings, you can, and probably should, go it alone. Be a complete *auteur*, and insist upon executing your vision without any intermediary between yourself and the recording console. Like a poet or novelist, you must embrace the solitary life.

Prince never wavered from these core precepts, and it is unlikely that any musician in the history of recorded sound has spent so many hours alone playing and writing. The takeaway for aspiring musicians is apparent: there is no need to be dependent on anyone.

     ***

Of course, there are aspects of Prince's legacy that ultimately must be wrestled with, rather than unapologetically celebrated. Specifically, there is the conundrum of his recordings from roughly 1989 through 2016, which have engendered endless debate about whether, or to what extent, Prince returned to the form that characterized his strongest work. Of course, Prince had erected for himself (and others) an impossible standard; his output from 1980-1988 constitutes one of the most prolific runs of brilliance in the history of pop music, one that rivals the heydays of the Beatles, the Rolling Stones, and Bob Dylan.

Few would disagree that Prince's efforts became less consistent from 1989-2003, and that the sheer volume of his output became at times overwhelming. But he nonetheless released plenty of indelible songs during that period, as well as several albums, such as *The Gold Experience* (1995) and *Emancipation* (1996) that were remarkably consistent and coherent.

Likewise, Prince's recorded output from 2004 to 2016 has spawned considerable debate, and he himself stoked this controversy by releasing material in a puzzling manner, such as via the sprawling three-album set *LotusFlow3r* (2009), which was initially available as a physical CD solely in the United States, and there only in Target stores. But in hindsight, one can more easily discern that the first disc of that collection features musicianship that is an extraordinary combination of looseness, discipline, and ingenuity. And it is also poignantly clear that Prince had brilliant music left in him, as shown, for example, by the cuts "Way Back Home," "June," and "Black Muse" from his final three albums, songs that some see as ranking with his strongest work.

Ultimately, the notion that Prince's career at some point entered into a steady downward trend is not only unsuited to the moment, but also frankly not accurate. For example, Prince's live performances during the past 15 years demonstrated that in this area, he remained an ascending talent, not one in decline.

Indeed, Prince played some of the most memorable concerts of his career in the last months of his life. These shows featured him alone at a piano, performing songs from across his canon and astonishing attendees with the expressiveness of his playing. Casual and hardcore fans alike were often literally brought to tears by renditions of "Purple Rain," "Condition of the Heart," and "Strange Relationship." That the shows took place in venues such as the Sydney Opera House underscored the once-in-a-lifetime quality of the events.

If only that had not been so true.

***

And then, there was that guitar playing. This element of Prince's repertoire – so incandescent from the outset – actually improved over the last decade of his life, showing greater focus, depth, and feeling.

In the immediate aftermath of his death, articles and television reports frequently recalled Prince's solo on "While My Guitar Gently Weeps" at a Rock and Roll Hall of Fame event in 2004. The performance of the song, by a Tom Petty-led supergroup, had been arranged to commemorate George Harrison's posthumous induction to the hall. Prince himself was inducted the same night, but his guitar playing delivered an emphatic message: formal accolades mean nothing next to the visceral act of creating music. Certainly, George Harrison would have approved of the supergroup's faithful rendition of his mournful composition. But in another respect, he was being blown off the stage.

In the days following his death, fans and critics also fondly recalled Prince's performance at the Super Bowl in 2007, which dominated that year's quintessentially all-American entertainment event. Indeed, the game itself proved forgettable in comparison to a performance that was immediately celebrated as the greatest in the history of the event.

Perhaps, then, Prince's last decade will be remembered as a time when he cemented his legacy as an entertainer of the masses, but in a manner that enhanced, rather than detracted from, his reputation as a musician. How many classic songs he created during this time, or at any time following his creative peak, may ultimately be beside the point.

***

While events like the Super Bowl confirmed him as a world-class attraction, it was Prince's famed "afterparties" that connected him most intensely with his fans. Typically, Prince would arrive at a small club in the wee hours following an arena show earlier in the night. Notoriously, it was this exhausting pace that burned through his band members and road managers so quickly. But Prince, feeding on the energy of his fans, delivered some of his rawest, raunchiest shows in these settings.

I saw one such show in Boston in 1988, in a club packed with people who had learned about the "secret" show. Joshing with us, Prince remarked, "I thought this was supposed to be a mellow little afterparty." We all went crazy. So much for that.

As usual, Prince wore a knowing, slightly arrogant smirk. But for a moment, I saw something else. There was a hint of vulnerability on his face and gratitude in his eyes. He was happy to be alive, loved his work, and appreciated being among his most affectionate fans.

"I never had so many buddies," Prince said.

He had that right.

Alex Hahn
Boston, Massachusetts
February 2017

PROLOGUE

THE LAST DECEMBER

"You will understand the action of the Thaumatrope….on turning around the card, the consequence is that you see both sides at once."

- John Aytron Paris (1827), describing the operation of the child's toy known as a Thaumatrope, which blends two contradictory images into a single picture.

"I like dreaming now more than I used to. Some of my friends have passed away and I see them in my dreams."

- Prince, January 21, 2016 at Paisley Park

"Only Prince had a key and he was the one who would let people in or out."

- Paisley Park Police Incident Report, 2013

1.

It cannot fairly be said that death preoccupied Prince Rogers Nelson, who preferred to celebrate communal experience, carnal pleasure, and the sheer joy of musical expression. More accurately, it was a dark subject that he kept at bay. This is not surprising; Prince had a lifelong pattern of pushing painful thoughts into the recesses of his psyche.

In December 1986, at the very peak of his creative powers, he legendarily erased "Wally," a song that his longtime engineer, Susan Rogers, felt was the most emotionally candid work he had ever created. About a year later, after completing the anarchic and graphic *Black Album*, he abruptly became frightened and repulsed by it and scrapped the record's release. And when making the 1986 film *Under the Cherry Moon*, he insisted upon the death of his character Christopher Tracy, whom he again felt represented an unacceptable part of his personality.

"It was a turning point for Prince – he was killing off this character who was part of himself," observed former associate Howard Bloom. In late 1980, Bloom engaged Prince in a lengthy series of psychoanalysis-like discussions which helped fuel the publicity campaign for the album *Dirty Mind*. But by the time of *Under the Cherry Moon*, Prince was beginning to disown those parts of his psyche that felt threatening. In one cut of the film, Tracy survived and achieved redemption; in the version that Prince adamantly insisted upon releasing, he was assassinated.[1]

This pattern of erasing pieces of his own personality that he deemed unacceptable extended even to his homes in the Minneapolis area. Rather than simply moving out or selling his residences, he was instead apt to destroy them. In 2005, in the midst of a divorce from Manuela Testolini, he bulldozed his large residence on a 149-acre estate in Chanhassen. This followed his demolition in 2003 of another former residence, the famed purple house on Kiowa Trail on Lake Riley in Chanhassen, where

Prince's father had been living until his death in 2001.[2]

Throughout his life, this tendency to excise unwanted things recurred in unusual ways. In 2014, he engaged a young photographer, Maya Washington, to shoot the image that would that year grace the cover of the album *Art Official Age* and would be adapted, in an illustrated form, for the covers of his final two albums. But those images themselves were nearly destroyed.

"He had a freak-out where he wanted me to delete everything," Washington related later. Only narrowly did she convince Prince that the photos should be saved.[3]

It is not clear what disturbed Prince about the images that Washington shot inside Paisley Park, although perhaps he was uncomfortable acknowledging his appearance as that of a man in his mid-50s. Even in the final airbrushed version of the cover, much of Prince's face is obscured by sunglasses, his large afro, and a turtleneck. But whatever its proximate cause, Prince's impulse to eradicate the photos is entirely consistent with his lifelong tendency to eliminate things that troubled him.

When tragedy occurred, this propensity surfaced again in the form of public denial and manipulation of narratives. The death of his son shortly after the baby's birth in 1996 – an axial event in Prince's life – was followed by repeated insistences that nothing was amiss. It would have been one thing to treat this calamity as an entirely private matter; it was another altogether to announce on *The Oprah Winfrey Show* that his son was fine and to show the host around a nursery that had been prepared for him.[4]

After creating counterfactual narratives, Prince would cope by escaping to the recording studio, where his solitude was complete, or to the stage, where adoration and applause drowned out negative feelings. But regardless of what method of retreat was chosen, he remained essentially alone; all crises in his life would be handled with neither assistance nor consultation.

This tendency towards social, psychological, and physical retreat had emerged from a very early age, and became more deeply entrenched over time. Prince, somewhere at his core, had a profound desire to genuinely connect with others, and to enjoy a sense of community. And yet, when his ties to friends, bandmates, or lovers strengthened to a point of deep intimacy, he would usually pull away, often decisively. "He always found a way to separate himself from people who cared about him or loved him," recalled Paul Mitchell, one of Prince's closest friends throughout his teenage years. "He could never be in a really meaningful relationship with anyone, be it male or female or relative."[5]

With all of this in mind, it is ironic that, in the final few years of his life, Prince began, albeit gradually and tentatively, to grapple with his own vulnerabilities and with an acceptance of mortality. In 2014, he wrote a landmark song, "Way Back Home," which acknowledged his tendency towards self-isolation and spoke of a struggle to find a sense of peace that had always eluded him. Despite his impulse to destroy the photographs taken by Maya Washington, he treated this young woman as a genuine collaborator throughout their sessions. And beginning in 2014, discarding some of his rock star pretenses, he opened his Paisley Park complex to fans on a regular basis and interacted informally with them at these dance parties, providing extraordinary access to himself and his home. Finally, the death in early 2016 of an old friend – the beautiful woman he had dubbed "Vanity" – would prompt much more public emotion than had previous losses in his life.

This was exactly what longtime associates had hoped for. If he could more forthrightly acknowledge his own feelings, creative wellsprings could be unlocked that Prince, despite all his talents, had not accessed frequently enough. Maybe his insistence on controlling every domain of his life could be relaxed, leading to more authentic relationships.

In the end, Prince would not let go of his obsessive self-reliance soon enough. Part of him wanted to be more revealing, but another part wanted to retreat to the literal and figurative cocoon that was Paisley Park. Despite his provisional movement towards greater openness, he would continue to insist on approaching crises as he always had – alone.

2.

Since 2013, Prince's primary touring band had been comprised of three young women: guitarist Donna Grantis, drummer Hannah Welton, and bassist Ida Kristine Nielsen. Together, he dubbed them 3rdEyeGirl. They divided fan opinion, with some feeling that Grantis, Welton, and Nielsen were competent but unimaginative musicians. Others argued that the chemistry between Prince and the band members was obvious, and that he seemed rejuvenated by their presence. The group's ability to lay down a funk groove was dubious; instead, anchored by Welton's thunderous drumming, their style veered more toward hard rock. At the same time, the trio operated with a spatial economy that opened a large, airy pocket where Prince's vocals and lead guitar sat comfortably and clearly.

Meanwhile, as Prince solidified his relationship with the band during 2014, he had also developed a creative partnership with then 24-year-old Josh Welton, Hannah's husband. Welton was a skilled producer of contemporary R&B music, and Prince saw the collaboration as a means of reaching a younger audience. For the first time, Prince was letting someone else – a very young man at that – in effect serve as co-producer. The results were sometimes pedestrian, but on cuts like "X's Face" and "June," Welton and Prince achieved a meaningful stylistic synthesis.[1]

Josh Welton's stamp was unmistakable first on *Art Official Age* (2014) and then *HitnRun Phase One*, which was released in September 2015. Not only had Prince forged a vibrant community among himself, Welton, and 3rdEyeGirl, but something fundamental had changed in his relationship to his musicians. Over the decades, many had left his employ feeling demeaned and underpaid. Some were troubled by his religious dogmatism and moral condescension, traits that also showed up in song lyrics.[2]

But these tendencies had gradually abated, and working with 3rdEyeGirl represented an important signpost on his path to a more inclusive approach. Onstage, he allowed each member of the band time in the spotlight, and sometimes even elevated them above him on risers. All told, Prince loosened his grip and became less of a dictator and more of a leader.

In late 2015, Prince reached out to another innovative young musician, the Memphis, Tennessee-based Dwayne Thomas, Jr., a bassist who worked under the stage name MonoNeon. Thomas' compositions and visual methods, such as wearing gas masks onstage, owed debts to the Dadaist and Surrealist art schools, making him the most brazenly experimental artist Prince had worked with.[3]

By this point in the year, 3rdEyeGirl was effectively on hiatus with Hannah Welton having become pregnant and Ida Nielsen pursuing a solo record. A new ensemble thus took shape with Dwayne Thomas on bass, Donna Grantis on guitar, and Kirk Johnson on drums. Prince rotated between guitar and keyboards. The result, particularly in comparison to 3rdEyeGirl, was loose, funky, and improvisational.[4] All told, Prince's compound percolated with new musical possibilities.

But if there was a downside to Prince's cultivation of so many younger musicians, it was the lack of a peer in his own age group who could do something other than look up to him. "Prince obviously wanted to do a lot of mentoring, but I think the problem became that no one was there to mentor him," said Jill Jones, a close friend and collaborator during Prince's earlier years.[5]

Indeed, Prince's inner circle was comprised primarily of people decades his junior. The exception was Kirk Johnson, 51, who had served as a musical collaborator for decades, primarily as a drummer. He had been a friend of Prince since childhood, served as the best man at Prince's wedding in 1996, and eventually became the estate manager of Paisley Park. An athletic individual who taught classes at a gym in Chanhassen, he also served as a de facto bodyguard.[6] And yet, despite the centrality of his position, Johnson was an employee rather than a true intimate, and certainly was not inclined to challenge any of Prince's more mercurial behaviors.

The same was true of Prince's romantic partners. With apparent sincerity, in 2014 he told *Rolling Stone* that he had become celibate, but he still continued to socialize publically with attractive young women.[7] These included then-24-year-old Damaris Lewis, a former swimsuit model who maintained to the media that the relationship was platonic, and singers Andy Allo, 25, and Judith Hill, 30, with whom he collaborated musically. But neither Hill, Allo nor Lewis, whether they were muses, friends, or something else, were able to meet Prince on equal footing.

One of the most obvious patterns in Prince's life had been his resistance to genuine romantic intimacy, as opposed to serial dalliances with much younger partners who often resembled one another. He had been twice divorced, following the pattern of his father, John L. Nelson, who had abandoned two wives with similar appearances, including Prince's mother, Mattie Shaw. Prince's paternal grandfather, Clarence Nelson, had also left his wife and family. Due perhaps in some measure to this multi-generational pattern of romantic strife, in 2016 Prince lacked a strong female partner – or a strong partner of any kind, for that matter – when one would be most needed.

***

During the autumn of 2015, even as he engaged in multiple collaborations at Paisley Park, Prince also began planning a solo piano tour. Shorn of the large bands, visual displays, and amplified sounds that typically characterized his shows, he would perform entirely alone. Although he had done solo piano segments before during conventional concert sets (such as during the 1988 *Lovesexy* tour), never had he attempted such sustained intimacy with audiences.

Energized by this impending challenge, Prince summoned a small group of European journalists to Paisley Park during the second week of November 2015 to describe his plans. Shortly on the heels of this meeting, it was announced that the tour would begin in Vienna, Austria on November 21.[8]

Within days, however, everything changed. On November 1, tragedy struck Paris in the form of a coordinated series of terrorist attacks by ISIL. Prince, along with many other American acts, cancelled European dates.[9]

A more personal note of mortality was interjected at home. On November 19, Prince's former girlfriend Kim Upsher died of a brain aneurism at Hennepin County Medical Center in Minneapolis. Upsher, with whom Prince had attended high school, had been one of his first serious lovers, and one of the few friends with whom he had stayed in touch over the years. It is unlikely the event did not shake him in some manner.[10]

After the European attack, plans were laid to undertake the piano tour in Australia instead. He began drilling on songs from across his canon, assembling a huge line-up of songs that he planned to pick and choose from concert to concert. The tour would in some ways be a return to his roots, as the piano had been the first instrument he had mastered as a child. But at the same time, he was planning a touring schedule that would take him almost as far from home as it was possible to go.

3.

Despite his bankability as a performer, money had long been a problem for Prince. His payroll and other expenses often outstripped revenues, and he sometimes failed to pay vendors. He took a casual approach to running his affairs, for example continuing to own – and pay property tax on – numerous pieces of fallow property throughout the Minneapolis area.[1] And none of the four albums he released during 2014 and 2015 (*Art Official Age*, *Plectrum Electrum* with 3rdEyeGirl, and the two *HitNRun* albums) had been a commercial success. He was hardly broke, but his funds were spread across a complicated sprawl of business entities and subject to various obligations. His personal cash reserves were low, and he was hesitant to liquidate his most readily available asset – a collection of gold bars worth nearly $1 million.

This precarious and confused financial situation prompted Prince to accept lucrative bookings such as the one that took place on December 31, 2015 on the tiny island of Saint Barthélemy (often called St. Bart's), the Caribbean's most elite and most expensive island. The Russian billionaire Roman Abramovich, who owned an estate overlooking a beach on the island, had commissioned Prince to perform the New Year's Eve show, and doubtlessly provided ample compensation.[2] The travel, however, would be onerous: three legs of plane travel to the island, and four on the return trip.[3]

On the afternoon of New Year's Eve, wearing a long zippered leather jacket and carrying a silver cane, Prince exited a helicopter at the island's airport and headed to the estate. He and the band performed an energetic 20-song set that, appropriate to the essentially commercial nature of the occasion, was heavy on hits such as "Let's Go Crazy," "Kiss," "1999," and "Purple Rain." The concert took place on a large patio overlooking the beach, and Prince, as if to take the edge off the night air, wore a black beanie cap, a vest and long sleeves, sporting sunglasses throughout.[4]

By this time, there were subtle signs that Prince's health was not perfect. His use of a cane had begun, some years ago, ostensibly as a fashion accessory. But it was an open secret among his larger circle of associates that he had long experienced hip and joint pain.[5] Meanwhile, his efforts to exude constant vitality and boundless energy were not always successful. During a lengthy interview with Arsenio Hall in 2014 he appeared drawn and tired, and his efforts at humor perfunctory. Meanwhile, Prince's chef, Ray Roberts, began to notice Prince frequently suffering from colds and flus, and requesting foods that were easy on the throat.[6]

The concept of a piano tour was itself perhaps an accommodation to aging. Indeed, this format by nature would place a minimum of strain on his 57-year-old body, allowing him to remain seated throughout the performances. The schedule that Prince created, however, was anything but restful. He could have limited the performances to the United States – and perhaps even the Midwestern states near his home – and still attracted ample audiences from throughout the world for these intimate shows. Instead, he planned a tour that would require staggering amounts of airplane travel across four countries. The 2,600-mile return trip from St. Bart's to Minneapolis was just the beginning.

***

Upon returning from St. Bart's, Prince began actively recording new music with Dwayne Thomas, Kirk Johnson, and saxophonist Adrian Crutchfield. A suite of up to seven songs was quickly completed, and Prince released the song "Ruff Enuff" to the TIDAL streaming music service in early January, just days after its recording was completed. By this time, Prince was also preparing to preview the piano show at Paisley Park. A sense of excitement pervaded Prince's compound and the Minneapolis area as fans anticipated the debut of this unique concept.[7]

Outside Paisley Park's gates, however, music and popular culture suffered an unexpected loss: David Bowie, one of rock's icons, died on January 10, 2016. Bowie had been a musical innovator, pop craftsman, and cultural pioneer in one package. And while he was one of the best-selling artists in pop history, his influence on other musicians was perhaps the most significant part of his legacy.

Ten days after Bowie's death, on January 20, Prince was immersed in meticulous preparations for his first solo piano show, which was to take place the next day. The main performance room of Paisley Park had been carpeted and generally rendered more atmospheric in preparation for the event. Prince spent hours testing sound as well as planning the set list together with sound technician Scott Baldwin.[8]

During these preparations, Prince advised Baldwin of a point in the set where he would be mentioning David Bowie, but made clear that the reference would be short and simple, and that he would not perform one of Bowie's songs. "I'll leave it to all of those other artists to do their tributes," Prince, said, rolling his eyes in disdain at the idea.[9]

Prince had always been congenitally resistant to eulogies. When asked by *Rolling Stone* in 2014 about Michael Jackson's death – which had occurred five years earlier – he simply said, "I don't want to talk about it. I'm too close to it." The same distancing occurred following the death of one of Prince's heroes, Miles Davis, in 1991. Rather than attending the funeral, Prince sent a friend to read a poem.[10]

And yet, events would soon show that Bowie's passing, and the subject of mortality, had been on Prince's mind perhaps more than even he himself had at first realized.

Even at the time, the historic nature of what would be Prince's final concert before an audience in his home state quickly became clear to the assembled fans. He began with a portion of the theme from the television show *Batman,* which was among the first pieces of music he had ever learned to play after gaining access to his father's piano at age seven. Next came a cover of the Jackson Five's 1969 song "Who's Loving You?", another song that served as part of the sound track of Prince's youth. And then came "Baby," a very rarely played number from Prince's debut album. It quickly became clear that Prince was leading the audience in a chronological procession through his musical and personal development.

Vocally, it was amply clear in this unmediated setting that Prince's falsetto had not been in the least diminished by age, with his lower register providing a rich, soothing counterpoint. The sound quality and balance in the room were immaculate, owing to the hard work he and Scott Baldwin had put in the day before. Prince even elicited a round of applause for Baldwin, a remarkable display of generosity to a behind-the-scenes figure.[11] Meanwhile, Prince's piano work displayed an oceanic depth that was surprising even to some longtime fans. It was not mere virtuosity that captured the audience; rather it was the triangular emotional bond that formed among Prince, his instrument, and his listeners.

Between songs, Prince revealed aspects of his interior life that he had seldom shared, such as by relating stories of his childhood. "I thought I would never be able to play like my dad, and he never missed an opportunity to remind me of it," Prince lamented ruefully prior to performing Ray Charles' "Unchain My Heart," a song he recalled playing with his father.[12]

The reference was surprising. Prince rarely ever mentioned his late father, the jazz pianist John L. Nelson, with whom his relationship had oscillated between estrangement and reconnection. But acknowledging him in this setting with wry fondness seemed like a gesture of reconciliation, as well as another means of bringing parts of Prince's life full circle. The visual and aural image of his father, playing a piano in the family living room, was likely one of Prince's earliest memories. And Prince was paying this homage before a local audience at Paisley Park, not far from the Minneapolis jazz clubs where his father played in the 1950s, nor from the community center where John had met Mattie Shaw, Prince's mother, late in that decade.

Prince performed two marathon sets that night, covering a remarkable amount of material across his nearly four-decade career. If there was any disconcerting element, it might have been Prince's appearance. According to longtime Prince follower Jefrey Taylor, who sat only five feet from the piano and who had observed him from close quarters several times before, the artist appeared to have shed a fair amount of weight from his already lean frame. "He looked gaunt and had lost some muscle tone, it was a noticeable difference," Taylor said.[13]

Midway through the opening set there was an unusual interjection. "How many of you have lucid dreams?" Prince asked the audience. "I like dreaming now more than I used to. Some of my friends have passed away and I see them in my dreams." Prince then segued into "Sometimes It Snows in April," the song that concludes his film *Under the Cherry Moon* and tells of the death of his alter-ego Christopher Tracy.[14]

The second set of the evening, which focused less on Prince's biography and more on rarely performed songs, concluded with "Free Urself," a fall 2015 single release. At the end of the song, Prince engaged the audience in a prolonged chant of the phrase "free urself." As the swell of the chanting grew, Prince stopped singing and playing, and simply listened.[15]

As the energy reached its peak, he stood up at the piano and abruptly left the stage with a single word: "Bye."[16]

26

February 15, 2016

After completing the Paisley Park preview shows in January, Prince soon left for Australia – a grueling flight of nearly 24 hours – where he was to play a number of tightly spaced shows before moving on to New Zealand. Mere hours before he took the stage for the first set of the tour in Melbourne, bad news arrived: Denise Matthews, the former female protégé whom Prince had dubbed Vanity, had died at age 57.[17]

Of all of Prince's muses, perhaps none was more inextricably linked to him than Matthews. Although she was replaced by Patricia Kotero as the female lead of *Purple Rain*, Matthews' erotic energy still loomed over the film. Prince's pained screams during "The Beautiful Ones" could not have been stimulated by the blank slate that was Kotero – Matthews was a much more likely catalyst for one of the most powerful displays of emotion in his career.

Matthews, who had long since left music to propound her Christian faith, died of renal failure, an illness linked to her heavy use of crack cocaine in the 1980s and 1990s. That substance abuse had begun during a 1982-83 tour in which she was the front woman for Prince's "Vanity 6" side project. The demands of her role and the intoxicating atmosphere around Prince's entourage overwhelmed Matthews' volatile psyche, along with those of many others.[18]

Prince began by telling his Melbourne audience that "Someone dear to us has passed away, I'm gonna dedicate this song to her." He delivered an anguished version of "The Beautiful Ones" and then proceeded, more lightly, to tell a story about ordering his bodyguard Chick Huntsberry to throw Matthews into a pool after a fight in which she taunted him for being too small to do it himself. "I probably shouldn't be telling this story," he said, "But she'd want us to celebrate her life and not mourn her."[19]

Although repression had always been Prince's favored means of coping with loss, something was different this time; at a minimum, the passing of this friend seemed to make death less abstract for Prince. And there was another element of poignancy; his mother, Mattie Shaw, had died 14 years earlier on the same date, February 15.[20]

"Vanity" was a concept and a template created by Prince, one that he would use in some fashion across most of his career. With great redundancy, Prince would bring sexually attractive women into his fold and then squander time and energy recording albums with them that were often forgettable. As Prince aged, the female counterparts did not, and the overall contrivance changed little. But with Matthews' passing, something became clear: while concepts such as "Vanity" are timeless and changeless, the same cannot be said of human beings.

***

From Melbourne, Prince travelled to Sydney, where he performed at the iconic Sydney Opera House on February 20. He and his small entourage then flew across the Tasman Sea to New Zealand, where he performed in Auckland on the 24th. Then, in a bizarre scheduling decision, the tour proceeded back to the far side of Australia for a show in Perth the next night. Prince had insisted on these arrangements simply because he had never played Perth before.

Because Prince's piano was too large for a private jet, it was impossible to get the instrument to Perth in time for the show. Undaunted, Prince ordered that another piano be flown from Chanhassen to Australia for the show.[21] When all was said and done, in the course of 24 hours, Prince played shows in two different continents and flew about 3,400 miles – greater than the length of the entire United States.

It had been ten days since Prince had received the painful news of Denise Matthews' passing. Now, it was time to return to America and to begin a proper, albeit brief, period of mourning.

February 27, 2016: Union City, California

The memorial service for Matthews in the Bay Area brought together many of Prince's former associates, united in grief and a sense that some profound demarcation in their lives had occurred. These included several women from Matthews' heyday – Apollonia Kotero, Jill Jones, Brenda Bennett, and Susan Moonsie. In fact, Moonsie and Jones had been among Prince's most significant romantic partners during the 1980s. The bouyant "Private Joy" (from the 1981 album *Controversy*) was about Moonsie, and Jones had inspired the blistering rocker "She's Always In My Hair," a 1985 B-side.

If jealousies had ever characterized the relationships of these women to one another – or to Matthews, for that matter – such feelings were either long gone, or had been rendered entirely irrelevant by their shared loss. None of Prince's girlfriends had exuded feminine vitality – and, more to the point, sexuality – in such a visceral manner as had Denise Matthews. She had inspired some of Prince's most salacious lyrics. A former Prince bandmate who had also dated Matthews still marveled, decades later, about the time he had spent three straight amorous days in bed with her. Now, this force of nature was gone.[22]

Prince himself was not present at the memorial. But his friends and former lovers consoled each other at the service, seeking to manage the memories and emotions that had surfaced. Kotero broke down after entering the church and was embraced in a group hug by Bennett and Moonsie. "Don't cry," both women repeated to her several times.[23]

The women and their friends managed to lighten the mood afterward by having dinner in San Francisco and sharing a midnight walk from Fisherman's Wharf to Ghirardelli Square. The next night, the reunion of Kotero, Jones, Bennett, and Moonsie took on another dimension as they attended Prince's performance at the Paramount Theatre in Oakland. The show quite literally brought them from laughter to tears over its epic length, and the sense of the women reconnecting – both with Prince and each other – deepened.[24]

Backstage, however, the atmosphere was more ambivalent. Jill Jones, now 54, had not been in touch with Prince for the better part of three decades. She had been both a musical collaborator and lover, but the relationship had not infrequently been characterized by friction. She eventually returned a friendship ring he had given her, effectively severing a once-powerful bond.[25]

For Jones, any resentment had drifted well into the past, and seemed moot against the backdrop of Matthews' death.

"Thank you for giving me all of these women," Jones said of her companions, all of whom she had met as a result of her association with Prince.

"So now you're okay with it?" he responded, a reference to past conflicts over Prince's womanizing.[26] The retort straddled humor and resentment.

Jones found herself concerned about Prince's appearance; he looked haggard and fatigued. His make-up – which Jones had known Prince to always apply immaculately – looked chalky and inconsistent. Most worrisome of all, Jones felt sure Prince was on some kind of drug. He was not visibly inebriated, off-balance, or slurring his words, but his manner palpably indicated the presence of something artificial.[27]

During her years with him, they had often stayed up for nights on end, but nothing stronger than coffee had fueled these activities. "I never want to do drugs, because I'm afraid I would like them," Prince had once told her during a discussion of Jimi Hendrix's excesses.

Later during the backstage encounter, when Prince's attention was drawn elsewhere, Jones huddled with Kotero, Moonsie, and Bennett to express her concerns. Prince quickly returned to the group, breaking up the conversation.

"What are you talking about?" he asked playfully.

"You," Moonsie replied.

The conversation became lighter, as Jones proposed that they all vacation together from time to time, and perhaps go skydiving. "I'm not gonna go skydiving, that's for sure," Prince responded.

By this time in the conversation, Prince had become genuine and gregarious; Matthews' death, while a loss for all of them, had created some renewed sense of community. But when the women asked Prince to join them for dinner, something in his manner shifted, and he demurred.[28] When they left, Prince told Jones he had some things to discuss with her, and would be in touch in a couple of months.

Jones later drove back to Southern California with Kotero and voiced her concerns about Prince. Kotero responded that Prince's hip pain provided a suitable explanation for the use of any medication that might be causing side effects. Jones harbored deeper suspicions, but she lacked sufficient evidence – let alone access – to confront Prince and try to render assistance. But the backstage interactions had made clear that Prince, despite his cocksure arrogance being intact, was vulnerable. And both Jones and Kotero remained hopeful that they could, in coming months, renew ties and offer him a form of unconditional support – to say nothing of seasoned advice – that Prince was missing in his small entourage of paid employees, female companions, and youthful bandmates.

4.

With the Piano and a Microphone tour having completed two full legs – Australia and California – it was increasingly clear that the tour was, in some tangible sense, about legacy. There was no reason to think that Prince did not have decades of performing left in him. At the same time, these shows were self-evidently a statement about Prince's entire body of work, his abilities as a musician, and his intimate bond with his audience.

So much of Prince's career had been a series of transitions – some of them abrupt and rushed – between concepts, styles, bands, and albums. But now there was a clear sense of pause. And as a result, an air of crystalline immediacy pervaded the theatres and opera houses where Prince performed.

"The space between the notes – that's the good part," Prince said at several of the concerts. And these words certainly could have served as a metaphor for these performances, in which he used silence as deliberately as any of the notes on his keyboard. Whether or not Prince was aware that the phrase "music is the space between the notes" had originated with the French composer Debussy, it was certainly apt. And the comment that often followed was pure Prince: "How long the space is – that's how funky it is or how funky it ain't."[1]

But for all the laudatory reviews and word-of-mouth that the tour was generating, signs of Prince's physical discomfort began to mount. On March 3, Prince appeared with companion Damaris Lewis at a Golden State Warriors basketball game. He made his way to a courtside seat with a cane and wore large sunglasses throughout the contest. Prince licked his lips repeatedly during portions of the game when he was shown on camera, an indication of dry mouth, and wore several layers of clothing, including a long-sleeved, collared shirt and gloves.[2] And while neither of these is necessarily abnormal in themselves, they are considered indicia of excessive use of prescription opioids.

His use of such drugs had, at various points in his career, been an open secret amongst his friends. He had first been exposed to them at the height of his fame, during the 1985 *Purple Rain* tour, when he suffered both a leg injury and ongoing orthopedic strain as a result of jumping from stage risers while wearing four-inch heels. Thus started a cycle of on-and-off use that would continue in some measure during the ensuing decades.[3]

Prince's use of the drugs again reportedly became heavy in the late 1990s and into the year 2000, leading to explosions of anger and consistent irritability that friends attributed to opioid overuse. While his use of these drugs had begun out of medical need, at least some of the time he acquired them illicitly, in one case using a girlfriend as a regular intermediary for several months in early 2000, paying her $100 per pill of Percocet.[4]

Still, Prince was again able to stop short of a crisis, and friends felt that his behavior moderated considerably starting with the 2004 release of *Musicology*, which also helped revive his commercial fortunes. Whether he ever stopped using the drugs entirely is unclear, but Prince's performances in ensuing years were never visibly marred by substance abuse.

***

In an even more explicit sense, Prince addressed the question of his legacy shortly after concluding the California shows. On March 18, appearing at the club Avenue in New York's Meatpacking District, Prince told a crowd of about 300 people that he had signed a contract with Random House to write a memoir. The idea seemed fanciful; Prince was notoriously resistant to introspection and was generally opaque in his written communications. But he seemed to embrace the idea with gusto. "The good people of Random House have made me an offer that I can't refuse," he told the audience, referencing a line spoken by Don Vito Corleone from *The Godfather*, a film that recurred in songs and characters across his career.[5] And just as the movie had told the saga of a family patriarch, Prince was now clearly feeling an impulse to tell his own story in some epochal fashion.

Shortly after this event, the tour resumed with shows in Montreal on March 21 and 22. Along with the many miles travelled on the tour, a great amount of emotional territory had been traversed as well. From the loss of Kim Upsher in November 2015, to the death of Bowie in January 2016, and then the passing of Denise Matthews in February, there was a sense of emotional gravity surrounding the tour, even apart from Prince's impassioned renditions of his songs. And gradually, those feelings were coming to the surface.

March 25, 2016: Toronto

During many of the shows on the tour, the audiences were raucous, resulting in a festive atmosphere and sometimes causing parts of songs to be drowned out by applause. Tonight, however, the crowd was reverently silent during many of the songs, allowing Prince to concentrate even more intently.

The openers on the 25th, "I Would Die 4 U" and "Baby I'm a Star," were typical set list choices, but Prince quickly veered off into the obscure territory that most delights his hardcore fans. "Four" (played fourth in the set, in a wink to aficionados) was taken from an instrumental jazz album recorded under the moniker Madhouse in 1986. The fifth number, "Dolphin," was better known, but primarily among serious fans. From *The Gold Experience* (1995), the song is partially a study of reincarnation.

Tonight's rendition of the song contained an unexpected twist. Midway through "Dolphin," Prince abruptly segued into David Bowie's "Heroes." This was just the sort of thing that Prince had spoken of dismissively in January when telling sound engineer Scott Baldwin that such tributes should be left to other

34

artists. But something had shaken loose, and Prince began to explore the meaning of Bowie's loss.

Then, continuing a literal and metaphoric cycle, Prince quickly transitioned back to "Dolphin," and then back to "Heroes" again. That he intermingled Bowie's song with "Dolphin," a song about reincarnation, seemed entirely deliberate, as if he were telling the audience that Bowie's spirit, in some manner, would return.[6]

Across his recorded canon, Prince's references to death usually came in an almost tragicomic manner, depicting hedonism as the only logical response to mortality, as reflected in songs like "1999" and "Let's Go Crazy." But rarely had he addressed this topic in an earnest and reflective fashion. In two such examples, he uses the same metaphor – the final month of the year – to evoke the end of life. The first, "The Same December" (from the 1996 release *Chaos and Disorder*) speaks of a "Same December" from which all of us originate, and where we all eventually return. The similarly titled "Last December" (from the 2001 album *The Rainbow Children*) raises the perennial question of a life's legacy – that is, what one feels they have accomplished when the end is in sight.

Both of these songs find Prince at his most vulnerable, grasping for a way to understand the human condition. And on March 25, moving from "Dolphin" to "Heroes" and back again, Prince returned to an emotional space he had only rarely visited.

And yet, despite the emotional impact of the Toronto show, something had shifted in his performances. Prince still hit his falsetto notes with ease, but his midrange – which had sounded relaxed, round, and full in Australia – at times began to sound rough, strained, and certainly more nasal.[7]

From January through late March, Prince had traveled nearly 30,000 miles, a greater distance than the earth's entire circumference. Multiple stressors were acting synergistically – drug use, travel demands, and generally weak health. Prince now weighed about 112 pounds, down from a peak of about 130 some years ago, meaning that he had effectively lost about 15 percent of his body weight.[8]

With the Canadian leg of the tour now complete, Prince returned to Minneapolis. The next stint had already been planned, this time to cover the American south, starting with an appearance in Atlanta on April 7. But instead, his tour coordinator contacted the show's promoter on the morning of the show with bad news: Prince had the flu, and needed to postpone. It was, by some accounts, the first time in at least a quarter century that he had cancelled a concert for health reasons.[9]

Determined to make up the show as soon as possible – and worrying above all about disappointing his fans – he directed his representatives to reschedule the concert for April 14, just a week after the initially scheduled event. At the same time, Prince was conscious that he needed medical help, and on April 7, he saw a Minneapolis doctor, Michael Schulenberg, who was reportedly treating him for opioid addiction.[10]

On April 11, following four days of public silence, he used Twitter to laud a new release by the singer Sidibe. Prince had been using this social media platform for several years, posting media articles about himself, promoting events, and occasionally communicating directly with individual fans. Now, he sought to shape public perceptions of recent events, including the cancelled show. On April 12, he tweeted about the arrival of a new purple Yamaha piano at Paisley Park, declaring that he had achieved a "resounding" sound while performing "Boom" from the album *LotusFlow3r*.[11]

The message was clear – notwithstanding the cancelled show, Prince was enjoying his new instrument, raring to play, and feeling fine.

Thursday, April 14, 2016: Fox Theatre, Atlanta

Upon taking the stage at the Fox Theatre for the first of two shows, Prince apologized profusely for the missed show a week earlier. He then did everything he could to make up for it, delivering yet another bravura performance.[12]

The Atlanta show again presented a sampling from multiple eras, giving serious and casual fans alike ample points of entry. "Muse 2 the Pharaoh," from *The Rainbow Children* (2001), made an extremely rare appearance. And funk workouts like "Controversy" and "Kiss" were translated eloquently for the piano.

A cane was visible near Prince during the show, but his mobility did not seem compromised; at various points, he stood up and took a lap around his piano, seemingly unable to contain the energy caused by his music.[13] However, he unexpectedly and uncharacteristically left the stage at several points during the set. "Sometimes I forget how emotional these songs are," he said after one of these breaks.[14]

Prince delivered a stirring performance of Joni Mitchell's "A Case of You," a song with special significance for him. He had attended her concerts as a young boy, and he would continue to emulate her lyrical approach throughout his career. And in the year 2001, the year that John L. Nelson died, Prince dedicated a recorded version of the song to his father.

But perhaps the greatest surprise was the reappearance of "Heroes" as a set closer. This time, Prince played the entire song, providing the emotional climax of the set. If his mixing of "Heroes" and "Dolphin" had constituted the beginning of a deeper connection with a recently passed musician, tonight his emotional immersion in Bowie's signature composition became complete. Singing at first in his most natural register, his midrange, Prince then allowed his voice to crack and briefly reached for his falsetto in the chorus. Aging, loss, sorrow – all of these things seemed bound up in the performance. His voice sounded strained and raw, and the performance came across less as a reflective remembrance, and more an act of will. Several minutes of sustained applause followed before Prince returned to the stage for an encore.

A second show followed at 10 p.m., and covered a similar range of territory. In fact, over the entire tour he had delivered at least a portion of some 130 songs – a staggering amount of lyrical and musical information to integrate and perform.

Prince himself was particularly pleased at how the late show had gone, and immediately expressed plans to release a live recording which had been made. But by the time the evening ended, he was again not feeling well, and changed plans in order to seek medical attention. He advised his tour coordinator that upcoming shows in St. Louis, Nashville, Tennessee, and Washington D.C. (which had been planned but not announced), should be postponed. He then left for Minneapolis on a private jet at 12:51 a.m. on April 15. On the flight were Kirk Johnson, singer and Prince protégée Judith Hill, and a pilot.[15]

Over a meal, looking across a table at Prince, Hill saw him abruptly lose consciousness, according to a report she gave to the *New York Times*. The plane was diverted to Moline, Illinois, where it landed on the tarmac at 1:17 a.m. Emergency medical technicians administered two shots of Narcan, a drug used to counteract opioid overdoses.[16]

Eighteen minutes later, Prince was taken by ambulance to nearby Trinity Moline Hospital. Seemingly convinced that the crisis had passed, he sought to leave immediately, but was prevailed upon by his companions and medical personnel to remain overnight.

According to Hill's account, Prince remained lucid and communicative throughout the night. At 8:33 a.m., he used Twitter to broadcast a message to his hundreds of thousands of followers: "I am #TRANSFORMED."[17] The tweet, which included a location stamp, indicated that it had come from

Chanhassen. According to Hill's account, however, it was not until 10:57 a.m. that the small entourage left by plane for Minnesota.

In all likelihood, Prince had deliberately sought to make it appear that he was already home. He reportedly did not use a cell phone, but rather used a MacBook to surf the Internet. When Twitter is used on the web (as opposed to on a mobile application), it is possible to make it appear that a tweet is coming from another location. It appears that this is what Prince did, the first of a series of highly coordinated actions to demonstrate to fans that nothing serious had happened. And indeed, almost his every move during the coming week would be in service of that goal.[18]

Friday, April 15, 2016

First, Prince laid plans for a "dance party" at Paisley Park the following day. Such events did not obligate Prince to perform, but he typically showed up to greet fans. And that was precisely what he planned – a short, discrete appearance that would indicate not to just the attendees, but also to fans and media outlets around the world, that any rumors about a serious health scare were unfounded.

Prince then contacted Jeremiah Freed, a blogger and podcaster who operated under the name Dr. Funkenberry. Prince had cultivated a personal relationship with Freed via email, phone, and in person in recent years, and had come to rely upon him as a means of disseminating information to fans. After assuring Freed that he had in fact only been suffering from the flu, he asked him to spread word of the dance party and also to attend.[19]

At 3:11 p.m., Freed took to Twitter at Prince's behest and began, in cryptic fashion, to let fans know that something was afoot. "Thinking @prince should just have a party at #PaisleyPark 2morrow n squash the story that way. Thoughts?"[20]

Some of Freed's followers expressed concern, suggesting that Prince should not push himself to make public appearances following a health scare. But plans went forward, including for Freed to be flown to Minneapolis.[21]

Saturday, April 16, 2016

At 5:33 a.m. on the 16th, Prince tweeted his support for National Record Store day and name-checked the local store Electric Fetus, where he was known to shop. Next, at 10:02 a.m., Prince tweeted an electronic flyer for the dance party. Later, during the mid-afternoon, Prince left his compound for a bike ride, appearing relaxed and carefree as he cruised around a local strip mall parking lot with a companion. And in the late afternoon, he visited Electric Fetus with Kirk Johnson and administrative aide Meron Berkure.[22] He purchased CDs by some of the musicians that had most influenced his work: Stevie Wonder, Joni Mitchell, and Santana. He tweeted that he had "rocked Stevie's Talking Book all the way home!"[23]

By the time nighttime arrived, however, Prince was struggling to maintain the illusion of good cheer. He arrived at the dance party at midnight, about two hours after it began. Freed made eye contact with Prince, and saw an unusual blank look. "He looked upset to me, [w]hen I saw him, there was no smile," he later told the *Times*.[24] Another fan, Nancy Anderson, told *The Star-Tribune* that "he looked pasty, weak and frail," and "[had] trouble walking up the steps to the piano."[25]

These reports were grimly corroborated by a photo taken of Prince at the event. Wearing a loose-fitting shirt and leaning against the new piano, his intent had clearly been to strike a mellow, relaxed figure. Instead, his body is stiff, and his eyes and face betray fatigue and sadness, with his impish smile nowhere to be found.

Still, Prince gamely tried to work the crowd for the mere five minutes that he remained present. He openly addressed concerns about his health, assuring people that these were unfounded rumors.[26] In an apparent effort at irony, he solicited a round of applause for his doctor. He played a snippet of "Chopsticks" on the piano, after which a recording of his April 14 Atlanta show began playing over the speakers. This, however, simply served a cover for an abrupt exit through a hidden door; as *Star-Tribune* reporter Sharyn Jackson put it, "Just as quickly as he had first appeared, he was gone."[27]

Shortly after leaving, at 12:37 a.m., Prince tweeted a photograph of happy fans at the party, an apparent way of giving thanks for their attendance. It was nearly 20 hours after he had begun his day.

   ***

On the morning of April 17, as if to mitigate the risk that his frailness at the party had been noticed, Prince yet again took to Twitter to again proclaim his good health. In response to a tweet about his Atlanta show, Prince stated that "I've barely slept since that nite." He placed this next to the hashtag "FeelingRejuvenated."[28]

The next day, April 18, Jeremiah Freed – who remained in the dark about Prince's actual condition – released a podcast that recounted the dance party. Freed had not spoken to Prince privately, and in fact had been abruptly sent back home the day after the party. But he used the podcast to shoot down rumors that drugs had played a role in the events of the 14th, dismissing such reports as innuendo.[29]

Also on the 18th, Prince spoke to another close friend, the television journalist Tamron Hall. Consistent with the narrative he had presented to the public, he assured her that he was fine. Hall was certainly among a small group of people he might have confided in, but the story Prince offered her was the same: all was fine.[30]

One person who had recently had intimations to the contrary was Prince's childhood friend Paul Mitchell. Although Mitchell had not seen Prince in decades, in recent months, following the death of their mutual friend Kim Upsher in November 2015, he had started to worry about his old friend. He had planned to make inquiries about how to contact Prince, such as by reaching out to Andre Cymone, another boyhood friend as well as a former band member. On the week of April 18, Mitchell had put a reminder in his phone to resume these efforts. "I wanted to try to get in touch," Mitchell said. "I felt like he was all alone."[31]

Wednesday, April 20

As Prince shaped a public narrative following the emergency plane landing of April 14, a handful of associates worked behind the scenes to provide the help that was so urgently needed.

Phaedra Ellis-Lamkins, 40, could not have been better suited to the role of orchestrating an intervention to address Prince's addiction to prescription opioids. A former labor union executive in the San Francisco area and sometime music manager, she had helped to accomplish his decades-long goal of obtaining his master recordings from Warner Bros. in 2014. Formidable and capable, she was also someone Prince might be willing to listen to.

And yet, she was on the West Coast, and powerless to do more than make phone calls. After becoming aware of the gravity of Prince's condition, and the profound risk that the overdose of April 14 would be repeated, she contacted Howard Kornfeld, a physician in Mill Valley, California specializing in addiction treatment. Kornfeld, unable to immediately travel, instead dispatched his son Andrew, a non-physician, on a red-eye flight to Minneapolis on the night of April 20. Andrew brought with him a small dose of the drug Suboxone, which is used for opioid detoxification, apparently for administration by a local physician.[32]

That same day, Prince received another visit from Dr. Schulenberg, who reportedly then prescribed medications for opioid withdrawal.[33] Prince picked up the prescriptions at a local Walgreens. From there, Prince returned to Paisley Park. He was greeted by his chef, Ray Roberts, who had prepared Prince a standard vegan meal. The chef was then discharged for the evening and went home.[34]

At night, Paisley Park was not just Prince's private sanctuary, but something akin to a solitary fortress. The facility had no overnight staff, and typically only one close aide was allowed to hold a key for entry, and usually only when Prince was out of town. A Paisley Park police incident report from 2013 put it this way: "Only Prince had a key and [h]e was the one who would let people in or out."

In terms of Prince's isolation, then, the night of April 20 was not atypical. But in other respects, it was unique. Over the previous two weeks, he had cancelled one show for medical reasons. At the rescheduled event a week later, he was not able to complete a set without leaving the stage for several breaks. He nearly lost his life on the return flight from that show, and had twice seen a physician. He had postponed additional shows, and had appeared in public looking frail and sad.

Despite all of this, on the night of April 20, amidst Paisley Park's 55,000 square feet of recording studios, rehearsal rooms, meeting areas, and offices, Prince remained entirely alone.

***

At 10:07 a.m. on Thursday, April 21, 2016, Prince Rogers Nelson was pronounced dead after being found in an elevator inside Paisley Park.

The cause was later determined to be an accidental overdose of a prescription painkiller, Fentanyl.[35] Whether Prince had known he was taking this extremely powerful and potentially lethal drug is unclear; subsequent reports indicated he had been in possession of mislabeled versions of ostensibly much more benign painkillers.[36] But these ambiguous factual threads would not be disentangled for months, if ever; for now, there was merely disbelief.

The event created shockwaves across the world. By midday, President Barack Obama had issued a statement of condolence and praise. The phones of hardcore fans erupted throughout the day with text messages of the news.

Outside Paisley Park, a common ritual of breathless media attention began. A row of white television vans formed, their satellite dishes pointed toward the gray sky. Reporters in full make-up wore trench coats for shelter from the rain, and practiced their lines using teleprompters which had been tucked under hastily assembled tents. The backdrop to their live reports was a massive, stark white building, surrounded by a chain link fence.[37]

A throng of grieving fans on Audubon Road was the first to begin a makeshift memorial, inserting flowers in the chain link fence. They faced the building expectantly, as if anticipating a message, the emergence of a spokesperson, or a signal – anything at all.

Every so often, the gate slid open, and a City of Chanhassen squad car would emerge. Helicopters hovered overhead. Grass became mud as fans trudged along the fence in the gray rain.[38]

As the day progressed, thousands of fans navigated their way around streets that had been cordoned off, many of them finding parking spaces some distances away. They then made their way to the perimeter of Paisley Park, wearing shirts bearing Prince's likeness and carrying offerings: bouquets of flowers, balloons, notes, stuffed animals, photos, clothing, and even boxes of Bisquick for the pancake-loving icon. The mementoes would soon swath the chain link fence.

At around 5 p.m., the rain slowed to a trickle. Suddenly, gasps arose from some of the onlookers, who gestured toward the sky.

Over Paisley Park, from behind the gray skies, emerged a perfect rainbow.

***

The last year of Prince Rogers Nelson's life left in its wake the same sort of contradictions and conundrums that characterized his entire career. With Prince, nothing was simple or self-evident. Mystery and misdirection were central to his personality, constituting a coping mechanism and a manner of being, and these same traits were central to his concluding months.

When examining the events of 2016, pictures swirl together in our minds in a manner not unlike that caused by a Thaumatrope, an optical toy popular in the 19th century, which uses a small disc with pictures on both sides. When twirled quickly, the pictures appear to blend into one – a dove is placed in a cage, or a happy face begins to weep.

The images from Prince's last months intermingle in just this way. The evidence can't be ignored that Prince was suffering from an escalating addiction to opioids that not only caused two overdoses but had, even before that, been playing havoc with his health. But does he exit the stage as stereotypical self-destructing star, his gifts deteriorating before our eyes? To the contrary, the piano tour only solidified Prince's reputation as arguably the greatest performing musician of his time. Despite the tour's retrospective qualities, it had far transcended mere nostalgia. He had not just played his standards, but had visited the most obscure precincts of his canon. In paying tribute to musical forefathers like Ray Charles and Bill Withers by covering their songs, he had shown gratitude and grace.

And of course there are other paradoxes of his last months, including the most central one: why had this happened? How can it be that Prince was allowed to erect a facade of robust health and sunny optimism in the last weeks of his life, when so clearly help was needed?

The answer may ultimately lie in Prince's own psychology, rather than some blameworthy failure to act by others. "If you were to stand up to him, he was the type that could easily shut you out," noted Samantha McCaroll-Hyne, a Minneapolis-based blogger who regularly attended events at Paisley Park and frequently observed Prince at close quarters. "I believe it's foolish to think that anyone else is responsible for his actions."[39]

There are also any number of fans who argue that Prince was conscious of, and even planned for, his impending demise. Why do the lyrics of "Way Back Home" seem like such an obvious goodbye? Why does "Big City," the final song on Prince's final album, end with the line "That's it!" Why did he, so soon before he died, reach out to old friends to whom he not spoken in over a decade, such as former bandmates Andre Cymone and Dez Dickerson?

Such coincidences and serendipities are haunting, but ultimately unsatisfying as an explanation. The blogger Jeremiah Freed, who was aware from his private communications with Prince of many specific plans ahead, used his podcast to dismiss out of hand the notion that Prince had foreshadowed his death. And Samantha McCaroll-Hyne was aware that Prince had planned to host dance parties each weekend of summer 2016 at Paisley Park. And even at the final event on April 16, she felt a sense of energy and hope emanating from him.

"He was in high spirits," she said, recalling the sense of wonder he displayed over his new guitar and piano. Indeed, as far she could tell, a happy summer lay ahead for Prince and his local fans. Paisley Park would percolate with new instruments, new musicians, and new ideas. The next classic song, the next searing guitar solo, the next ethereal piano line, the next patented Prince scream, were all just around the corner.

46

"He seemed extremely excited for the future," she said. "He was looking forward to it."[40]

My Lord calls me;
He calls me by the thunder;
The trumpet sound within my soul,
I ain't got long to stay here.

-"Steal Away" (Negro Spiritual)

1. MIGRATION

"10,000 Lakes," the phrase that graces Minnesota license plates, evokes the pristine landscape discovered by the Franciscan friar Louis Hennepin in 1640. The state's name, which means "sky-tinted water" in the language of the Dakota Indians who once lived there, reflects its natural beauty. Even today, the state's main urban center, Minneapolis, retains a surprisingly unspoiled aspect.

The phrase also evokes a semi-mythical Midwestern heartland – a wholesome and healthy place governed by traditional American values and earnest hard work. It is not surprising that such territory would produce, as it did, a sincere folksinger like Bob Dylan. Nor is it an unlikely origin for a quintessentially American novelist like F. Scott Fitzgerald or a populist politician like Hubert H. Humphrey, both Minnesota natives.

Far less expectedly, it would also serve as the home and lifelong base of a mercurial, meteoric African-American composer, singer, and instrumentalist – a protean talent who would become the most prolific pop composer of his era. Ultimately, no pop musician of the past one hundred years would be more associated with his home state than Prince Rogers Nelson, known to the world simply as "Prince."

But while Bob Dylan left Minnesota at a young age and only rarely returned, Prince held tightly to his home state, becoming its favorite son. Touring the world as an international superstar, Prince would over time purchase or rent homes in Marbella, Spain; Toronto, Canada; Los Angeles; and Turks and Caicos, but he never cut ties with his home state. To the contrary, every milestone in Prince's life took place in a tight geographical radius around Minneapolis. The state played an outsized role in his life, much as the local nightclub First Avenue essentially became a character in his film *Purple Rain*. Minnesota's qualities, however contradictory, would over time become Prince's own: he was guarded, yet authentic; welcoming, yet insular; steady, yet unpredictable. As perplexing as his loyalty to his home state might have seemed to outsiders, fellow Minnesotans saw no such contradiction. He was one of their own.

Once he had achieved fame and fortune, Prince could have established his base in any major cultural capital. Instead, he used the largesse generated by *Purple Rain* to create a sprawling studio compound in southwest suburban Chanhassen; he called it Paisley Park, after a song of the same title. Prince had the building's stark white exterior lit so that it was surrounded by a soft purple aura, stamping the facility with his signature color.

At first, Paisley was a commercial facility open to other musicians for recording. By the last years of his life, it had become Prince's home, where he generally spent his evenings in isolation, and where he continued to compose, rehearse, and perform at a frenetic rate that had continued almost unabated for decades.

"I will always live in Minneapolis," Prince once said. "It's so cold, it keeps the bad people out."

***

To understand what made Prince one of the most original and seminal figures in the history of popular music, however, one must look beyond his home state. In the mid-1990s, Prince would describe himself as a "slave" to the exploitative record companies who owned his master tapes, emblazoning the word on his face in protest. Widely criticized for seeming to equate struggles with Warner Bros. to actual human bondage, he eventually calibrated his claims. But his anger was authentic, and in some measure can be traced to the suffering of ancestors who bore the full brunt of American racism.

Prince's roots stretch back to territory discovered in 1682 by the French colonist Robert Cavelier de La Salle, who dubbed it "La Louisiane" to honor France's absolute monarch, Louis XIV. Over the coming centuries, French cultural, social, and legal traditions were embedded in what became known as Louisiana.

Colonists like de La Salle also brought with them the noxious institution of slavery, placing thousands of Native Americans in bondage as they arrived. The French brought other slaves from Africa, and it was not uncommon for plantation owners to own a combination of African and Native American slaves.

In 1803, the United States acquired the state from France in the Louisiana Purchase, expanding the country by some 828,000 square miles. Suddenly, many Louisiana slaves were transferred to American owners. One such slaveholder was John Nelson, who had a substantial plantation in Louisiana's Lafourche Parish.[1] He would become the great-great grandfather of Prince Rogers Nelson.

Sometime in the years leading up to the Civil War, Nelson developed a relationship with a Cherokee woman, a freed slave, whose name is unknown to history. She gave birth to a boy named Edward, a rebellious spirit who as an adult emphatically rejected the heritage of his slave-owning father in favor of his dark-skinned mother. For all of his adult life, Edward referred to himself as either mulatto or black.[2] In 1880, he married a black woman named Emma Hardy and then became a traveling minister for the Colored Methodist Episcopal Church, visiting parishes throughout his state and elsewhere, advocating for the rights of African-Americans.

In January 1882, Emma gave birth to Clarence Allen Nelson, Prince's grandfather, who would be the first of at least 10 children. The Nelsons made their home base in Louisiana's Cotton Valley.[3]

Clarence was just 16 when he wed Carrie Jenkins, who was a year younger. Like Clarence's parents, the couple settled in Cotton Valley, where they owned and worked on a farm, tilling the same fields that their forebears had worked as slaves.[4] On June 29, 1916, Carrie gave birth to their fourth child, John Louis Nelson, who would become Prince's father.[5]

John was only a toddler when Clarence became involved with another woman, prompting his parents' divorce. Carrie remarried a man named Charles Ikner, bringing her four children with her to Ikner's home when John was three years old. Soon after, her new husband died; she left Louisiana in search of a fresh start, travelling northward with her children and other members of her extended family.

The family became part of the largest internal movement of people in the history of the United States. Between 1910 and 1970, in what came to be called the Great Migration, some six million African-Americans would re-locate from the South to urban centers in the Northeast, Midwest and West, seeking to escape segregation, racial violence, and Jim Crow laws, and in search of the good wages and better living conditions promised by encouraging reports in African-American newspapers.

Some took a circuitous route through the Deep South and ended up in cities such as Washington D.C., Philadelphia, and New York. Others moved in a straight Northerly line up the middle of the United States. For Carrie and her family, this led to Minneapolis, Minnesota.

The City of Minneapolis had grown up around Saint Anthony Falls, the only waterfall on the Mississippi River. The falls were named by the Franciscan Friar Louis Hennepin, who had been selected by Robert Cavelier de La Salle – the same explorer who named Louisiana – to help bring religion to Native Americans. The county that included Minneapolis eventually bore Hennepin's name, as did one of city's most important streets.

Long favored by Scandinavian immigrants, Minneapolis also

had a small but growing black community. And like so many other American cities that became destinations during the Great Migration, it reaped a side benefit from the arrival of African-Americans: the blossoming of jazz and blues. These African-American musical forms had developed in New Orleans and other southern cities, and began to permeate the cities of the East and Midwest during the Migration. And among those who would bring this music to the Midwest was John Nelson.

John was left without any parent before his 18th birthday when his mother Carrie died at age 49. By about age 20, he landed a job as a doorman at the Andrews Hotel on 4th and Hennepin Avenue in downtown Minneapolis, a large brick building that had opened in 1911. A somewhat drab establishment, the Andrews catered mainly to visiting businessmen, and Nelson's wages were substandard.[6] But despite his humble existence, there was a confidence, even a brashness, in the young man that helped him move through the world. He was relatively short, about five feet six inches, but spoke with a deep baritone.

Even as he worked long hours at the hotel, Nelson learned the piano and began to play in local clubs at night. The city's musical scene was vibrant, with clubs like Peacock Alley, the Blue Note, and Jet Away popping up around town. Soon, using the combined income from his job and his gigs, Nelson purchased a small single-family home on a tree-lined street at 2929 5th Avenue South, less than three miles from the hotel.[7]

Now 22 years old, he started a romance with 18-year-old Vivian Howard, a light-skinned African-American woman whose family had come to Minneapolis from Missouri. They married in 1938 and settled into a new home at 334 E. 38th Street. Two years later, Vivian gave birth to a daughter, Sharon, followed in the next several years by Lorna and Norrine.[8]

Nelson's economic fortunes soon improved as a result of a wartime boom. Following the bombing of Pearl Harbor in 1941, which brought the country into World War II, the United States needed not only combat troops, but also laborers to manufacture war machinery. Nelson went to work at Honeywell, a prominent employer in Minneapolis since the early 20th century. The family's standard of living rose, and in 1944 they had a fourth child, John Rodgers, Jr.[9]

The Nelson home became a festive place where the young patriarch would entertain his family and friends by playing the piano and singing songs. Nieces and nephews, who called him "Uncle Johnny," remembered his impromptu performances as the highlight of their visits.[10] They also enjoyed a family dog that Nelson named "Prince."

Nelson formed a jazz trio that became a fixture of the city's music scene. Combining the name he had used for his dog with a version of the middle name he had given to his son John Jr., he adopted a stage moniker, Prince Rogers Nelson.[11]

The band not only played standards but also Nelson's original compositions, which were abstract, nonlinear pieces that sometimes evoked Thelonious Monk or Duke Ellington. Along with their unconventional structures, the songs utilized odd phrasings and minor-key voicings. In a city full of talented musicians, Nelson's ingenuity and skill nonetheless stood out.

Nelson also became prominent in the social life of his neighborhood. Often dressed in a suit and tie, he cut a dapper figure and was known for a sense of humor that was offbeat and not infrequently profane. He joined a lively scene where men would hang out in bars, barbershops, and at barbecues, wisecracking and swapping stories.

The family continued to do well as a result of Nelson's employment with Honeywell, and in 1952 they purchased a new home at 3278 5th Avenue South. From outward appearances, the Nelsons' story was nearly perfect – early adversity had been vanquished and a share of the American dream claimed.

The reality was somewhat different. As Nelson approached

his 40s, his marriage to Vivian became strained. Unbeknownst to his family, Nelson was pursuing a woman who looked much like Vivian – beautiful and light-skinned – but who was considerably younger. She also had a mercurial personality that intrigued Nelson. What's more, she shared Nelson's love for music, and could even sing.

When Nelson left Vivian and his four children in 1956, it came as a shock to his friends and extended family. Sadly, this was almost exactly what Nelson had experienced as a toddler in Louisiana when his own parents separated.

In March of the following year, Vivian initiated divorce proceedings. A nervous Sharon Nelson, then 16 years old, testified before the court concerning the hardships that had ensued following her father's departure.

When the proceeding concluded, a child support order had been entered against Nelson, and Vivian was awarded the family home. Still, Vivian now faced life as a single woman with four children ranging from ages 12-16.

During the divorce proceedings, one important person was missing from the courtroom: John Nelson himself. After leaving his wife, Nelson had settled into a non-descript, three-level apartment building at 2201 Fifth Avenue South. With his family responsibilities diminished, he could spend time on music, as well as with the new love of his life.

For Nelson, it was as if life had started over.

***

Whereas John L. Nelson's parents had lived an agrarian existence in Louisiana's Cotton Valley, the next generation of African-Americans in the South began to fill urban centers, like New Orleans, that were rapidly industrializing. But as would so often be the case in the United States, an influx of darker-colored persons would be perceived by some whites as a threat. And in late 19th century America, the response far too often was violence.

A signature event of this kind was the 1895 New Orleans dockworkers riot, in which non-unionized black dockworkers were attacked by a mob of white unionists. By the end of the two-day melee, six of the African-American workers had been murdered.

The year 1895 also marked the birth of an African-American boy named Frank Shaw in Arcadia, Louisiana, which was about 45 minutes by car from John L. Nelson's birthplace in Cotton Valley. As an adult, Shaw did what a great many blacks in Louisiana and other states did in the face of such virulent and violent racism: he left, becoming part of the same Great Migration that had led John Nelson's family to Minneapolis. For Frank Shaw, this relocation led him to Iowa, another Midwestern state with a reputation for racial tolerance. There he married 19-year-old Lucille Barnell, herself a former Louisiana resident. The couple eventually moved north, arriving in Minneapolis in 1930.

The Shaws lived at 821 Dupont Avenue in predominantly black North Minneapolis, a working-class neighborhood that everyone called "the Northside." Shaw found work as a car washer. He was 38 years old and his wife 30 when Lucille prematurely gave birth to twin daughters, Mattie Della and Edna Mae, at Minneapolis General Hospital on November 11, 1933. They were believed to have been the first black twins born on the Northside.[12]

It might have seemed that stability was within the grasp of this young family. Unfortunately, as the Great Depression took hold in the United States after the 1929 stock market crash, Minneapolis was not spared its impact. Shaw was unemployed when the twins were born, and he and Lucille faced the struggle of raising two babies during a national economic meltdown. Being part of the Great Migration had led them to greater safety, but not to prosperity.

***

Mattie Shaw, after growing up poor in a Minneapolis project,

lived for a time in Missouri, where she married a man named
Alfred Jackson, Sr. Shortly after Mattie gave birth to a son
named Alfred Jr., the couple separated and Mattie returned to
Minneapolis. By her early 20s she was working as a clothing
inspector at a local coat manufacturer and living at 1031 Bryant
Avenue North.[13]

Mattie and many other local residents socialized frequently at
the Phyllis Wheatley Settlement House, the cornerstone of North
Minneapolis' cultural and social life, an all-purpose recreation
center where people played sports, took music lessons, and
attended concerts. While the center served a diverse ethnic
population, it was in particular a sanctuary for African-
Americans, and a site of frequent musical performances. During
the 1950s, a notable local jazz bassist, Oscar Pettiford, gigged
there on a regular basis, and national artists like Duke Ellington
also passed through.

Mattie was a woman of striking beauty, immaculately
groomed and stylishly dressed despite her limited means. Both of
"the Shaw twins," as Mattie and her sister were called, were gifted
athletes and known in particular as talented basketball players.
And Mattie's Southern roots, like those of John Nelson, showed
up in the form of musical talent. She became an amateur jazz
singer, with a voice that reminded listeners of Billie Holiday, and
would sometimes perform with other musicians at the Phyllis
Wheatley. And it was here where she met a handsome, dashing
jazz musician named John Nelson, with whom she quickly fell in
love.

John and Vivian's divorce became final on March 15, 1957.
By Minnesota law, he could not remarry for at least six months,
but John and Mattie were unwilling to wait. They sidestepped the
problem by travelling to the neighboring state of Iowa, which
lacked a similar law. In the town of Northwood, no more than 10
minutes from Minnesota's border, they were married on August
31, 1957 before a Justice of the Peace, with the Justice's family

serving as witnesses. Within weeks of this date, they conceived their first child.

**

John Nelson, the great-grandson of a slave owner, had made it through a chaotic childhood marked by loss, geographical relocation, and economic struggle. He now had a new wife, steady employment, and a sideline musical career that seemed full of promise.[14]

On June 7, 1958, some ten months into her marriage with Nelson, Mattie Shaw gave birth to a son. They bestowed on him the same name that Nelson used as his stage name, calling him Prince Rogers Nelson.

2. DANDELIONS

From the start, family, friends, and neighbors all called Prince "Skipper." The Northside of Minneapolis, where he grew up, was a place of contradictions and inconsistencies. With its tree-lined streets and quaint houses, it almost felt more like a suburb than a city. But blight, crime, and drugs were obvious on gritty boulevards like Hennepin Avenue.

John Nelson's substantial income at Honeywell allowed the family to live in one of the nicer parts of the neighborhood. About six months after Prince's birth, John and Mattie left their apartment on 5th Avenue and purchased a home on quiet and pleasant Logan Avenue.

All told, the marriage of John L. Nelson and Mattie Shaw seemed to fulfill the passionate promise that had prompted their elopement to Iowa. A second child, Tyka, was born in 1960. Music was central to the Nelson household, as it had been in his previous family. Although childcare responsibilities kept Mattie from joining her husband in the clubs, she helped him rehearse in the living room. The children looked on as their parents made music, a joyful ritual that bonded the family.[1]

From an early age young Prince warily eyed his father's piano and eventually felt emboldened enough to clamber up and explore the keys. But Nelson zealously kept the piano off limits, and Prince soon learned better than to touch it.

Nelson was a strict disciplinarian in all respects, and physical punishment was not unheard of, any more than it was in most other households throughout Minneapolis and the country at that time. But Nelson's approach was not extreme when measured against those norms, and Prince did not experience it as traumatizing; instead, he largely revered his father.

John Nelson himself began to feel urges of rebelliousness as the 1960s got under way, specifically against the constraints of his job at Honeywell. Seeking to move towards a professional music career, he frequently gigged out of town on weekends. His absence from his family was also felt on weekday nights, when he played in clubs until the early morning hours. This placed a strain on Mattie, who had to watch over the children without assistance.[2]

Despite all of the work he put into it, Nelson could not help but feel the prospects of a musical career fade. Pop and rock gradually changed the texture of the city's musical community and made jazz less central. The audience for quirky musicians like Nelson shrank; some of the places he played were now literally nothing more than strip clubs, where his skills were ignored as he played behind women in lingerie.

Nelson began to scapegoat the demands of family life for his inability to advance his career. Mattie's resentment grew as the burdens of childcare fell almost entirely on her. The smoldering anger between the couple began to erupt into occasional physical violence. Between the fights, there was mainly tension; the separate silos occupied by the spouses within the household hardened, and the differences soon became irreconcilable. Finally, the marriage fractured, prompting John Nelson to move out when Prince was just seven years old.[3] For the second time in his life, John Nelson had ended a marriage and left his family.

Ironically, many years later, Prince would recall feeling some sense of relief at his father's departure, perhaps because the pervasive hostility in the household had finally broken.[4] But at the same time, Prince had lost his primary role model and source of guidance.

One benefit of his father's departure, however, was that Nelson had left behind his piano. Previously, Prince had only been able to longingly look at the instrument, but now he could play whenever he wanted. Following Nelson's exit from the household, Prince developed an almost immediate aptitude for the instrument. One of the first songs he learned was the theme to *Batman*, one of his favorite television programs. In the absence of his father's affection the piano provided an outlet, a means of soothing the conflicted emotions that were increasingly taking hold in young Prince's psyche.[5]

For her part, Mattie Shaw was plunged back into adverse conditions not unlike those she had faced growing up in a Minneapolis project. Shorn of John Nelson's substantial income, she worked several jobs in order to care for her children, causing a palpable strain on everyone in the household.

Nonetheless, the community around the family was a tightly knit place where neighbors looked out for one another, ensuring a steady supply of friends and neighbors as Prince grew up. The family now lived at 2620 8th Avenue North, a home that John and Mattie purchased shortly before their separation. Prince started at John Hay Elementary School at 1014 Penn Avenue North, only a half mile from his home. Hay, which was part of a strong public school system, served about 700 students and had a relatively diverse population.[6]

Prince was turning out to be a small and thin boy, taking after his father. In class photos, he was routinely placed in the front row so as not to be obscured by other students. He wore a closely cropped, well-groomed Afro, and dressed impeccably. His mother, no less than John Nelson, earnestly sought to have her son make a positive impression on the world.[7]

Among Prince's classmates and early friends was Terry Jackson, who lived on Russell Avenue North, also a short walk from Hay Elementary. Jackson's family, unlike Prince's, was strong and stable, with his father Leroy being the first black prosecutor for the City of Minneapolis. Even as a child, Jackson immediately noticed seemingly contradictory personality traits in Prince. Around teachers and adults he did not know well, he appeared to be shy and almost meek. But among friends, he was talkative and playful, as well as someone who liked to pull pranks.[8]

The shy persona, Jackson detected, reflected his distrust of

60

adults and served as a way to avoid unwanted attention from authority figures. In truth, Prince was not an inherently quiet or withdrawn child. Instead, he oscillated among multiple personality traits to achieve his goal in a given situation.[9]

Prince remained free to visit his father, who moved into a one-bedroom apartment at the Glenwood Terrace Apartments at 1707 Glenwood Avenue on the Northside. But Nelson continued to spend large swaths of time on the road, and while he regularly provided Prince a small financial allowance, emotional support was another matter. And Nelson's absence would be even more glaring when a radical shift took place in Prince's home.

In 1968, with Prince now ten, Mattie Shaw married another Minneapolitan, Hayward Baker, who also had children of his own. This improved the household's economic fortunes, but was jarring and disruptive for Prince.

While there was little chance that Baker ever could have served as a substitute for John Nelson in Prince's eyes, he failed to connect with his stepchildren on any level, and perhaps failed to even try. He would occasionally give Prince and his sister expensive presents, but these efforts came across as crass rather than heartfelt. His interest was in Mattie, not the children; Prince began to feel more and more alienated from the adults in his home.

***

As John Nelson continued to try to forge a professional jazz career and his son showed early signs of musical talent, major changes were afoot in African-American music. Moving away from the straight 4/4-time signature that was standard in blues and jazz, a young James Brown and other musicians began to use syncopated rhythms to create a new idiom, one that would become known as funk.

In 1967, this style had what might be considered its definitive birth with the release of James' "Cold Sweat." Over the next two years, as improbable as it seems in a city with a very small black community, Minneapolis became one of the more important outposts of this new style outside of the old South. A local station, KUXL, became a key part of the scene, playing Minneapolis artists like Mojo Buford, Willie Walker, and Maurice McKinnies, all of whom had helped develop this new musical form.[10]

Prince, now ten years old, became particularly enamored with a KUXL deejay named Jack Harris, who went by "Daddy Soul" on the radio.[11] Harris was also a musician, and developed an outsized influence by writing music for other artists as well as recording his own. Songs like Harris' "Get Funky, Sweat a Little Bit" helped define the Northside's unique form of funk.

Meanwhile, a local record label called Black and Proud Records emerged in 1968 and released a series of notable 45 RPM records by Harris and other artists. Prince was growing up in a minor funk hotbed, and nearly half a century later, the sounds he heard in those days, including the voice of Harris emanating from a radio, would remain fresh in his mind.

***

As the 1960s continued, the social changes that were convulsing the United States – including efforts to fight racism and widespread protests against the Vietnam War – began to penetrate the Northside. Economic opportunities for African-Americans had begun to shrink, and some felt that Jewish-owned businesses in the neighborhood treated blacks in a discriminatory manner. Simmering anger over these issues boiled over on July 19 and 20, 1967, when a protest against economic inequality turned violent. Acts of arson occurred, including the outright destruction of several Jewish-owned businesses.

It is unclear how, or if, these events impacted Prince and his family, but other social upheavals affected him directly. The Minneapolis public school system, like so many others around the country, began to undertake active efforts to desegregate its schools. For Prince, this resulted in being bussed several miles away to Kenwood Elementary School, which was predominantly white. Fortunately, close friends like Terry Jackson were bussed with him to Kenwood, and the relatively short distance between his home and the new school allowed him to keep his social life centered around the Northside.[12] And only a year later, both Prince and Jackson were back at Hay Elementary.

Prince and his friends began to see important musicians perform live. He and other friends, including his cousin Charles "Chazz" Smith, surreptitiously entered a Sly Stone performance through a fence. Terry Jackson's mother, Glenda, took the boys to a James Brown concert, where they were treated to the stage moves and microphone mastery of the greatest funk master of the era.[13]

At the Brown show, Prince startled his companions by jumping on stage. "He started doing the mashed potato," Jackson recalled, referring to a dance style popularized by Brown that involves stepping backwards with one heel turned in. Prince's friends – and Brown himself – looked on incredulously as the small ten-year-old grabbed the crowd's attention. Eventually a stage hand peaceably removed Prince, who rejoined his friends near the front of the stage.

In the summer of his sixth grade year, when he was 12, Prince attended a summer camp program at Camp Ojibway in Siren, Wisconsin. The Rev. Art Erickson, a community leader who worked with the Minneapolis school system to create afterschool programs, supervised Prince and other students there, and found him to be a happy and unguarded child, filled with playful energy. In a video taken by Erickson, Prince is seen riding on the shoulders of a peer, his face full of joy.[14]

But in the coming academic year, Prince's relationship with Mattie Shaw's new husband began to deteriorate. In order to punish Prince for some transgression, real or imagined, Baker would frequently lock him alone in a room, often for long stretches of time. The only saving grace was that there was a piano in an adjacent room that remained accessible. Prince began to associate the instrument with loneliness, and the rudimentary improvisations he created reflected this.[15]

Baker continued to inflict other forms of punishment on Prince, some bizarre. Among other things, he would force Prince to pick dandelions in the yard for long stretches of time. By doing so, Baker deliberately isolated Prince from his friends and his music.[16]

Years later, in January 1993, Prince wrote a song "Papa," which makes reference to a four-year-old boy being locked in a closet and beaten. It describes an abusive father who "crucified every dandelion in the yard." But in "Papa," the strange punishment that Baker applied is inverted, with the abusive father picking dandelions.

At the conclusion of "Papa," the father shoots himself. Something similar happens in an early draft of *Purple Rain*, when Prince's father's character murders his wife before committing suicide.

The next year at summer camp, Prince bore the emotional scars of this mistreatment, and seemed a very different person to the Rev. Art Erickson. "He went from a smiling kid to a deeply introverted kid," Erickson recalled. "You could see it in his looks."[17] Erickson took another video, and this time Prince stared blankly and without expression into the camera.[18]

Concerned, Erickson approached Prince privately and asked what had happened. Prince responded that his stepfather had been locking him in his room for long stretches, letting him out only briefly to eat. Erickson, while stunned, did not believe there was anything he could do, as the norms and laws of the times made it difficult to intervene in family affairs. He did, however, take Prince under his wing and encourage his scholastic and athletic development.[19]

Prince described the same details of being locked in a room by Baker to Paul Mitchell, a close friend during high school. And later, shortly after Prince was signed to Warner Bros. Records in 1977, Erickson encountered him at local movie theater. Erickson reached out to say hello, and in a brief conversation, brought up the past.

I said to him, 'You told me a story in 7th grade about being locked in your room and all that stuff. Are you going to stick with that? Did that really happen?'" Erickson recalled. "He said, 'Yeah, that really happened.'"[20]

Did Prince also suffer abuse at the hands of his biological father? Prince during some interviews made passing references to physical punishment by John Nelson, but was never specific. And at the very time when Prince was reporting Hayward Baker's abuse to Erickson, no reference whatsoever was made to any problems with John Nelson.[21] In short, there is little evidence that Prince experienced traumatic abuse at the hands of his father.

There is, however, ample evidence that Prince was locked in a room for long periods of time by Baker, and that this deeply scarred him, along with various other punishments meted out by Baker. But he shared this with relatively few people. Despite all that he revealed during his life, this tremendously formative and traumatic experience would remain largely hidden.

3. BASEMENTS

Fred Anderson, surely one of the very few African-Americans to be born in Fergus Falls, Minnesota during the 1920s, would become, like John Nelson, something of a frustrated jazzman. A skilled stand-up bassist, Anderson eventually moved to Minneapolis and began performing with local groups. Eventually, however, Anderson's dream of becoming a professional musician would become secondary to family responsibilities.[22]

In 1948, Anderson married Bernadette Early, a lifelong Minneapolis resident with a civic-minded personality, boundless energy, and a radiant smile. Their family grew rapidly, prompting Anderson to focus on his job with the U.S. Postal Service. Still, he played in downtown clubs whenever time allowed, and became a respected member of the city's vibrant jazz scene of the 1950s.[23]

The Andersons eventually divorced, leaving Bernadette in economically challenged circumstances not unlike those experienced by Mattie Shaw after her separation from John Nelson. Bernadette worked as a maid for a Jewish family, and aspects of her family life were troubled; one of her sons would end up in prison and another would suffer mental health problems as a result of serving in Vietnam.[24] But she obtained a college education and would come to play an outsized role in urban Minneapolis.[25]

The youngest of Bernadette's six children was Andre, who as a boy became a mixture of a hooligan and neighborhood hustler – someone who took cars on joy rides and boosted bicycles to make some cash. Such activities were known in the neighborhood as "the five-fingered discount," and Andre became an expert at it. Andre combined a wide variety of traits;

he was garrulous and profane – a tough neighborhood kid who was nobody's fool – but also had a softer, more reflective side.

As a youth, Andre Anderson's life in many respects moved in parallel to that of Prince Rogers Nelson. Like John Nelson, Fred Anderson kept his musical instrument off limits to his son, but Andre took liberties in this area as well, playing his father's bass after school and quickly becoming proficient. One day, however, Andre dropped the instrument and broke it, justifiably enraging his father. To avoid further trouble, Andre acquired an electric bass. He also began to learn guitar and several brass instruments while attending Harrison Elementary School.[26]

After living for many years in a rougher part of Minneapolis, eventually the Andersons moved to 1244 Russell Avenue in the more middle-class Northside, where Andre could attend Lincoln Junior High starting in seventh grade. Terry Jackson, Prince's longtime friend and elementary school classmate, lived next door 1248 Russell.

Lincoln Junior High was far enough from Andre's old neighborhood that he expected few if any of his friends to be enrolled there. He thus started school that year with a mixture of expectation and apprehension.[27] On his first day, upon reporting to the school gymnasium to be assigned a homeroom via a roll call, Andre looked for familiar faces, but saw none as he scanned the large group of students lined up against a wall. Spying a small student at the end of the line, Andre somewhat arbitrarily decided to stand next to him and strike up a conversation.[28]

Prince Nelson, who was now trying to shed "Skipper" in favor of his birth name, was quickly charmed by Andre's casual humor, and their mutual interest in music was quickly established. The two even shared the same birth month and year, with Prince having been born on June 7, 1958, and Andre on June 27.

Within days of meeting Andre, Prince invited his new friend to John Nelson's apartment. The tight space was dominated by a large piano and an impressive stereo system; there was no couch. There was also a guitar, and the youths began to tentatively play together, taking turns on the two instruments. Both discerned the other's talent, and they developed a rapid synergy, both musically and personally, as they began to play together in the days and weeks that followed.[29]

During one of these afternoon sessions, Andre saw a photograph of John Nelson's band on the mantelpiece. He noticed that one of the musicians looked like his father, albeit with more hair. Prince, not sure who it was, said they could ask his father when he returned from work.

When John Nelson arrived, all three were stunned to learn the coincidence – Andre's father had once been part of the Prince Rogers Trio, and the fathers had been close friends. Yet another parallel had been established between Andre and Prince.[30]

***

As Prince's relationship with Andre Anderson began to flourish, his situation at the Shaw-Baker household had reached a point of crisis. No longer willing to accept punishments from Baker that ranged from petty to severe, and worrying that things might further escalate, Prince decided to leave.

He appealed to his father to let him move into John Nelson's one-bedroom apartment, and Nelson grudgingly agreed. But the small space was ill-suited to cohabitation. And Nelson remained ambivalent at best about being a father.[31] When he came home from work early one afternoon to find Prince in bed with a girl from school, Nelson used this as a pretext to declare that his son would have to live elsewhere.[32] Nelson arranged for Prince to be taken in by his older sister Olivia Nelson, who was in her mid-60s and living on the south side of Minneapolis.[33] But this was an ad hoc, unsatisfactory option; Olivia was a disciplinarian who required him to focus on his schoolwork, and there were no instruments available at her residence.[34]

Prince remained close friends with Terry Jackson, with whom he had attended elementary school, and he now asked to move in with the Jackson family at 1248 Russell Street on the Northside. This arrangement would have been perfect; John Nelson's apartment was nearby, and Andre Anderson lived next door.[35]

But Terry's mother, Glenda, rejected the idea. Prince had been a regular playmate of Jackson's over the years, and Glenda had seen his behavior become increasingly arrogant and rebellious; she felt that reining in these impulses would be too difficult. "She was worried she would have to physically discipline him, and she didn't want to do it," Jackson recalled.[36]

Next door, Bernadette and Fred Anderson had separated, but Bernadette had emerged as a central figure in the life of the Northside, becoming known as "Queen Bernie" in the community. Her radiant energy filled the residence, and her benevolence was well known throughout the neighborhood. Prince, perceiving an opportunity in her generosity, asked Andre if he could move in.[37]

Bernadette readily welcomed Prince despite her large family. He and Andre shared a bedroom on the second floor, with each carving out a portion for themselves. The varying temperaments of the boys showed up in the room's arrangement; Prince folded his clothing and made his bed meticulously, while Andre's side was usually cluttered and disorganized.[38]

After months of playing music at John Nelson's apartment in the afternoons, Prince and Andre reached out to Prince's cousin, Chazz Smith, as a potential drummer. Chazz set up his drums in his family's back yard and invited his friends to bring over their equipment. The impromptu jam session attracted an audience of neighborhood kids, but also created such a din that the police were called. Chazz's father was adamant that the incident not be repeated, and told the group to find another space.[39]

The Andersons had a basement that conceivably could be used as a rehearsal space, but after years of disuse it was decrepit and filthy. Andre, Prince, and Chazz spent weeks clearing it of spiders, cobwebs, and centipedes before bringing in their equipment.[40]

An exuberant chemistry emerged among the trio as they developed cover versions of songs by Santana, Grand Funk Railroad, and others. Chazz, who had previously known Prince to be a skillful piano player, was shocked at how quickly he had picked up the guitar. In a clear attempt to show off, one afternoon Prince played Carlos Santana's complex solo on the 60s classic "Soul Sacrifice" note-for-note.[41]

Meanwhile, the dankness of the basement remained an issue, as did Bernadette Anderson's complaints about the noise. Seeking a backup option, they approached Terry Jackson about using his family's basement. The lanky and intense Jackson, who had played drums and percussion instruments since age ten, got his mother's permission and then asked to join the band. The others agreed, and the band, now a four-piece, began to seek its first gig.[42]

                                        ***

Starting with 8th grade, school bussing took Prince to Bryant Junior High School on the south side of Minneapolis. On weekdays Prince would often stay at the home of his aunt Olivia Nelson, which was much closer to school. On weekends he slept at the Anderson residence, and by day the band rehearsed in the Jackson basement.

At school, Prince adopted an approach not unlike that of his father at Honeywell, accomplishing his duties efficiently and avoiding scrutiny. The impish and sometimes combative behavior

70

he demonstrated around friends and some of their parents disappeared, and he was deferential to authority figures.[43]

Prince, like his fellow adolescent males, also began to develop an interest in their female classmates. He compensated for his nervousness around girls by writing lines in a spiral notebook that he memorized and then used when approaching them.[44] But these scripted efforts not surprisingly came across as ham-handed. Prince's small stature added to his insecurities, particularly with girls who were experiencing growth spurts and thus towered over him.[45]

With his efforts at teenage romance largely stymied, he spent long hours in the school's music rooms, where he caught the attention of one of Bryant's outstanding teachers, Jim Hamilton, who had played piano in Ray Charles' touring band. The Bryant music program was robust, so much so that all students were required play an instrument. Many had both innate talent and musical pedigrees like those of Prince and Andre; keyboardist Jimmy Harris, for example, was the son of well-known local pianist Cornbread Harris. Among this talented and motivated student body, it was typical for students to play multiple instruments – in fact, it was relatively unusual for them not to.

Hamilton observed that while Prince was not musically head and shoulders above his peers, he demonstrated discipline that was perhaps even excessive. But Hamilton warmly encouraged Prince's efforts, assigning him complicated pieces and even providing him a private practice room.[46]

The competitive atmosphere prompted Prince to engage in one-upmanship by mastering more instruments than any of his peers. One day, student Terry Lewis, himself an extremely skilled bassist, heard from outside a practice room what he thought was Jim Hamilton playing the drums. When he entered, he saw it was Prince.[47]

Hamilton also taught a class called the Business of Music, where students learned the legal and financial basics of the industry. Here again, Prince demonstrated rigor, showing an unusual interest in arcane topics like publishing rights. Prince also sought information on this topic from Pepe Willie, a musician and the boyfriend of one of Prince's cousins. Now living in New York, Willie was peppered with questions about copyrights and other legal matters during a lengthy phone call. Perplexed at the interest of a teenager in such issues, Willie demurred and said they would speak when he was next in Minneapolis.

Music was not, however, Prince's singular focus; he tried out for the junior varsity basketball team and made the squad despite his small stature. His shooting was below average, but his speed and ball handling skills were effective on the court. As with music, he was fiercely competitive.

The Afro that Prince had kept closely cropped in grade school was now becoming massive, which seemed like an effort to compensate for his height. But in the eyes of some friends, his hair only underscored the slightness of his frame. One afternoon, as Prince and his friends walked down the street with the sun at their backs, Terry Jackson noticed that the shadows cast in front of them caused all of their Afros to appear abnormally large.[48] Jackson laughed and teased Prince for looking like a character from the *Flintstones* television show known as "The Great Gazoo," who wore a huge helmet that made his head disproportionately large to his body. Jackson began using the nickname "Gazoo" for Prince, which caught on among some of their friends. Some extended family members continued to call him Skipper. He tolerated both nicknames cheerlessly, but such shifting appellations were commonplace in the neighborhood, and a standard part of the way young men in the city joshed with each other.

Chazz, Andre, and Terry Jackson were very much denizens of the Northside, and Prince's ties with these friends, through the band and sometimes living at Andre's home, continued to strengthen. At the same time, he developed two other friendships with people who lived on the south side of Minneapolis, and who could not have been more different than his bandmates.

Paul Mitchell and Duane Nelson, themselves best friends from a young age, were both outstanding young athletes with imposing frames. Mitchell was handsome and charismatic, the classic big man on campus. The more reserved Duane Nelson was in fact Prince's half-brother, the son of John Nelson and his first wife Vivian. Duane, who had been born about two months after Prince in August 1958, had grown up in Vivian's home after his father left to live with Mattie Shaw. (It would eventually be revealed, decades later, that Duane's father had actually been another man, but by the time of this revelation, Duane, John Nelson, and Prince himself were all deceased.)[49]

Owing in part to their mutual interest in sports, Prince became close friends with Duane and Paul. Because Prince's abrasive behavior tended to provoke fights and his small stature invited bullying from other students, Duane and Paul began serving a protective role in a manner not unlike bodyguards. "He was a little guy with a big mouth," Mitchell recalled of Prince. "It was good he had someone to take care of him." There was also a reflective side of the Mitchell-Prince relationship, with the two enjoying long, relaxed conversations in Mitchell's home.[50] At yet other times, they had boisterous fun, such as when Prince and Mitchell pretended they were professional wrestlers and staged their own matches in Aunt Olivia's basement.

Prince was anxious to join Duane and Paul on the football team, but his size inhibited his progress. Prince waited game after game to be put on the field, with Mitchell typically sitting beside him to offer comfort. Mitchell recalls that while Prince's love of basketball was genuine, his interest in football was more pragmatic. "He just wanted to be on the team to be around us, and he saw that girls liked it," Mitchell recalled.

Prince's opportunity seemed to have finally arrived during one game as the coach called his name. Prince grabbed his helmet and ran down the bench. But the coach, rather than putting Prince in, instead ordered him to wave his hands around the coach's face to prevent him from being bitten by mosquitoes. Crestfallen and humiliated, Prince walked away. "He came back and sat down and said, 'I'm done,' Mitchell recalled. "He never came to football practice again – he would just sit in the stands and wait for us."[51]

Incidents like these caused Prince to become even more provocative, which could have led to violence absent the protective presence of Duane and Paul. "He would say some of the meanest things to people," Mitchell recalled. "A lot of it was pent-up anger and frustration, and feeling like his parents didn't want him."[52] Prince's accumulating resentments led him to sometimes be abrasive even towards his friends, resenting their success in athletics and football. "As much as he liked us, he felt envious that things were easier for us," Mitchell said.

Prince developed a strong crush on classmate Kim Upsher, who happened to also be Mitchell's steady girlfriend. For Prince, this only underscored that Mitchell, by now the football team's quarterback, had the size and magnetism that he lacked. While Prince did not try to steal Mitchell's girlfriend, he channeled his feelings into a film script for a high school class. The screenplay cast Mitchell as a malign version of himself, an athletic bully who shoved Prince whenever he made overtures towards Upsher's character. In the end, Prince's character employed Kung Fu fighting moves to vanquish Mitchell's character and then head off into the sunset with Upsher.[53]

The subtext of the film script – Prince's frustration and desire to win – could not have been more obvious, and Prince's behavior toward Mitchell continued to oscillate between warmth and resentment. But they were also in some sense best friends, two very different characters with a powerful emotional connection.

***

When not spending time with Duane and Paul Mitchell on the south side, Prince busied himself in the Jackson basement with Andre, Terry Jackson, and Chazz. Chazz, by virtue of being the oldest member, emerged as the leader of the group.[54]

Minneapolis was a competitive hotbed of young musicians from high schools throughout the city. "There was a band on every block," Terry Jackson recalled. The group played a wide range of cover songs, but focused on rock artists such as Chicago, Santana, and Grand Funk Railroad.[55]

As the leader, Chazz took it upon himself to name the band, but he was fickle and changed it several times before settling upon Soul Explosion.[56] The band began playing gigs, which were easy to find. Bernadette Anderson was a leader at the local YWCA and also became a proud booster of the band, eagerly booking slots for them. People throughout the neighborhood enjoyed seeing the competition between young local groups, which became part of the Northside's lively atmosphere.

After honing their skills at casual gigs, the group entered a "battle of the bands" competition. The performance went well, and Terry Jackson delivered a stirring vocal on a rendition of the War song "Slippin' Into Darkness" to close the set.[57]

Soul Explosion left the stage feeling they might have prevailed. But after the votes were tallied, a group named Phoenix was announced as the victor. Prince and Andre looked at each other despairingly. Moments later, an ebullient Chazz ran up to them and exclaimed that they had won. He had changed the name of the group to "Phoenix" immediately before the competition.[58]

***

Now having completed ninth grade and reached age 15, Prince felt a strong sense of community in the band, and had two other close friends in Duane and Paul Mitchell. Yet the wounds he had experienced as a result of effectively being rejected by both of his parents remained raw. Prince was equal parts anger and charm, and seemed torn between a desire for friendship and an urge towards solitude. And these seemingly contradictory impulses would remain on full display as Prince and his friends prepared for the next phase of their lives.

4. GRAND CENTRAL

What Prince now craved was greater privacy, and he sought to reorder arrangements in the Anderson household to fulfill this goal.

To Bernadette Anderson, the idea seemed ludicrous – Prince wanted to swap the bedroom that he shared with Andre for a basement that was only marginally fit for human habitation. She resisted, uncomfortable with the idea of banishing her surrogate son to lesser quarters. But Prince remained adamant, and Bernadette finally relented. Andre, seeking in some manner to follow suit, also abandoned the second-floor bedroom for a room in the attic.

Prince set up a bed in the dank space, arranging his clothing and guitar around him. At night, the basement became a sanctuary where he could noodle on his instrument and write down the lyrics that were starting to take shape in his mind.

Meanwhile, dynamics in the band started to shift, with Chazz relinquishing his leadership role and decisions becoming democratic. A permanent name was finally chosen: Grand Central. Singing duties were shared, with each member handling lead on songs that were best suited to their voices. Prince, who usually sang in a low register, was able to effectively emulate Sly Stone, a favorite of all of Grand Central's members.

The brilliant and creative Sly, together with his band the Family Stone, served as a key influence for the group but also a cautionary tale as a result of his self-destructive drug use. "I'm not going to be like Sly – I'm going to practice my ass off like James Brown's band," Prince boasted to his bandmates one day in the basement. But Sly and his band provided tremendous inspiration through their innovations of the funk form. Among other things, bassist Larry Graham pioneered "slap bass," a technique of attacking the strings with one's forefinger and thumb to create a percussive sound, on the group's 1970 single, "Thank You (Falettinme Be Mice Elf Agin)." Andre incorporated the technique into his sound, and Prince was strongly influenced by the rhythm guitar playing of Sly's brother Freddie as well as Sly's vocals.

As Prince and his compatriots assimilated influences and developed their sound, the competition between the many bands in the neighborhood became fiercer. The level of talent in the community was not only exceptional, but other bands typically had more experience. One group, the Family, was led by a bassist named Sonny Thompson whom many considered the best pure musician in the community. The Family was also visually intimidating, wearing long black jackets onstage that looked like a gang uniform. Another prominent group, Flyte Tyme, boasted an outstanding roster of more seasoned players, including Jimmy "Jam" Harris on keyboards and Terry Lewis on bass, and was fronted by a powerful vocalist named Cynthia Johnson.

The competition motivated Prince and Andre, who also began to write original material, often creating songs more quickly than they could teach them to each other. They practiced on their instruments in their respective precincts of the Anderson household – Andre in the attic and Prince in the basement – developing embryonic riffs. Then, they would come together to hear each other's ideas and, more often than not, meld them together.

The band soon added a new member: Linda Anderson, Andre's sister. The move was prompted in part by John Nelson's purchase of a compact Farfisa organ for use in the basement. This added a new dimension to the sound and, just as critically, allowed Prince to translate his own keyboard ideas into the band's repertoire. He often instructed Linda on exactly what to play.

The band developed a tremendous cohesion through hundreds of hours of rehearsing and gigging, and its reputation in the neighborhood and across Minneapolis grew. The dream of becoming professional musicians was common among young local musicians, just as it had been for many of their parents. And for the Grand Central members, that notion began to seem plausible as they received more praise.

One afternoon, during a reverie in the Jackson basement, Prince and Terry mused about what would happen if either of them became famous. A pact was made: if anyone made it first, that person would come back and include the rest of the Grand Central members.[1]

At such moments, there was a powerful sense of shared mission and even destiny among the band members. But at other times there were intimations that one member, Prince, had started to chafe at the democratic and communitarian elements of Grand Central. This emerged more clearly when the notion of expanding the group was proposed.

The idea was broached by Andre, Chazz, and Terry Jackson, who all favored adding David Eiland, known as "Batman" in the neighborhood, as a saxophonist and rhythm guitarist. Eiland sometimes played with Flyte Tyme, and this offered a potential means of poaching a member from a rival.

Prince, however, was adamantly opposed, and went so far as to threaten to quit the band. The depth of his resistance was surprising, but even more so his willingness to issue an ultimatum. Grand Central typically made decisions by majority vote, but in this case, one member was seeking to exercise a veto, thereby threatening the band's structure and even its very existence.

Despite all other members of the band favoring Eiland's addition, they finally acquiesced to Prince. "That was his first power move," Jackson recalled. We let him have his way."[2]

***

Prince and his close friends engaged in adolescent games and explorations, testing their imaginative powers and sometimes incorporating surreal elements. Among other things, Prince, Andre, Chazz, and two other classmates formed a private clique based around a fantasy of being space aliens who had been given human form at birth. One member showed Jackson detailed charts of the star system from where the aliens had originated, as well as a diagram of a space ship they intended to build.[3]

Jackson, dismissive of a concept that he considered juvenile, declined to join but remained curious where the idea would go. One afternoon, Jackson surreptitiously followed them back to Chazz's house after seeing them picking cattails near Bassett Creek on the Northside. In the Smith family kitchen, the group boiled the cattails in a cauldron on a stove and declared that they were creating "survival food" for their alien race.

Jackson, as a result of refusing to participate in the clique, became somewhat ostracized by his friends. Adding to Jackson's resentment was that Prince and Andre, taking advantage of the fact that his family never locked the door, frequently entered his family's kitchen and took food. One afternoon, when Jackson found Prince and Andre stuffing themselves with snacks in the kitchen, he became enraged, prompting Prince to remove a rake comb that he kept in his Afro and throw it at Jackson. Prince then fled the home with Jackson in pursuit.

Jackson grabbed a golf club in the hallway and chased Prince down the sidewalk, hoisting the club at Prince as he ran. The club bounced off the ground and did not appear to hit Prince. But while Jackson viewed the incident as an example of adolescent squabbling that got out of hand, Prince felt differently; he began to nurse a grudge against Jackson that would never entirely heal.[4]

***

The high school nearest the Anderson household was North High School; it had an almost 50 percent minority population, which was a legal trigger for desegregation. As a result, after completing his studies at Bryant, Prince was assigned to attend Central High, almost half an hour away from the Northside by bus.

Prince retained an affection for basketball, and successfully tried out for a very strong junior varsity team at his new school. But despite being a solid six or seventh man, the overall quality of the team – it was in fact one of the best high school squads in the state – kept him out of the starting five. He vocally complained to coach Richard Robinson about a decision he deemed wrongheaded and unfair, but to no avail. Despite his skills, his size had become a factor; he remained well below average in height among his peers, no more than five feet, two inches.

Over at North, Andre found himself frequently buttonholed by classmate Morris Day, a flamboyant personality who also played drums. Aware of Grand Central's growing reputation, Day pestered Andre about replacing Chazz as the band's drummer, claiming that he would take them to the next level. Chazz was frequently late to rehearsals as a result of his commitment to the Central High football team, but Andre's loyalty to his friend for the moment outweighed such considerations, and he rebuffed Day's overture.[5]

Undaunted, a few days later Day pulled Andre into a band room and climbed up onto a set of drums elevated on a riser. Intent on impressing him, Day tore into the drums, which he had not known were unsecured. The set came crashing down, and Andre, worrying that he might be blamed for damaging the equipment given his reputation as a troublemaker, quickly fled.

Within days, an undeterred Day again insisted upon auditioning for Andre. Taking Andre to his home, where he had his own kit set up, Day played along with the Tower of Power's 1973 hit "What is Hip," a song with exceedingly complex syncopation. Day nailed it flawlessly, and Andre soon reported back to Prince and Terry Jackson that they should consider replacing Chazz with Day. Prince and Jackson, meanwhile, had also been evaluating yet another drummer, a classmate named Keith King. King's talents were outstanding, and he also sang, making him a suitable replacement for Chazz in this respect as well. Prince and Terry decided to evaluate both King and Day as candidates. Chazz, meanwhile, remained oblivious to this swirl of activity.

Day and his mother, LaVonne Daugherty, lived on the northwest side of town, and King on the south side. Both locations could be reached via a bus that travelled up and down Hennepin Avenue; Prince and Jackson decided to take whichever bus came first. They ended up catching the northbound bus, and arriving at Day's home, they were treated to the same rendition of "What Is Hip?" that had impressed Andre. Stunned, they told Day on the spot that he was Grand Central's new drummer. Keith King, meanwhile, never received his chance.

Decades later, Terry Jackson saw King on a Minneapolis bus, disheveled, smoking a cigarette, and speaking unintelligibly. When Jackson got closer, he was shocked to hear him mutter something about Prince.

Startled at King's state, Jackson found himself wondering how much of a role luck had played in Day having more than his share of success as a musician, while King had ended up in such a sorry condition. As Jackson put it, "History was determined randomly by which bus came first."[6]

***

Morris Day had achieved his goal of being Grand Central's drummer. Now the problem was how to tell Chazz Smith that he had been thrown out of the band. The situation remained fraught, particularly because of the family relationship between Chazz and Prince. The group began secretly practicing with Day when Chazz was not available, and pondered what to do. An important talent show was rapidly approaching, and Chazz himself had been responsible for booking the event.[7]

Believing firmly that Morris' superior skills would help them win the competition, Prince told the band they had to act. When Chazz arrived at rehearsal late after football practice one afternoon, Morris stepped out from behind a staircase, and it was announced that Chazz was being replaced.

"Who sold me out?" Chazz shouted as tears flowed from his eyes. A silence filled the room. Then, one by one, the other band members pointed at Prince. A crestfallen Chazz retreated, his social and musical bond with his companions largely severed.[8]

When practice finally began amidst a subdued atmosphere, it was clear that something fundamental had changed, even beyond the band's membership. Emotional considerations had been cast aside, and what had been an afterschool band had taken a major step towards becoming a professional ensemble. And in the process, Prince Rogers Nelson had forcefully and definitively seized the mantle of leadership.

***

As the reconfigured Grand Central developed its sound, Prince began exploring a technique that would have profound implications, not only for himself but ultimately for the very direction of pop music in the 1980s.

The idea emerged after Prince and Jackson attended another Sly Stone concert in Minneapolis. The event itself was spectacular and dramatic, with Sly arriving in a helicopter and taking the stage with his massive band. Prince remained relatively impassive as he studied the group's sound. He focused in particular on the intricate trumpet work of Cynthia Robinson, which provided a melodic counterpart to the band's gritty bottom end.[9]

Seeing the concert prompted Prince to think more about the use of horns in R&B music. His conclusion was an unusual one – he decided that a keyboardist such as Linda Anderson could imitate, for example, the lines that Cynthia Robinson played in Sly Stone's band. "Prince came up with the concept of horn lines on keyboards after that," Terry Jackson recalled.

Because horns were such a mainstay of R&B, Prince's conscious elimination of this element was a declaration of his intention to innovate. Writing rock and funk songs in a manner that borrowed from others was not enough; at only age 16, he was already thinking of ways to develop new stylistic concepts.

***

The Grand Central lineup was completed by another percussionist named William Doughty, who went by the nickname "Hollywood." The band had a strange appearance; two of its members, Prince and Doughty, were extremely small, drawing an odd contrast with the other members, and particularly with Terry Jackson, who was about 15 inches taller. Prince's attire stood out; while his bandmates dressed either casually or with elements of '70s garishness, Prince emulated his father with neatly pressed pants and button-down shirts.

John Nelson himself was now an increasing presence in Prince's life, having been galvanized by his son's success with music. Nelson attended many of the band's gigs, giving members pep talks before and after shows, as well as shooting photos.

Soon, a formal patron emerged for the group: Day's mother, LaVonne Daugherty, who became the group's de facto manager in 1974. Andre immediately developed an unrequited crush on the sexy and confident woman, who in turn viewed Grand Central as a potential route to a career in show business. Daugherty had an elaborate contract drawn up by an attorney that established the band as a legal entity called "Grand Central Corporation." Each band member signed on their own behalf, although their parents' signatures were also required to give the document validity. Following the contract's execution, the band itself was renamed Grand Central Corporation.

Daugherty was assisted by Pepe Willie, who had returned to Minneapolis from New York, now ready to answer Prince's questions about the music business. Willie attended some of the group's rehearsals, and quickly noticed Prince's increasing dominance. He would often stop the band mid-note, put down his guitar, and impatiently demonstrate to keyboardist Linda Anderson what to play.

Impressed by Prince's instrumental skills, Willie asked him to serve as a guitarist on a series of recording sessions for his own band, 94 East. The sessions, which took place in late 1975 at a Minneapolis studio called the Cookhouse, gave Prince his first look at a recording studio. His work ethic stood out; when the group took a break, Prince kept practicing. Upon their return, he scoffed at their indolence.

The day after the session, however, Prince had lingering doubts about his performance. He asked Willie to be allowed to re-record one guitar part; Willie acquiesced, making arrangements for an engineer to meet Prince at the studio while he played golf.

While Prince's precision was greater this time, the net result was less positive. The equipment settings at the studio had been changed from the previous day's setting, and Prince's part no longer sat comfortably into the mix. The perfect had turned out to be the enemy of the good.

***

All of Grand Central's members were anxious to record the band's own demo, and LaVonne Daugherty agreed to pay for time at ASI studio, a small 16-track facility on the Northside. The group proceeded to cut six original songs, a mixture of compositions by Prince, and Andre. The sessions were engineered by David Z. Rivkin, who would play an important role for Prince in years to come.

With the demo complete, Daugherty contacted funk musician Isaac Hayes, best known for composing the soundtrack to the movie *Shaft* in 1971. Hayes had recently formed his own label, Hot Buttered Soul, and liked the idea of signing a band of teenagers who might be able to follow in the footsteps of the Jackson Five. He began making grand predictions of success to Daugherty, who passed them on to the Grand Central members.

Andre, believing that financial success was imminent, dropped out of high school. Prince, hedging his bets, elected to continue his studies at Central. And as days turned to weeks without a formal contract being proffered, it soon became clear that Hayes' lavish promises had been illusory. In fact, he was in dire financial straits that would soon lead to bankruptcy.

Prince's wariness had been vindicated, and as a result he began to develop confidence in his instincts relative to business matters. And indeed, starting with this event, his decisions in this area would be unfailingly accurate – even when extremely unconventional – for the better part of a decade.

For the time being, however, those instincts had merely helped mitigate a setback rather than improving his fortunes. His frustrations about the lack of progress grew.

Shortly afterward, Prince was interviewed about his musical activities by the Central High School student newspaper in February 1976; he informed the reporter that a record was being readied, hopefully for a summer release.

In truth, the band's path forward was anything but clear. Confounded by the constraints of the music industry's structure, where the power to make or break a band sat in the hands of remote potentates, Prince needed someone to "discover" him in order to break through. Instead, he found himself stuck in land-locked Minnesota, where access even to a professional recording studio seemed unattainable, and where local amateurs were guiding his career.

"I think it is very hard for a band to make it in this state, even if they're good," Prince complained to the high school newspaper. "I really feel that if we would have lived in Los Angeles or New York or some other big city, we would have gotten over by now."

5. GRADUATION

As his final year at Central High School continued, Prince spent more time during the week at the home of his friend Paul Mitchell, who lived on the south side of Minneapolis, near school. Mitchell's family, like Andre Anderson's, welcomed Prince. And while Prince continued to show a caustic streak, his warmer, more playful tendencies prevailed in the congenial atmosphere of the Mitchell home. "I felt he kind of wanted a family. He would argue with my mom, mess with us and laugh," Mitchell remembered. "My sister would get mad at him for eating all of the food."

His friendship with his half-brother Duane Nelson also remained strong, and although Prince's formal involvement with sports had ended, he, Duane and Paul remained frequent visitors to local basketball courts and football fields.

In some ways, life in the neighborhood where Prince, Duane and Paul lived was idyllic, with a strong sense of community and wide interest in both sports and music. And yet both the south side of the city and the Northside remained working class neighborhoods where crime and, in particular, substance abuse remained uncomfortably close to the surface.

Examples abounded. Prince and Tyka Nelson had grown up noticing that their grandparents were conspicuously heavy drinkers, something that Tyka attributed to socio-cultural issues. "It goes back to slavery – when you finally get to come in from the fields, you want to sit down and relax and have a drink, and that's kind of the way we were brought up around my grandparents," Tyka recalled later.[1] John Nelson's first wife, Vivian, had become an alcoholic and died in 1973, leaving Duane Nelson devastated.[2]

Regrettably, what had taken hold among parents and grandparents would often re-emerge among children. Tyka

Nelson ended up addicted to drugs before eventually repairing her life.[3] Duane Nelson developed a drug problem that would make him a recluse and lead to an early death.[4]

In short, despite the hardiness, resourcefulness, and talent of so many of this community's residents, none were immune to the darker forces that plagued most urban centers during the early and mid-1970s. In many cases, the psychic and physical wounds suffered during that period would carry forward for decades.

***

With the potential Isaac Hayes deal having evanesced, the atmosphere around Grand Central became glum. This disappointment had impacted not only the band, but also their large community of family members, supporters, and fans. Grand Central was by now one of the most notable young bands in the entire state, which was what had seemingly led them to a cusp of a record deal in the first place. At the same time, it was clear that without a professional demo tape, the success of the group would be no better than regional. "It was always to the point where the band was going to take off, and then it didn't happen," Tyka later recalled.[5]

Obstacles abounded. First, they lacked the money to book time even at low-end studios. LaVonne Daugherty was unable to provide additional funds after the Hayes fiasco, and Pepe Willie was focused on his own plans and interested in Prince as primarily a studio musician or sideman.

For all the community and friendship Grand Central offered, Prince quickly began to see its limitations. He tired of playing cover songs, and new musical and lyrical ideas were rapidly taking shape in his mind as he played guitar and piano in the Anderson and Jackson basements in early 1976.

Prince began employing an ingenious, if extremely rudimentary, method of multi-track recording that allowed him to explore these ideas – specifically, by using two cheap cassette machines that he had signed out from the Central High music

88

program. He began by recording a vocal and guitar part. Then, while playing the performance back, he recorded it onto the second cassette machine while singing and playing another part. This process continued at least one more round.

The results were atrocious from the standpoint of fidelity, but the process demonstrated what could be accomplished in a professional studio, if only Prince had access to one. Because Prince was a proficient singer in three ranges – falsetto, mid-range, and low range – combining them in a single mix opened up immense possibilities.

One of Prince's first recordings using this primitive process was a cover of the 1975 hit "Sweet Thing" by the funk group Rufus, which featured a young singer named Chaka Khan. Prince's version evoked the original, but his vocals had a wider range than Chaka's, even as they displayed a similar femininity.

In recording original material, Prince began to explore heavier guitar work in addition to layered vocals. All told, this work in the basement constituted an explosion of creativity in which Prince explored a myriad of styles, themes, and approaches. The music evoked the late 1960s at times, showing elements of psychedelia and even folk.

It was not possible to record drums using the cassette recordings, or even to effectively amplify guitars. But given access to a studio, Prince began to believe that he could create full recordings without the assistance of other musicians. This approach had been tried rarely on major commercial records, and typically by much more seasoned musicians. For the most part, R&B and funk were considered communal forms of music; this was certainly the approach of Sly & the Family Stone and most groups who followed in their footsteps.

At the same time, it was fairly well known that at least one prominent African-American R&B musician, Stevie Wonder, recorded his songs track-by-track in the studio, playing drums as well as keyboards. This presented a clear template for what Prince wanted to accomplish.

For the time being, however, his fate was linked to that of Grand Central, which now adopted a new name, Shampayne. The change was in part to avoid confusion with the national funk group Graham Central Station – an offshoot of Sly & the Family Stone headed by bassist Larry Graham – and also because Chazz Smith claimed that the name "Grand Central" had been his creation.

The band continued to perform gigs around the city, and by spring 1976 had saved enough money to purchase recording time at an inexpensive studio. They chose Moonsound, run by a lanky Englishman named Chris Moon.

Moon, whose personality was equal parts laid-back and fanciful, had moved to Minneapolis as a teenager and opened his studio after graduating high school. His interest was less in making money and more in working with interesting musicians, as well as exploring new recording techniques. He was also a frustrated songwriter who wrote lyrics copiously but lacked skill on any instrument.

As the Shampayne sessions began, Moon became intrigued by several aspects of Prince's personality. First, there was the discipline; he would usually arrive early for the sessions to practice on various instruments. Second, he was shy and quiet, in contrast to the boisterous personalities of Andre, Terry Jackson, and Morris Day. This reticence caused Moon to speculate that Prince had less of an ego than his bandmates, something that might make him an appealing collaborator.

One afternoon in the studio, Moon approached Prince with an idea: if he would provide instrumentation for Moon's lyrics, Moon in turn would provide free studio time for the young artist to work on his own material.

Prince pondered the offer for a few moments, and then he grunted; it was hardly a definitive answer, but Moon chose to interpret it as a yes. "Let's shake on it," Moon said, and Prince agreed. He was then given a key to the Moonsound studio, meaning he had free rein to work on music after school.

When his Grand Central mates found out what had happened, their pride was injured, and they issued Prince an ultimatum: he had to choose between Moon and Shampayne. A deeply conflicted Prince phoned Moon and expressed hesitation about leaving his friends. Moon calmly told Prince that he was free to make whatever decision he wanted. Two hours later, Prince called back and reaffirmed his commitment to the Englishman.

Shampayne continued without Prince, and the Twin Cities' lively community of young bands continued to thrive. But it had become clear to Prince that this local scene did not present any commercially viable path. Record executives were not going to come to Minneapolis to discover acts; another approach had to be found.

Moreover, despite the city's many seemingly up-and-coming groups, Minneapolis' indigenous funk community was waning. The golden years of KUXL were over, and Black and Proud Records lasted just two years. Maurice McKinnies, one of the leading lights of the local R&B community, became disillusioned by the lack of opportunities and left for California. Against this backdrop, Prince saw clearly that working alone in a recording studio would offer more opportunity than gigging with his friends.

Since Moon had to work a day job, Prince was usually alone in the studio in the afternoons. Working with lyrics Moon had left for him, Prince would sit at a piano to create melodies. Moon taught him how to use the studio equipment, and soon Prince started to construct full-fledged songs, playing one instrument after another just as he had planned when experimenting with those rudimentary recordings in the Anderson basement. And although Moonsound itself had limitations, it was a quantum leap forward for Prince.

When the weekends arrived, freeing Prince from school, he worked virtually around the clock at the studio. Like his father, he needed very little sleep to refresh himself. As the sessions continued in coming weeks, he became more sociable and talkative with Moon. Still, his work habits were relentless; when Moon smoked a joint or cracked open a beer, Prince shot him disapproving looks and insisted that they return to work.

Prince graduated from Central High in the spring of 1976, giving him even more time to spend at the studio. Prince was a quick study on the studio equipment, and could soon run the controls with ease. He and Moon competed to control the faders, their combined hands like an octopus on the mixing board.[6] Nonetheless, Moon saw that Prince had an innate understanding of how sonic frequencies could be arranged to create a professional sound.

Moon liked to experiment, and found that Prince did as well. Tricks were employed such as playing instruments backwards in the mix, a technique often used by Jimi Hendrix. The songwriting was relatively collaborative, with Moon providing lyrics, Prince creating musical riffs, and the two then negotiating how to combine them.

While he enjoyed exchanging ideas with Moon, it became clear that Prince's ultimate goal was to control the recording process and work primarily on his own material. Moon, while hoping to play an ongoing creative role, recognized that Prince would be the public face and driving force of the project. Both were committed to creating a demo tape that could get Prince signed to a record label.

After several months, 14 songs were completed, far more than necessary. All of the instruments were played by Prince, but just as he had hoped, the results sounded remarkably like a full band. While many of the songs ended up being meandering creations, the catchy funk-pop number "Soft and Wet" emerged as the obvious flagship choice for a demo tape.

One afternoon Moon invited local drummer Bobby Z. Rivkin to the studio to meet Prince. Rivkin was the brother of David Z. Rivkin, who had engineered Prince's sessions at API Studio earlier in 1976. (The brothers' shared middle initial was a nickname coined by their grandmother). When he arrived and saw Prince playing piano for the first time, Rivkin was stunned. "It sounded like he had four hands; he was filling out more chordal information on the piano than I've ever heard," Rivkin remembered. In the weeks to come, Rivkin kept hanging around Moonsound. He had already decided that this young musician was worth devoting his entire career to.

　＊＊＊

Prince Rogers Nelson was now 18 years old. Over the past six years, he had gone from being a shy youth to a member of an important local band, eventually becoming the band's leader. Now, among a tremendously talented community of musicians, he had been singled out for special attention in a manner that might lead to a professional career.

With his friends, Prince was still a source of practical jokes and easy laughs, and continued to enjoy the congenial atmosphere of the Northside. At the same time, a distance was forming between himself and that world, one born of his need to dominate every phase of his music. His ambitions, discipline, and drive outstripped that of any of his colleagues. And the results of his solitary work in the studio – which showed him to be an emerging songwriter as well as an extremely capable multi-instrumentalist – made him even more committed to the principle of self-reliance. Thus, despite a growing group of loyal patrons and supporters, Prince was by choice becoming more alone.

6. DEMANDS

With high school complete, Prince had ample time to play music and an increasing sense of destiny about his future. The primary concern now was money. Day-to-day survival was not an issue, as he remained sufficiently cared for at the Anderson household. But to advance his career, he needed financing, recording time at a superior studio, and promotional machinery.

Having finished a slate of demos at Moonsound, Prince felt he had essentially outgrown the need for Chris Moon as a collaborator, and asked him instead to begin serving as a manager. But Moon, wanting to be a creative collaborator rather than a business functionary, declined. "The piece I don't do," he told Prince, "is booking your hotel, making sure you're wearing the right kind of clothes. I'm not interested in that."

So Prince flew alone to New Jersey, where he stayed at his half-sister Sharon Nelson's apartment and began reaching out to Manhattan music executives. But he had wildly overestimated his ability to proceed without representation, and his calls to labels went unreturned.

Disappointed and frustrated, he contacted Moon in Minneapolis. Not wanting to see Prince fail, he agreed to make some phone calls and present himself as Prince's manager. Unfortunately, almost to the extent of his client, Moon lacked either business experience or music industry contacts; just as Prince's had, his efforts to penetrate New York's executive suites went nowhere.

Unwilling to admit defeat, Moon resorted to extreme measures. Upon reaching an administrative assistant at Atlantic Records, he claimed to be Stevie Wonder's manager and insisted upon speaking to her boss. After the assistant nervously patched him through, Moon sheepishly admitted that he actually represented an artist named Prince.

"If you like Stevie Wonder, you're gonna love my artist,"

Moon blurted out. "He's only eighteen and he plays all the instruments. And he's not blind!"

For all its chutzpah, Moon's stunt led to a meeting and an airing of the demo tape, but nothing more. Atlantic passed, and other labels remained unwilling even to meet. Still hunkered down in New Jersey at Sharon's apartment, Prince found his options waning.

Back in Minneapolis, a likewise gloomy Moon continued to circulate Prince's demo tape among music industry acquaintances. Among those he approached was Owen Husney, a Minneapolitan with a small but thriving advertising agency that also provided marketing services for musicians. Idealistic and passionate, Husney had been the guitarist for a local group called the High Spirits during the 1960s. His agency was located in Loring Park, a charming green space in downtown Minneapolis. By this time in his career, Husney combined the energy and verve of a former musician with the savvy of an experienced businessman, making him an ideal candidate to assist Prince.

Moon, consistent with his flair for the dramatic, decided to spring a surprise on Husney after intimating that he had identified an unheralded local band. Husney, busy with other projects and viewing Moon as well-meaning but naïve, rebuffed him for several weeks. But eventually Husney gave Moon an audience at his office. Moon threw on Prince's demo tape, and Husney agreeably tapped his foot to the rhythm of "Soft and Wet."

"Who's the band?" Husney asked.

Moon then dropped his big surprise: this was no band, but rather an 18-year-old local musician playing every instrument. Husney, immediately recognizing the opportunity in front of him, jumped on a phone call with Prince and offered to be his manager. Striking a paternal note, he warned Prince that given his age, people were going to try to manipulate him. "I'm going to be the protector of your creativity," Husney told him.

Not even waiting for his client to return home, Husney

entered into a whirlwind of activity. He undertook a capital campaign, forming a corporation and talking up Prince's talent to wealthy friends. Quickly, $50,000 was raised off the demo's strength. When Prince returned to Minneapolis, he learned that Husney had rented him an apartment and placed him on a fifty-dollar-a-week allowance. He entered his first home as an adult, leaving behind the Anderson basement forever.

Next, Husney identified two core tasks – developing a live band for eventual concerts and recording a new demo. The Moonsound tape had already made the rounds at most major labels, and a more polished product was needed. Husney cautioned Prince that before they re-entered a studio, he needed to write additional catchy songs in the vein of "Soft and Wet."

The interpersonal chemistry between Prince and Husney was both strong and combustible, with tempers occasionally flaring. There was also a tenderness to their bond; after one loud argument over strategy, Prince stormed out, but later in the day invited Husney over to hear a new song. He played Husney a plaintive ballad called "So Blue."

"It just was his way of saying, 'I know what happened between us and I'm sorry,'" Husney recalled. As he listened to the song, Husney's eyes filled with tears.[1]

Husney also purchased new instruments and converted a room in his office suite into a rehearsal studio, which became a place to jam on new ideas with local musicians. Andre Anderson, whose resentment about the end of Shampayne had passed, typically handled bass duties. Bobby Z. Rivkin, who had been awed by Prince's piano skills at Moonsound, sometimes made his way into the drummer's chair, in part due to being employed with Husney's agency as a gofer.

Prince also began recording material in a makeshift studio in the office, trying to write tighter and catchier songs as Husney had suggested. One was entitled "Hello, My Love," written about Husney's secretary, whom he had developed a crush on. Prince's romantic life had not yet flourished to any meaningful degree; because he remained nervous around women, music constituted an alternative means of flirting.

While the studio in Husney's office was fine for jams and recording basic ideas, it was insufficient to the task of creating a professional demo. Husney thus booked recording time at Sound 80, an important local studio where Bob Dylan, a fellow Minnesotan, had recorded portions of *Blood on the Tracks* in 1974. David Z. Rivkin was brought back in to engineer the sessions.

Many local funk artists were circulating through Sound 80 during this period, and one afternoon Prince was recruited to play guitar and add backing vocals on the song "Got to Be Something Here" by The Lewis Connection. Adding to the friendly, collaborative atmosphere, David Z. was simultaneously producing records by other local groups at the studio, including the notable recording "Thieves in the Funkhouse" by Band of Thieves.

As had been expected, Prince continued to perform all instruments by himself. David Z., by this time a veteran engineer, found himself stunned by the efficiency and relentlessness of Prince's process. Prior to beginning a recording, he would hum into a hand-held cassette recorder the basics of each part he intended to record. He would then scamper around the studio and pick up various instruments, recording the individual parts and using the cassette player to provide prompts as needed.[2]

All told, the early part of 1977, with Prince still only 18 years old, became a period of immense productivity. Prince's fluency with studio equipment improved by the day, as did his musicianship. Between sessions, Prince continued to jam with Andre and Bobby Z. at the Loring Park rehearsal space. The trio began exploring sounds that were radically different than the pop material that Prince was recording at Sound 80. Among other things, the group stretched out into long-form instrumental grooves that straddled funk and jazz, with Prince shifting between guitar and a Moog synthesizer.

Prince, intrigued by the results, enlisted Husney to bring in basic equipment to record the ongoing sessions. The intent was not to release the long jams that were recorded – they contained neither vocals nor traditional pop hooks – but rather to document Prince's explorations into different musical realms, and perhaps to save ideas for further work down the road.

The primary focus, however, remained on creating a professional demo at Sound 80. Husney was insistent on a high-quality collection of just a few songs, as opposed to the sprawling Moonsound demo that had been rejected by Atlantic early in the year. Progress was made quickly, and by April, a slate of songs was completed that included the re-recorded "Soft and Wet" along with the ballad "Baby" and the mid-tempo pop number "Make It Through the Storm."

After assembling a glossy promotional kit to go with the songs, Husney prepared to approach record labels. Brimming with confidence about the demo's strength, Prince and Husney decided that, rather than lower their expectations after Prince's disappointing trip to New York, they would issue certain non-negotiable demands to any interested labels. A three-record deal was essential so that Prince had time to build an audience and hone his style. They also would insist that Prince play all of the instruments. And most audaciously, they would require that Prince produce the album himself.

This final demand was in all likelihood an unreasonable reach. Most major artists relied on outside producers who were typically seasoned pros with decades of technical experience and hit-making savvy. Prince was still a teenager, with less than two years of working in recording studios. But he deeply feared that his creativity would be stifled by a producer, a concern shared by Husney. And he was highly resistant to the idea of answering to any authority figure.

Next, using tactics only slightly less brazen than Chris Moon's

Stevie Wonder gambit, Husney used subterfuge to drum up interest. He had a solid contact at Warner Bros. Records, an executive named Russ Thyret. Rather than simply asking for a meeting, Husney told Thyret that Prince already had active interest from other labels, and was being flown out to Los Angeles by CBS Records. He suggested that Thyret get Warners into the mix before a deal was inked.

Enticed, Thyret agreed to meet when Prince arrived in California. Husney then called CBS and A&M Records and continued the charade, emphasizing that two other labels were actively interested. Quickly, Husney had booked a full slate of meetings.

Husney and Prince flew to Los Angeles and visited five labels: Warner Bros., CBS, A&M, RSO, and ABC/Dunhill. The manager made the initial pitch by himself, after which Prince came in and said just a few words. The intent was to portray Prince as a mysterious and elusive wunderkind, and it worked; following the meetings, Husney's phone began to ring with follow-up queries.

One of the potential suitors, CBS Records, expressed interest but remained skeptical that Prince had created the demo without other musicians. Calling what they thought was a bluff, executives from the label offered Prince a day of free studio time, asking him to re-record a song from scratch. Prince re-cut "Just As Long As We're Together" at a local studio as the executives watched. Unfazed by their presence, Prince methodically moved from instrument to instrument and produced a pristine recreation of the track. The notion that the demo was some sort of hoax was dispelled within the hour.

With enthusiasm suddenly high, the executives began to court Prince and Husney in typical Los Angeles fashion. Lavish dinners were lubricated with expensive wine, and Prince was regaled with promises of fame. But if the duo was not entirely immune to such charms, they appreciated the contrasting approach of Warner

Bros.' Russ Thyret. He took them to low-key lunches rather than high-end dinners, and also invited Prince and Husney to his home. "He sat down on the floor and just talked music with us," Husney remembered.

With their presentations to the labels complete, Prince and Husney returned to Minneapolis, hoping that formal offers would soon arrive. Although RSO and ABC decided to pass, the other three labels all remained interested. Husney then began issuing the demands he and Prince had settled on. A&M would offer only a two-record contract, which ruled it out from the start. Warners and CBS were offering lucrative three-record deals, but both were hesitant to let Prince produce himself. CBS proposed what it thought was a wonderful concept: Verdine White, bassist of Earth, Wind & Fire, would produce the first album.

Prince angrily rejected the idea, seeing it as a sure sign of heavy-handedness to come. It also seemed obvious to Prince that A&M's executives wanted to ghettoize him by pairing him with a well-known black artist. He also felt that Verdine White's syrupy R&B sound was a thing of the past, and certainly not one that he wanted to emulate.

This left Warners. Thyret was on board, but the final decision lay in the hands of chairman Mo Ostin and president Lenny Waronker. These executives' careers had been linked since 1966, when Ostin, a thirty-nine-year-old vice president at Reprise Records, hired the younger Waronker as part of his artist development team. When Ostin became chairman of Warners in the early 1970s, Waronker joined him as an executive. Both men developed a sterling reputation within the industry; under their stewardship, Warners became a company that signed interesting artists and carefully nurtured their creativity.

Waronker, who had also met Prince during the courtship period, had been floored by the demo tape and his preternatural confidence. Still, Prince's slate of demands, and in particular the insistence on a three-album package, continued to divide company officials. Prince's talents were undeniable, but could he deliver a hit record? This, as with all things in pop music, was nearly unknowable, but such questions loomed even larger given Prince's youth and the hard bargain he was driving.

Waronker and Ostin solicited input from all levels of the company, ranging from business affairs lawyers to talent scouts. Finally, the executives reached a decision that was as much intuitive as analytical: Warners would meet nearly all of Prince's demands. They would only go so far as to allow Prince to coproduce the first album, but otherwise he would function autonomously in the studio. And Prince and Husney would have their three-album commitment.

Prince, still just 18, had achieved a dream that had eluded thousands of other brilliant musicians from his hometown, spanning multiple generations. These included his own father, Andre Anderson's father, and countless others. Indeed, going back to the earliest African-Americans of Minneapolis who had arrived during the Great Migration to form a vibrant musical community, a great many had come to nurture hopes of having professional careers. Somehow it was the shy, slight Prince Nelson —who had been effectively abandoned by both of his parents, causing him to suffer disruptions, dislocations, and traumas throughout childhood – who was now better positioned than any member of this community before him to achieve national prominence.

After accepting Warners' offer over the phone, Prince and Husney flew to Los Angeles to formalize the relationship. A flurry of congratulatory meetings took place, and Waronker brought Prince to a studio to explore some of the equipment. "We didn't want him to feel like he was auditioning, we just wanted to see him do his thing," Waronker recalled.[3] Prince quickly immersed himself in recording a song, moving from guitar to bass as the executives watched. Eventually, Waronker suggested that they conclude the session.

"No, let me do a bass overdub," Prince said quietly. Waronker, surprised, said that Prince was free to take the tape with him so that he could continue work later. Then, for the first time, Waronker saw a flash of anger on Prince's face, and his voice became firm. "No, I need to finish the track," he responded.[4]

Later in the impromptu session, Prince sat in the narrow recording booth and listened to a playback of the song. As Waronker walked past him to speak to the session engineer, Prince looked up at the executive and spoke up again, this time delivering a message about how Warners needed to handle his career. "Don't make me black," Prince said, and went on to describe white rock artists he admired, demonstrating a deep knowledge of popular music.[5] The message was clear: Prince would refuse to be pigeonholed as an R&B artist.

For Waronker, it was yet another positive sign. Prince had not only had talent, but a clear vision. And the studio session demonstrated that his focus on achieving his goals was likely to be monomaniacal.

Prince signed a three-album contract with Warner Bros. on June 25, 1977, just weeks after turning nineteen. At a final celebratory luncheon with company executives, Prince reverted to behaving in a shy and awkward manner; with the business details concluded, there did not seem to be a great deal to say. Not long afterward, he returned to Sound 80 in Minneapolis to record a song that represented his own way of communicating with his new patrons; called "We Can Work It Out," the song's charming and unassuming lyrics express hope that the Prince-Warners partnership would be a happy one. The peppy song, easily as catchy and assured as anything on the demo tape that had led to Prince's signing, seemed to portend a fruitful and happy relationship.

The song abruptly ended, however, with the sound of an explosion.

7. RECORD SENSE

Prince with Warners' Marylou Badeaux on June 25, 1977, the day of his signing to Warner Bros. (Courtesy Marylou Badeaux)

Only weeks after Prince inked his contract with Warner Bros., questions began to arise over who would control the relationship.

Although the company had agreed to at least let him coproduce his first album, left unresolved was the choice of the co-producer and, more fundamentally, how large a role Prince would play in shaping the album's sound. Not long after they returned to Minneapolis, he and Husney tried to place the issue of Prince acting as a solo producer back on the table. Their argument was a simple one: he had demonstrated beyond question that he could function on his own in the studio. A co-producer would do nothing but get in the way and stifle Prince's creative energies.

Still, the issue was one on which Warner Bros. was reluctant to yield. Despite their belief in his talents, Mo Ostin and Lenny Waronker weren't sure they could entrust Prince with this complicated and expensive task, which required both technical knowledge and an intangible known in the industry as "record sense" – that is, the ability to create a radio-ready sound. Throughout the 1970s and well into the 1980s, the role of the producer remained paramount, and skilled professionals were almost always brought in to shape the work of new artists. Giving a 19-year-old such authority was unprecedented in Warners' history.

The executives faced a dilemma. Already having a keen understanding of Prince's personality, they realized that a dispute over such a fundamental issue could poison the relationship in its nascent stages. Treading delicately, Ostin called Owen Husney in summer 1977 to discuss the co-producer issue, and to suggest names that might appeal to Prince. The chairman's initial suggestion was one of the biggest names in R&B music: Maurice White, the leader (and drummer) of Earth, Wind & Fire, which had released a stream of successful albums during the 1970s. The group's danceable songs showed considerable songwriting craft, and its slick sound helped define 1970s urban radio. Singles like "Serpentine Fire" and "Shining Star" scored big on the charts and were also widely influential among R&B producers. Ostin saw White as someone who could both provide cachet and serve as the perfect mentor for a young artist.

Husney knew that Prince would be mortified – he had, of

course, already rejected CBS Records' bid to have Maurice's brother Verdine produce his first album. But Husney, while expressing his doubts to Ostin, agreed to take the proposal to Prince.

As expected, Prince rejected the idea emphatically, and then wrote a detailed memo to Husney that marshaled arguments against it. Earth, Wind & Fire's sound was dated and generic, he contended, and White's input would detract from, rather than enhance, his own highly original vision.

When Ostin and Husney spoke again, the chairman backed down regarding Maurice White, but argued that Prince was too green to be sole producer. In response, Husney floated the same idea that had worked so well with CBS: Prince would undertake an in-studio audition to prove his readiness.

Prince had already passed this test with Waronker during the impromptu studio session that had occurred after his signing in June. But company executives who had not been present viewed the idea as a good one. This time, though, Prince would not be informed what was happening; Husney would simply say that Warners wanted to give him a weekend of free studio time, and the executives would surreptitiously view the session.

Prince was flown to Amigo Studios in Los Angeles and set up with a studio engineer. The officials discretely drifted in and out as Prince recorded yet another version of "Just As Long As We're Together." "He thought these people were janitors," Husney later recalled.

The executives, after watching Prince construct the song in the better part of a day, decided it would be folly to force a producer upon him. Although his studio production skills remained raw, an artist this talented and determined would simply have to learn on the job.

But Warners added an important caveat. An "executive producer," someone with ample technical experience, would have to be present to oversee the recording process. Prince and

Husney agreed, realizing that they were unlikely to wrest further concessions. Selected for the role was Tommy Vicari, a veteran recording engineer who had worked with Carlos Santana, Billy Preston, and others.

Prince wanted to record in Minneapolis, and work thus began at Sound 80, where he had made his first professional demo. Vicari had favored a more sophisticated facility, and when technical problems interrupted the sessions, he proposed relocating to a sleek Los Angeles studio. Husney disagreed, arguing that any 19-year-old, even one as disciplined as Prince, could be distracted by the city's party atmosphere. They compromised on the Record Plant in Sausalito, a pleasant northern California city near San Francisco. A beautiful house overlooking the San Francisco Bay was rented in nearby Corte Madera, and Prince, Andre Anderson, Vicari, Husney, and Husney's wife, Britt, all moved in.

On the surface, the environment seemed idyllic. The Record Plant was a venerable studio where many important albums had been made, including much of Fleetwood Mac's smash 1977 album *Rumours*. In truth, the facility's acoustics had caused problems for many artists, including Fleetwood Mac itself. Studio designer Tom Hidley had pioneered the concept of a "dead room," in which natural reverb was stifled by extensive padding and other insulation. The intent had been to capture a band's sound more accurately and transparently, but in practice it robbed the studio's two main rooms of any natural character. "It was horrendous; the room was so dead, it just sucked up all the sound," recalled engineer Betty Cantor-Jackson, an engineer at the Record Plant in the 1970s.[1] Indeed, during the recording of *Rumours*, Fleetwood Mac and its producers had struggled for months to achieve a robust drum sound in Studio B, the very room where Prince would be recording.

As the sessions began, Prince felt the pressure that came with being the youngest producer in Warner Bros.' history. He insisted on an atmosphere that was monastic – "no guests, no phone calls, no pizzas, no dogs, no hangers-on, nothing," recalled studio manager Michelle Zarin.[2] This was in stark contrast to business as usual at the Record Plant, which was notorious during the 1970s for the large amount of cocaine and other drugs consumed on the premises by famous artists.

As usual, Prince recorded each song himself, creating a foundation of bass and drums and then adding other instruments. But while the recording of his demos at Sound 80 had been marked by moments of lightness and good humor, Prince was now deadly serious. Making sure every note was right, he burnished the songs into a state of perfection. But this was not all to the good; Prince's deliberate process, as well as the sterility created by the insulation in the studio, made many songs sound like an aggregation of overdubs, as opposed to an organic whole.

At first, Prince barely spoke to Vicari or assistant engineer Steve Fontana. Eventually, wanting to bring a sense of familiarity to the sessions, Prince asked that David Z. Rivkin be flown in from Minneapolis to record vocals; this lightened the mood and loosened his behavior. When he, David Z. and Vicari had dinner one evening at an upscale Sausalito restaurant, Prince took out a squirt gun, and the trio took turns surreptitiously shooting water at the ceiling. "People three tables away were looking up, wondering if something was leaking," Rivkin remembered. "We tried not to laugh."

Back in the studio, however, the atmosphere remained hyper-focussed, with Prince perhaps overly intent on proving his ability as a young wizard of the studio. "He was definitely out to make a statement: 'I can do it all, and you can kiss my ass,'" recalled assistant engineer Fontana.

The vocals proved most difficult and time-consuming of all, as Prince insisted on recording the parts countless times to achieve harmonic perfection. As a result, Rivkin felt any sense of spontaneity drain from the sessions. "The pressure caused him to keep doing things over and over and over," he recalled.

Another problem was that various songs had previously been recorded multiple times in different studios; Prince was largely bored of songs like "Just as Long as We're Together," which further robbed them of any freshness. And surprisingly, for all of his insistence that he would chart an original artistic path, the music he created was mostly straightforward R&B, with an emphasis on ballads. Prince had discarded strong material that had been recorded in primitive conditions on Russell Street North, such the Joni Mitchell-influenced "Nightingale," and the ethereal piano ballad "Leaving for New York." These works were more original than anything Prince was recording in Sausalito. Despite his surface brashness, Prince seemed to have suffered a loss of nerve that caused him to steer clear of more experimental material.

"Soft and Wet" was one of the songs that had been recorded countless times in various settings; in Sausalito, Prince dropped some of the interesting touches that had been present on the Sound 80 version, such as the prominent funk guitar in the song's final chorus. And only one rock number was recorded, the overdub-drenched "I'm Yours," further undermining Prince's stated goal of being a stylistically diverse artist.

As a result of the glacial recording pace, the album went well over budget. Although Warner Bros. did not complain, Waronker did fly in one afternoon for a progress check. The chill in the air could be felt from the moment he arrived, with Prince obviously viewing his presence as corporate meddling. When Waronker suggested adding more bass to the song "So Blue," Prince erupted and insisted that the executive leave the studio. Waronker returned to Los Angeles, realizing even more clearly that the label had on its hands an artist who, for better or for worse, would never be satisfied with anything short of total command over his career.

As work continued, Prince also showed less and less interest in the input of the executive producer, Tommy Vicari, who had hoped to play a significant role in shaping the album. Recalled Fontana, "He kind of looked at Tommy like, 'Oh, the babysitter's here, Dad's home.'" After several weeks of quizzing Vicari about how to run the equipment, Prince started ignoring him. When Vicari offered substantive suggestions, the responses were curt and dismissive.

One evening, Prince's resentment of Vicari's presence was underscored through a bizarre practical joke. When everyone else was out, leaving Prince alone in the Corte Madera house, he stuffed an outfit of Husney's clothes full of leaves, placed this makeshift dummy on Vicari's bed, and stuck a knife in its back, Rivkin recounted. "Vicari came back at four in the morning and thought Owen had been killed," he said. "He was really screaming."

As the hostility of the prank reflected, Prince recognized no further need for an executive producer. "He had absorbed everything he needed out of Tommy Vicari's brain," Husney noted. "Prince already wanted him out by that time, and Tommy was heartbroken, because he had just been treated like shit."

Another frequent presence in the studio was Andre Anderson, who also wanted to contribute. But while Prince appreciated his friend's company, the bassist's creative assistance was not welcome. "He got left out, because Prince wanted to make the whole album himself," remembered Husney. While Prince recorded, the bassist chattered impatiently about how he would soon be making his own album, Rivkin recalled. "He kept saying, 'I'm going to do my thing, I can't wait to do my thing.'"

Throughout most of the sessions, Prince cordoned off Studio B from other activities at the Record Plant via a sign on the door limiting access, as well as through a bodyguard at the door. Tony Saunders, a 21-year-old session bass player working on a project with the rock guitarist Greg Brown in Studio A, was surprised at such behavior from an obscure artist no one had heard of. "I was like, who does this little dude think he is?" Saunders recalled. Eventually, Saunders began socializing with Prince in the Record Plant's rec room, and they talked about their respective histories with music. Prince was particularly interested to learn that Saunders had been friends with Sly Stone since age ten, when Sly had bought him an organ as a present.

Sly himself was a regular Record Plant client, and worked in a special studio room known as "the Pit," which had been designed to Sly's specifications, with the mixing board submerged below the musicians to achieve unusual acoustical effects. Once, Sly and Prince encountered each other at the studio and briefly played together; among other things, Sly tutored Prince on the "slap bass" technique used on the pioneering funk song "Thank You (Falettinme Be Mice Elf Agin)."

Eventually Prince somewhat relaxed the security outside Studio B, allowing Saunders and others in to watch him work and make small talk between takes. But the socializing did not last long; as soon as Prince began to feel distracted, he cleared the room out. "I had never seen somebody so focused," Saunders recalled.[3]

After several months of sessions, Prince and his team left for Hollywood in January 1978 to add the final touches at Sound Labs Studios. After the album was pronounced complete, cover art was quickly prepared and Warner Bros. slotted the album for release in early spring.

For those who had observed the process, such as David Z. Rivkin, it was clear that not all had gone as planned. The excessive overdubs had led to an album that lacked emotional depth and energy, and the Record Plant's "dead room" insulation had compounded this problem. At best, Prince had created a document of his musical skills and technical ability in the studio; he had not, however, made a particularly engaging album. If his intent had been to emulate Sly Stone and Stevie Wonder – both of whom had recently recorded records that were full of grit and energy – he had instead let his perfectionist impulses overwhelm his artistic passion.

These problems with the record, however, were not nearly as apparent to Prince as they were to Rivkin and others. To the contrary, he was convinced that his diligence had led to the creation of a brilliant debut. Media attention and hit singles would surely follow. Anything other than this would be a shock to a young artist for whom so much had come so quickly.

Recalled Husney, "I think that by that point he had been told so much that he was fantastic that he believed he was going to be successful right away."

8. BANDMATES

Sueann Carwell in Minneapolis (Courtesy Vaughn Terry Jelks and SueAnn Carwell).

Upon returning to Minneapolis in early 1978, with *For You* complete but not yet released, Prince's first order of business was to create a touring band. To replicate what he played on the album, he would require two guitars, two keyboards, a drummer and a bass player. Husney rented a rehearsal room at a local store called Del's Tire Mart for auditions and rehearsing, and Prince began to ponder the group's composition.

For his bassist, Prince settled on Andre Anderson, who now adopted the stage name Andre Cymone. Despite their up-and-down history, one marked by competitive tensions, the connection between the boyhood friends remained strong.

Prince connected with other neighborhood musicians on his return, including Terry Jackson, the former percussionist of Grand Central. Prince showed Jackson a six-figure check he had received from Warner Bros., proudly handing it to his friend to hold. Afterwards, he took Jackson to the rehearsal space and invited him to sit down behind a drum kit. The duo jammed frenetically for several hours, with Prince handling guitar duties. After the exhilarating session, it looked like Jackson had a place in the band. "I thought I was in," he recalled.

But Prince soon decided upon Bobby Z., who by now had been drumming with him on and off in what seemed to be the world's longest musical tryout. "I auditioned for about 18 months against everybody in town twice," Bobby recalled. "Persistence is a trait that Prince admires, and I certainly had that."[1]

Bobby had shown his ability to stretch into different styles during the 1977 Loring Park sessions, but above all Prince appreciated his ability to lay down a backbeat. His approach was almost diametrically opposite from the intricate, syncopated style of Grand Central drummer Morris Day; by now, Prince had decided that the drums in his live act should be solid but unobtrusive.

After the choice was announced, Prince bluntly told Jackson that his management team had discouraged him from hiring neighborhood friends. Shocked that Prince would allow such considerations to hold sway, Jackson asked what had happened to their boyhood agreement about including each other in any future musical successes. Prince remained impassively silent.

Prince did, however, leave open the possibility of his friend playing a different percussion instrument in the group. Jackson brought over his congas and continued to join in on jam sessions. Grand Central's other former percussionist, William Doughty, was also sometimes invited to join in.

From there, Prince wanted to diversify the band, both in terms of race and gender. In many respects, the template for what he wanted to accomplish with his live act was provided by his longtime influence Sly Stone. Sly's large group included men and women, as well as blacks and whites, most of whom wore flamboyant attire. The group included two guitarists and two keyboardists, giving Sly a varied instrumental palette.

Applicants for the keyboard and guitar positions were recruited via advertisements in a local newspaper. The artist was not identified, but the ads referenced the existence of a major label contract, guaranteeing a slew of applicants.

Among the local musicians who saw the notice was St. Paul native Dez Dickerson. Good humored and boisterous, he was also emotionally centered, well spoken, and had a keen intellect. Interested in fashion, social trends, and subcultures, he also followed a traditional Midwestern code of morality and trust.

For some months, he had been hearing rumors around the Twin Cities area of a local musical genius – supposedly still just a teenager – who was the next Stevie Wonder and had recorded an entire album on his own. Conversations took place in hushed tones at local record stores, creating something of an urban legend that Dickerson had hoped to get to the bottom of.[2] Now, Dickerson inferred that the wunderkind must have been behind the advertisement, and threw his hat into the ring.

Weeks later, as he was about to leave town for a gig, Dickerson received a surprise phone call for an immediate audition. After hustling to a local warehouse where the tryouts were occurring, Dickerson jammed with Prince for only 15 minutes before the session was abruptly concluded. Prince then took the guitarist outside for a lengthy conversation in the parking lot. "He asked me deep, long-term-oriented questions," Dickerson recalled. "I could tell he was a thinker – he wasn't just saying, 'Gee whiz, we're all going to be rock stars.'"

No definitive offer was made, but Dickerson was invited back and made a regular part of the rehearsals. Soon, one of Prince's representatives handed him a check, thus solidifying Dickerson's status. A musical and personal bond quickly developed between Prince and his new guitarist. Dickerson's technical skills were reasonably strong, but his great strength was the sheer joy he took in playing. His style when soloing was not dissimilar from Prince's, but Dickerson's sound was warmer and looser, a contrast to Prince's more studied fretwork.

Meanwhile, Terry Jackson, feeling that he and William Doughty were duplicating each other on congas, decided to bring over his timbales, which he had played in Grand Central.

"What are you doing?" Prince asked Jackson curtly.

"Man, I'm setting up," his friend responded.

"I don't like timbales," Prince responded. "They're not going to be part of the future of R&B music." Prince then turned away from his friend.

Jackson, hurt and also frustrated after months of being strung along relative to a place in the band, packed up his equipment and left.[3]

***

As the nucleus of Prince, Andre, Bobby Z., and Dickerson formed, the band's sound took a definitive turn away from the gossamer-thin R&B that dominated *For You*. Dickerson, a fan of hard rock groups like Led Zeppelin as well as a follower of punk and new wave, brought a heavy guitar sound into play. Andre's bass work was also oriented more towards rock than R&B.

Auditions at the warehouse continued, and Gayle Chapman, a quiet young woman and a devout adherent of a Christian sect called The Way, was tapped for the first keyboard slot. Chapman's playing was unobtrusive, but she had an innate sense of how to use the space between notes to create rhythm. Finding a second keyboardist took longer, with Prince finally settling on Matt Fink, an acquaintance of Bobby Z. With four of the group's members – Prince, Andre, Dez, and Fink – all being aggressive and intense musicians, the group's sound became raw and rough as each of them vied for space within songs. Prince and Dickerson sometimes played guitar solos simultaneously, and Fink laid down wild keyboard solos influenced by jazz-fusion artists like Jan Hammer and Keith Emerson. For now the group was almost comically unpolished, but the outlines of a powerful rock-funk ensemble could be seen.

While usually cordial with his band members, Prince was at first more reserved than friendly. "If he didn't know you well, he came across as very shy, and sometimes people would read it as being anti-social," Dickerson observed. Bobby Z., meanwhile, noticed that Prince used silence as a means of exerting control in social and professional settings alike. "He talked to you or he didn't talk to you," Bobby Z. recalled. "You felt honored if he did and you felt shunned if he didn't."[4]

Still, his new colleagues also influenced his development in various ways. Chapman's religiosity was intriguing to Prince, especially given her frequent remarks that God had endowed him with unique gifts. "She did tell him he was blessed, and he did eat it up," recalled Bobby. Dickerson, meanwhile, wore colorful, sometimes outlandish attire that caught Prince's attention. Indeed, image was very much on Prince's mind; when Husney told him how the Beatles had shocked a generation by wearing haircuts that touched their ears, he seemed drawn to the idea of visual sensationalism.

In general, Prince remained especially receptive to anything that would distinguish him from other R&B artists. In many respects, his first album fit squarely in the tradition of singers like Al Green and Smokey Robinson, who wrote primarily love songs and rarely challenged their audiences with new musical directions. Already, though, Prince was considering how to break out of this mold. "He was very clear that he wanted the band to be an amalgam of rock and R&B," Dickerson remembered.

Rehearsals took place between four and five days of the week, and typically lasted several hours. For Dickerson, the schedule was demanding but hardly backbreaking, and it was clear that some of Prince's attention was elsewhere. Among other things, Prince also continued to visit local clubs, both as a means of checking out the local competition and assessing further

116

candidates for the band.

One evening, Andre took him to see a group known as Enterprise, fronted by a sixteen-year-old singer named Sueann Carwell, whose astonishingly powerful voice had been winning talent shows around Minneapolis. As Andre had expected, Prince was stunned by her skill. Far from simply considering her as an addition to his group, Prince quickly formulated the idea of building a side project around Carwell.

The notion was audacious and potentially even counter-productive; Prince's new album had not yet hit the streets and his live band was still jelling. Constructing a project around a young, unproven singer could be costly and time consuming. But Prince didn't care, and merely days after seeing Carwell perform, he visited her at her mother's home and described his plans.[5]

Like so many talented young musicians in Minneapolis, Carwell had a musical pedigree; her father Bobby was a noted percussionist and drummer, and went by the nickname "Sticks." But he – like far too many other jazz musicians during the 1950s and '60s – succumbed to a heroin addiction that eventually landed him in prison. Emerging from the shambles of these events, Carwell ran away from home at age ten and grew up primarily in foster homes.

She and Prince, in addition to sharing difficult childhoods, discovered a family parallel; Sticks Carwell had gigged with Prince's father John Nelson in the Minneapolis jazz scene, as had Andre's father Fred.

As Prince explained his plans for the Carwell album in the coming weeks, it became clear that the project would have few genuinely collaborative elements. Prince would not only write the material and play all of the instruments, but would also record guide vocals for her to sing over. He would then present a finished demo to Warner Bros., presumably resulting in a record deal.

Prince by now had moved into a rental home at 5215 France

Avenue in the Minneapolis suburb of Edina, and brought with him a four-track, reel-to-reel machine. This allowed Prince to copiously record new ideas without the technical limitations he had faced in the Anderson basement, and he now began active work on Carwell's project.

Although Carwell often spent entire nights with Prince working on material, the relationship never took a romantic turn. "I was young and sexy and could sing, but he said he would never mix personal with business," Carwell recalled.

As he wrote for her, he consciously sought to adopt a female perspective, both in terms of the lyrics and the sound. The coy and bouncy "Wouldn't You Love To Love Me?", for example, was sung from the viewpoint of a woman being pursued by a male suitor. In truth, the song had been re-configured for the purpose of Carwell's project; it was one of Prince's earliest original songs, having been initially recorded in the Anderson basement using the tape-to-tape technique.

Prince also spoke to Carwell about the business aspects of music. His roadmap for success remained tentative, and Carwell became another person to test out ideas with. "He had a vision, but not a plan," Carwell recalled. Above all, Prince made emphatically clear the importance of forging an independent path from other R&B artists. "He would always say to me, 'Whatever you do, go the other way – go against the grain,'" Carwell recalled.

Between sessions, Prince occasionally sat in with Carwell's group Enterprise, a group led by renowned local musician Sonny Thompson. The group performed for almost entirely black audiences in rougher parts of the city, including at the legendary Nacerima Club. "We played in front of pimps and robbers," Carwell remembered. The band included old friend Morris Day and veteran guitarist Jeffrey McRaven, who also played with the iconic local funk group Band of Thieves.

The Carwell sessions shifted between the humble home

studio and the sleeker Sound 80 in Minneapolis. At the latter location, Prince was enthralled by a vocal melody that Carwell improvised before the tape machine at the studio had started running. At the next session, Prince became surprised and angry when she was unable to recreate the improvised part.

"You sit there until you remember it," Prince fumed. Predictably, this did nothing to help Carwell recall the part. This prompted an enraged Prince to end the session – and perhaps, the project itself.

"I'll bring you home," he told her angrily and hustled Carwell into a car.

Carwell left in tears, and become even more disconsolate when Prince did not call for two weeks. The sessions eventually resumed, but the psychic cost of working with Prince was now clear to Carwell, and their work had been drained of much of its vitality. But Prince remained invested in the project, and sent the completed demo to Russ Thyret at Warner Bros.

Thyret's response, perhaps predictably, was that the album sounded too much like Prince's music to constitute an independent project. If Prince's hope had been to create a fascinating parallel project that bore no traces of his fingerprints, it had not been realized. And while Carwell's vocals were impressive, Prince's heavy hand had stifled her creative energies.

Apparently sympathetic that Carwell's big break had not materialized, Prince sought to integrate her into the band as a percussionist. Former Grand Central percussionist William Doughty was called back to the rehearsal space to tutor Carwell, and she began rehearsing with the group.

For Carwell, a tertiary role in a sprawling ensemble was hardly what she had hoped for at the beginning of her dealings with Prince. But her fortunes abruptly shifted again; Owen Husney, who had been managing her career as well as Prince's, obtained a sight-unseen deal for Carwell at Warner Bros., one that would involve another producer. The prospect of a career breakthrough again loomed for Carwell, and she excitedly prepared to move to Los Angeles to begin recording.

Upon hearing of these plans, Prince flew into a rage and made clear that her departure would be considered a betrayal. From his perspective, he had supported and mentored her and was now being abandoned. That Carwell stood to lose a once-in-a-lifetime opportunity if she stayed in Minneapolis was not in his mind a relevant factor.

Shortly before Carwell left for Los Angeles, another twist occurred. A local group called Lipps, Inc. wanted her to sing lead in the studio on a song called "Funkytown." The opportunity interested Carwell, but Owen Husney warned that this might make waves at Warner Bros. before work on her album had even started. Frustrated, she told Husney he would have to pay her something for foregoing the opportunity.

"What do you have in mind?" Husney asked.

"How about $75?" Carwell responded with the first figure that popped into her head. Husney readily agreed.

Carwell was asked by Lipps, Inc. if she knew of another good singer, and she suggested Cynthia Johnson, who was part of the local group Flyte Time. Johnson soon performed a memorable vocal on "Funkytown," which would become one of the biggest disco hits in history, charting at No. 1 in 28 different countries. Meanwhile, Carwell's debut album, *Sueann,* unfortunately did little to boost her career after its release in 1981; she came back to Minneapolis exhausted, emotionally depleted, and essentially broke. "I felt so hopeless after that album," Carwell recalled.

Shortly after her return in 1981, Carwell bumped into Prince at the First Avenue Club in Minneapolis. He strode up, his face a mask of anger. "I hate everything on your album," he said. He then paused. "Everything except 'Company,'" he added, referring to a cover of a Ricki Lee Jones song on the album.

This was a particular twist of the knife – the only good thing on her album was a song Carwell had not written. Clearly,

Prince's grudge from nearly three years earlier remained fresh.

Another strange epilogue to their collaboration would occur. After the lacerating encounter at First Avenue, Carwell had not expected to hear from Prince again. She was thus surprised when, about a year later, she received an out-of-the-blue phone call from Prince, asking if she wanted to open for him and his side project the Time at a local concert. Hoping that bygones were finally bygones, and anxiously seeking a career boost, Carwell happily agreed. At the show, she performed songs from the very same album that Prince had a year earlier disdained. Not only did he seem to enjoy the show, but he handled mixing duties from a backstage soundboard.

Afterward, Prince exuded warmth and encouragement, a reminder of the better times they had enjoyed during the long nights of recording at his home studio. Carwell, aware that Prince was about to go on tour with the Time in support of his *1999* album, wondered if she might be included as a second opening act. Perhaps, she thought, her fortunes had again taken an unexpected turn.

But in the weeks after the show, there was no phone call from Prince or any representative. As months went by, it became clear to Carwell that Prince's overture had, in the end, meant essentially nothing. Her inclusion at the Minneapolis concert had been the product of some whim, and his brief interest had waned into indifference.

***

Notwithstanding her many setbacks – some involving Prince, others not – Carwell righted her career and became a sought-after session singer for artists ranging from Rod Stewart to Christina Aguilera, as well as a successful live performer in her own right. Remnants of Prince's sessions with Carwell exist: "Wouldn't You Love To Love Me?" was later recorded by another protégée, Taja Sevelle. Unreleased versions of that song and another Carwell number, "Make It Through The Storm," are in existence, including one with her vocals.

Prince and Carwell continued to run into each other from time to time over the years, but his curt manner demonstrated that resentment over her leaving his band had never healed.

"He was still mad," she recalled. "I think he was pissed at me for about twenty or thirty years."

9. Against the Wall

As April 1978 arrived, Prince's live band was complete and his first album was about to hit the street. Consistent with the marketing strategy that he and Husney had followed from the start, the album was prominently billed as a one-man production. Chris Moon was credited as cowriter of "Soft And Wet," and Tommy Vicari received his executive producer title, but the credits otherwise stated that the album was "produced, composed, arranged, and performed by Prince."

Unfortunately, the buzz that Husney tried to create with journalists failed to mask the lack of compelling material on the album, and few publications reviewed the album, positively or otherwise. The commercial performance of *For You* also fell short of what Prince and Warners had hoped for; it initially sold just 150,000 copies in the United States, reaching a respectable No. 21 on Billboard's Soul Chart but only No. 163 on the Pop Chart. Prince remained far from the public's radar screen as pop music was dominated throughout 1978 by the soundtracks of two blockbuster films, *Saturday Night Fever* and *Grease*.

Nonetheless, Husney continued to pour his energies into promotion, which eventually began to bear fruit in select urban markets. During a promotional appearance in Charlotte, 3,000 boisterous young fans showed up, creating a scene that at once thrilled and perturbed Prince. "All of a sudden you get thousands of screaming kids saying that they love him – he didn't understand that," observed his friend and mentor Pepe Willie. "He felt like a piece of meat being carried around." These activities did not meaningfully boost the fortunes of the album, which remained stalled on the charts.

Prince refused, however, to acknowledge any deficiencies in the work. Believing that the album was simply not being effectively promoted, Prince started griping to Husney and Russ Thyret, the official at Warners with whom he had the most contact. A frustrated Thyret, who had energetically pushed the album to radio stations, complained to Husney that Prince had unreasonable expectations and didn't understand the music business. It was hard for the manager to disagree.

Seeking an outlet for his frustrations, Prince began to barrage Husney with all manner of unusual demands, including that he repair broken toilets and sinks. Husney, justifiably incensed that his hard work on much more important issues was going unrecognized, began to feel like a glorified gofer.

Things finally came unglued over Husney's refusal to perform yet another menial task. While he was awaiting a phone call from the William Morris Agency about a potential concert tour, Prince called and insisted that he immediately bring a space heater to the rehearsal studio. The manager explained the importance of the William Morris call and asked if Pepe Willie or someone else could handle the chore. Prince became indignant.

"You know what, fuck you," Husney told him. "Just go get your own goddamn space heater. I'm not going to do that."

Later, even after tempers had cooled, Husney felt matters had reached an impasse and told Prince that they should part ways. Prince seemed surprised and said he wanted Husney to stay, but he made no concessions as far as what the manager's role should be. He wrote Husney a three-page letter outlining his duties; it was filled with just the sort of demands Husney felt were beyond the pale. Uninterested in such a role, Husney stood by his decision to quit.

The rupture left Prince in managerial limbo. Pepe Willie stepped in to help on a temporary basis, but lacked the time or experience to serve as a full-time manager. With a full band on the payroll and the commercial fortunes of *For You* petering out, it was obvious that help was needed, and quickly.

Indeed, concerns were now developing at Warner Bros. about Prince's progress, the increasing chaos in his business affairs, and the large amounts of money he had burned through. His capital at Warners was being depleted, literally and figuratively. Now, the replacement of Husney with Willie set off further alarm bells.

Above all, touring support for the album was needed, and the label executives were anxious to see the progress of Prince's live act. But seemingly little had been accomplished – with nearly six months gone by since the release of *For You*, the band had not even played a show.

As the label executives made their candid concerns known, the stakes for Prince quickly came into focus. Although his contract was not in jeopardy, he did face the prospect of falling out of favor with his key supporters at Warners, which could in turn doom the chances of his second album. "Prince's feeling was, 'We've got to put on a show, or this thing is going to fade away,'" recalled Bobby Z., who shared these fears. "We felt like, we'll charge three dollars a ticket or whatever, but we've got to do something, get out of the basement and play."

Unfortunately, the band had not fully cohered. Grand Central had taken years to develop into one of the strongest groups in Minneapolis; Prince had overconfidently assumed that he could accomplish something similar with his new ensemble in a matter of months. But with the complaints of Warners Bros. mounting, there was no further time for delay; Prince's opportunity to develop his band more gradually had come and gone.

Pepe Willie hastily organized two shows at the Capri Theatre in north Minneapolis for January 5 and 6, 1979, the second of which was to serve as a showcase for Warners executives who would be flying in from California. This would in effect be an audition: unless Warners offered a green light and the necessary financing, a national tour would not take place.

The temperature on the night of the show turned out to be 20 degrees below zero, a kind of metaphor for Prince's current fortunes. Only about 300 people showed up, who were primarily friends, family members, and other local supporters. They responded enthusiastically out of loyalty, but Prince, playing live for the first time with his new band, seemed tentative and hesitant. He kept his back to the audience at times and fumbled his stage banter.

Matters worsened as the much more important second show took place. The bitterly cold weather, atypical even for Minnesota, felt arctic to the Warners executives who were accustomed to the balmly warmth of southern California. Prince and the band, already feeling less than confident after the first show, squirmed as the executives watched grimly from the balcony. "The show was very tense, very awkward," recalled Bobby Z. Causing further problems, Dez Dickerson used the occasion to experiment with a wireless guitar; it malfunctioned, creating embarrassing gaps in the set. Even worse, his wireless transmitter picked up signals from local radio stations and police radios, causing bizarre noises onstage.

Prince's cousin and former bandmate Chazz Smith, who drove home with Prince after the show, found him nearly in tears. "He thought the show was shit," Chazz recalled. "I kept trying to talk to him, and he wouldn't even talk." Husney, upon speaking to Warners' officials afterward, faced a grim reaction. "They told me that the show was a complete disaster," he said.

The official decision came within days: Prince was not ready for a major tour. While not surprising in light of the weak performance, it was a devastating message. "He was crestfallen," Dickerson remembered.

The implications were many. This also meant that Warners viewed *For You* as beyond rescue. And without a tour, Prince had no way of recouping some of the huge sums of money that he had expended over the past year. "There was quite a bit of debt to the label, and his back was against the wall," recalled Bobby Z.

Prince's trio of key supporters at Warners – Mo Ostin, Lenny Waronker, and Russ Thyret – had by no means given up, but they viewed the need for a professional management team as critical. Casting about for options, they contacted the Los Angeles firm of Cavallo & Ruffalo, which had handled Little Feat and other acts. Prince, anxious for help and understanding that by this point he had little choice, agreed to give the firm a try.

The move brought two important figures into Prince's orbit at a critical moment: firm employee Steve Fargnoli, who became Prince's day-to-day manager, and principal Bob Cavallo. Prince felt an immediate personal synergy with Fargnoli, a lofty thinker who percolated with ideas and enjoyed a hedonistic lifestyle. Bob Cavallo was in many ways Fargnoli's polar opposite, an avuncular family man with a crisp, calm manner. He took over the business side of things, aided by his considerable financial expertise.

As his ties with these new arrivals strengthened in the coming months, Prince's spirits lifted. The sting of the botched showcase at the Capri wore off, and Prince redoubled his efforts to get the band in touring shape. His mood was further improved by a romance with Kim Upsher, the former captain of the cheerleading squad at Central High who had then been dating Prince's friend Paul Mitchell. Upsher had an all-American kind of attractiveness – as Mitchell put it, "very cute with the sweetest smile and beautiful dimples."

Despite having a crush on Upsher throughout his years at Central, Prince had deferred to Mitchell. Now, with his friend no longer in the picture, he and Upsher became passionately involved.

Mitchell, who had moved away to Missouri to attend college on a football scholarship, had not kept abreast of Prince's activities since high school. He now received a phone call from Prince with several pieces of news. "I signed with Warner Brothers Records, and by the way, I'm also dating Kim," Prince told him. The call seemed like a gesture of respect towards Mitchell, as well as a means for Prince to demonstrate what he had accomplished.

It was indeed obvious to Mitchell how much had changed. During high school, Prince relied on friends and relatives for food and shelter, and had turned to Mitchell and Duane Nelson, his half-brother, for protection from students who otherwise would have bullied him. Mitchell had seen Prince humiliated by the football coach, outclassed at basketball by his taller friends, and turned down by potential girlfriends.

All of this seemed to have been turned on its head. Prince had a major label record deal, was dating the high school cheerleader, and even had a shot at stardom. Mitchell, who at Central High had seen Prince's competitive fires burn stronger as his frustrations accumulated, found himself not particularly surprised at how things were turning out.

"Yeah," Mitchell chuckled to Prince upon hearing that he was dating Kim Upsher. "I figured you would be."

10. No Girls Allowed

In April 1979, with his business affairs having been stabilized by the arrival of his new managers, Prince flew from Minneapolis to Los Angeles to start work on his second album. He was joined by Bobby Z. Rivkin, who continued to function as a combination of bandmate, friend, and logistical aide.

Following the tepid performance of the first album and the disastrous showcase concerts in Minneapolis, the pressure on Prince to improve upon *For You* was tremendous. But Warner Bros. officials, despite their concerns about his progress, nonetheless agreed to dispense with an executive producer for the second record. They had no worries about Prince's professionalism or technical abilities, and realized he was impervious to feedback from authority figures. Having ceded Prince an immense amount of control from the start, there could be no retreating from this approach.

Prince, while pleased that he would endure no meddling from a villain like Tommy Vicari, was nonetheless open to the views of a handful of band members and technical staff, including engineer David Z. Rivkin, with whom he had now been working for years. He had come to agree with Rivkin and others that *For You* suffered from overproduction, and was determined not to repeat that mistake. Prince thus planned to take a radically different approach to production; he would work quickly and efficiently, with far less attention to technical perfection.

The sessions took place at the little-known Alpha Studio, a humble facility in the home of engineer Gary Brandt, a friend of Bob Cavallo's. A far cry from the iconic Record Plant, it in fact was much more suited to Prince's needs and work style. Although the studio had a 24-track recording machine, Prince elected to use its 16-track board instead, which by nature restricted his ability to clutter the songs with overdubs. The sessions typically lasted at least 12 hours, with intrusions kept to a minimum. "No girls were allowed in the studio," Brandt recalled. "That was one of his requests."[1]

Andre Anderson also flew out from Minneapolis for the sessions and was allowed to contribute the occasional idea. Bobby Z., who did not perform, watched the album take shape day by day. He offered light feedback when asked, but above all knew how to be unobtrusive. "You don't get in the way of him recording," he recalled. "You can suggest things and do things, but if he's hearing it in his head, just get out of the way."

Prince approached the task of songwriting with renewed vigor, creating strong, simple melodies. Funk numbers like "I Wanna Be Your Lover" and "Sexy Dancer," were taut and infectious. Their lyrics, meanwhile, bristled with emotional and erotic energy. Going back to his days with Grand Central, Prince's intention had been to straddle the worlds of rock and R&B. That approach had been somewhat discarded with *For You*. Now, Prince felt confident enough to create an album that covered a fairly broad range of territory. He recorded two guitar-heavy rock songs, "Why You Wanna Treat Me So Bad?" and "Bambi," both of which improved greatly upon "I'm Yours," *For You*'s token rock number. There were also several ballads,

130

including "It's Gonna Be Lonely," which was enhanced rather than overwhelmed by its layers of vocal harmonies. Another ballad, "When We're Dancing Close and Slow," took its title from a lyrical passage in the Joni Mitchell song "Coyote" (from *Hejira*, 1976), hinting at the subtle but outsized influence her work had on Prince.

Indeed, since his childhood Prince had been an avid listener of this eclectic and inventive folk-rock artist. When Prince was about ten years old, he attended one of Joni's performances and sat in the front row. She noticed him perhaps because young African-Americans were relatively rare at her concerts – particularly in predominantly white cities like Minneapolis – but also because his strange, intense eyes remained locked on her throughout the show.

The standout track from the Alpha Studio sessions was clearly "I Wanna Be Your Lover," which featured strong hooks and a remarkably crisp sound, in part due to Gary Brandt's use of a customized AKG microphone for the snare drum. Prince loved Shure 57 microphones – a widely used but lower-end tool – and insisted, after learning what Brandt had done on "Lover," that the 57 be used for the remainder of the sessions. As a result, the snare sparkled less on other numbers, with the contrast between "Lover" and numbers like "Sexy Dancer" being clear. But aside from this questionable decision, Prince and Brandt created an album with a consistently bright and pristine sound.

After principal tracking was complete, scheduling issues at the studio prompted a move to Hollywood Sound Recorders in Los Angeles, where staff engineer Bob Mockler was assigned to work with Prince on overdubs. The album was completed by July, and Warners began preparing a publicity campaign.

The next task was to improve the strength and cohesiveness of Prince's live band so that Warners would authorize a tour in support of the second album. But rather than drill on the new material, he and the band flew to Boulder, Colorado and began work on a side project he dubbed "The Rebels." They settled into the Mountain Ears Studio in Boulder and began working on ideas that included substantial input from other band members, in particular Dickerson and Andre.

As with the Sueann Carwell project, Prince's goal – a lofty one for an artist with only one release under his belt – was to create an album that Warners would release and promote. Work continued over an eleven-day period, with the results ranging from Rolling Stones-style blues rock ("Hard 2 Get") to a more ambitious funk-rock hybrid sung by Andre ("Thrill You or Kill You").

Dickerson, for one, found himself doubting the material and wondering why the band wasn't rehearsing songs from *Prince*. "What are we doing? Where are we going with this?" the guitarist later recalled thinking. But there was some method to Prince's madness; the collaborative ethos built up the band's morale and improved its chemistry. By the end of the sessions, Prince himself had largely lost interest in the notion of the Rebels as a separate project, but his band was unquestionably stronger than when it had arrived in Boulder.

By the time of Prince's return to Minneapolis in late-July 1979, Warners' campaign in support of the second album, to be called *Prince*, was set to get underway. "I Wanna Be Your Lover" was selected as the first single, and it rose quickly up the Soul Singles Chart following its release in August 1979. Meanwhile, two new showcase concerts for label executives were arranged for the same month; this time, the band's assured performance impressed the executives. "After the first song, I could see that we had them," Dickerson recalled. "They left the place absolutely buzzing." Warners agreed to bankroll a tour, and Prince's career again became a priority for the label.

Prince hit the streets in October, and a short U.S. swing began in November 1979. Prince had changed his stage image radically in the course of less than a year; by the time the *Prince* tour began, he was wearing skin-tight spandex pants with no underwear beneath the pants, an outfit so form-fitting as to leave almost nothing to the imagination. Dickerson gleefully did the same. "We were trying to dress as outrageously and outlandishly as we could," the guitarist recalled.[2]

Bob Cavallo, whose personal tastes veered towards the conservative and who worried about a line being crossed into obscenity, hurried backstage after the opening show at the Roxy in Los Angeles to insist that Prince and Dickerson wear underwear going forward. When the manager left, Prince looked slyly at his guitarist. "Bob wants me to wear underwear? Okay, I'll wear underwear."[3]

At the next show, Cavallo was aghast to see Prince wearing nothing but a shirt and what could have passed for a pair of women's black panties. But what had begun as a practical joke on Cavallo became something more serious. A shirt and black underwear remained Prince's stage outfit for the rest of the tour, and became a perfect means to express his increasingly subversive sexual energies. And above all, he felt more comfortable wearing less clothing and showing off his body.

As the band played shows in Texas and Louisiana, "Lover" continued to speed up the charts, and would hit No. 1 on the Soul Charts in December. At a stop in Denver, the concert's promoters installed Prince and his team in a mobile trailer outside of the venue to serve as their dressing room. After the show, band members began to notice loud noises around the perimeter of the trailer. Peering out the windows, they saw that they were surrounded by fans who were clamoring for the band's attention. The throng grew and eventually began pushing the trailer, causing it to rock.[4]

Prince and the band started to panic, and their road manager somehow cleared a path outside and hustled them into a limousine. The vehicle pulled away, but many of the rabid fans piled into cars and gave pursuit.[5]

Worried about the danger of a high-speed chase, the road manager instead pulled in front of a hotel and told the band members to enter the lobby and pretend to be checking in. Meanwhile, he drove behind the hotel; the band members slipped out through the rear exit and piled back into the vehicle.

Many of the pursuing fans fell for the ruse, but several cars remained in pursuit. His patience fraying, the road manager stopped the limousine, exited, and jumped on the hood of a fan's Volkswagen that had stopped next to the limo. The Volkswagen driver started his car and drove off, flinging the road manager off the hood. The horrified band members rushed him to a local emergency room, where his injuries fortunately proved minor.

The crazy scene demonstrated that, at least in certain parts of the country, fame had arrived for Prince, although some of its elements had turned out to be as disconcerting as they were intoxicating. As Andre recalled, "That's when I realized, this is what the big time is all about."[6]

***

At other times being on the road was tedious, with long stretches of time on buses and short bursts of sleep at humble hotels. But Prince had thoroughly loosened up around his band members, and his pranks kept the atmosphere lively. "During those early days, we were just laughing all of the time," Dickerson remembered. In one recurring joke at airports, Prince would don a pair of dark sunglasses and then sit in a wheelchair with a blank look, appearing to be passed out. The band members then retreated into the background, making it seem that this odd figure had been abandoned. Prince slumped forward in his chair and even drooled, attracting shocked attention from passersby. At that point the band members re-emerged, trying to suppress their laughter as they pretended to come to his assistance.

The tour was unfortunately cut short when Prince suffered a real malady after a show on December 2, 1979 in New Orleans, coming down with a slight case of pneumonia. But following his recovery his management secured a prime opening slot with Kool & The Gang in San Mateo, California. Prince's band largely blew away the more veteran funk group, further increasing their confidence.

Prince's team also booked appearances on two prominent television shows, *Midnight Special* and *American Bandstand*. These would not be live performances as such; on both, the band would simply lip-sync to recorded versions of songs from *Prince*. The bandleader thus stayed focused on visual elements, using the appearances to begin fashioning a public image.

Making his television debut on January 8, 1980 on NBC's late-night rock and pop show, *Midnight Special*, Prince wore an ensemble of zebra-striped briefs and a coordinating zebra-print fringed top, with a cheetah-print guitar strap. He completed the outfit with heeled, thigh-high black suede boots and a single, large hoop earring in his right ear.

The group managed to generate a frisson of energy as they lip-synced to "I Wanna Be Your Lover." The imposingly tall Andre Cymone wielded his bass like a weapon; Matt Fink wore a jailbird suit; and Gayle Chapman had donned a red negligee. The interactions of the group members were loose and friendly, suggesting an almost democratic approach to performing, notwithstanding the bandleader's primacy. "Why You Wanna Treat Me So Bad?" was also performed, with the pre-recorded track giving the audience a sense of Prince's lead guitar chops.

During the next appearance two weeks later, on *American Bandstand*, Prince upped the ante by deliberately taunting the show's host, the revered veteran Dick Clark. In a setting where obsequiousness was the rule, Prince decided to opt instead for insolence. "He knew he wasn't going to suck up to Dick Clark and act like other idiots that go on that show," said one band member, recalling the meeting where Prince told them how to treat the host.

An unwitting Clark listened as Prince and band lip-synced to

"Lover." The host then moved into what he expected to be a formulaic interview before the second song. Instead, Prince remained mute, gazing contemptuously at Clark. Asked about his age, the 21-year-old Prince replied that he was 19. Clark, his nerves fraying, responded nonsensically, "Well, then you have another year to go before you graduate."

Next, when Clark asked how many instruments he played, Prince answered, "Thousands." He held up four fingers in response to a question about how long he had been a musician. Embarrassed and frustrated, Clark truncated the segment.

In the immediate aftermath, it was unclear whether the event had been a fiasco or a triumph. In the short term, Prince had alienated a powerful television host and surely made no friends in the entertainment industry. But he was also throwing down a marker, and declaring that the media establishment existed to serve his needs, not vice versa.

Just the same, the wisdom of this approach was far from clear at Warner Bros. "His early interviews were really awkward," said Bob Merlis, a former company publicist. "We thought maybe he just shouldn't do them – they were bizarre, risqué." In one interview, for example, Prince taunted a print reporter with questions about her pubic hair.

Prince, however, was not only comfortable with these methods, but saw a purpose in them that others did not. He wanted to shock, and felt that this was much more likely to make him famous than ingratiating himself with television hosts. Most appearances on *The Dick Clark Show* were forgotten almost as soon as they were over; Prince's would be discussed for weeks if not years. "Prince was saying, 'Dick Clark, you're gonna remember me,'" Bobby Z. observed. "And he did."

11. BATTLE I

Rick James on the *Fire it Up!* Tour

After Prince's first two television appearances, his managers seemed to have stumbled upon another perfect opportunity – an opening slot on a tour headlined by Rick James, a powerhouse in the R&B market. Prince's first solo tour, despite occasionally rabid audience responses like that experienced in Denver, had been spotty in terms of ticket sales. The presence of James atop the bill would solve that issue, and there would also be less pressure on Prince as a performer while his young band continued to come together.

For Rick James' management team, the presence of Prince – given in particular his growing popularity with young female fans – also offered a benefit. And the pairing offered an enticing opportunity to have two funk artists, one well-established and the other up-and-coming, to duel for fan attention. Promoters thus billed the concerts as "The Battle of Funk." And James and

Prince, both competitive spirits, were only too happy to play along.

Although James was only a decade older and had achieved fame fairly recently, Prince saw him as an ossified figure, a drug-addled buffoon whose funk stylings were derivative and whose image – which included almost comically long, heavily braided hair – was cartoonish. James, meanwhile, saw Prince as an effeminate, overhyped upstart.

James entered the fray with debits and advantages – he was a confident performer, but in many respects an artistic mediocrity. But Prince and his comrades would be tested by the tour as never before. Forty-two shows would occur over two grueling months, taking the bands on circuitous swings through the Midwestern and Southern United States, with occasional stops in Eastern cities. Gigs would often take place four or five nights in a row, each usually in a different city. Lip-syncing on television shows was one thing; performing night-after-night in these demanding circumstances was something else altogether. And the presence of Rick James nearly guaranteed that any number of unexpected and bizarre events would occur.

James, born James Ambrose Johnson, was 30 years old and already a hardened veteran of the music industry when his debut album, *Come and Get It!* appeared on April 20, 1978 – the same month that Prince's *For You* debuted. James was determined to at long last achieve fame and music industry fortune, which appeared to have occurred as two hit singles, "You and I" and "Mary Jane," skyrocketed up the charts.

Come and Get It! had ended up as a double-platinum smash, and its successor, *Bustin' Out of L Seven*, had gone platinum. By the time his third album, *Fire It Up!*, was released in autumn 1979, James was a potent commercial force.

Born in Buffalo, New York, James was raised as one of eight children by a single mother in a strict Catholic household. Music ran in the family: James' uncle was Melvin Franklin, bass vocalist of the Temptations, and James himself earnestly pursued a music career from an early age, first by singing on street corners.

James' teenage attempts to launch a musical career were ultimately thwarted at every turn, and from there his life careened wildly between unbelievable strokes of good fortune and extreme bad luck. First, his efforts to avoid being drafted into the Vietnam War prompted him to join the naval reserve. When this eventually appeared unlikely to keep him out of combat, he hightailed it out of his hometown of Buffalo to Toronto, Canada, becoming a refugee from the draft. There, James managed to connect with future musical luminaries including Joni Mitchell, who in turn introduced James to Neil Young.

Unlikely as it might seem, James entered a hippie phase, joining up with Young and other gifted musicians including Bruce Palmer to create a folk-blues band called the Mynah Birds. Given the immense level of talent in the Mynah Birds, it was unsurprising that the band landed a recording contract with Motown Records. Unfortunately, after the band was on the brink of releasing their first single, Motown discovered that James was a fugitive from the law and nullified the contract.

The military finally caught up to James, and he was arrested for desertion and thrown in the brig in the U.S. After serving a year, James moved to Los Angeles and continued with his musical career, along the way also variously acting as a pimp, running drugs, and writing for Motown.

Of all the stories that emerged from James' colorful run of legal and illegal activities in California, the most famous may have been his incredible good fortune on the night of August 9, 1969. James, after being invited to a party at the film director Roman Polanski's Beverly Hills home, got blasted the night before and ended up too hung over to attend. This enabled him to avoid the fate suffered by Polanski's wife Sharon Tate and four other guests, who were murdered at the party that night by disciples of the cult leader Charles Manson.[1]

By the time his tour with Prince rolled around, James had finally established himself as a major R&B artist on the strength of his first two solo albums. But with decades of hard living behind him, coupled with serious drug addiction issues, he could not have stood in starker contrast to the younger Prince. Unchastened by his brushes with the law and violence, James treated the road as a haven for excess and substance abuse. But Prince, as he had throughout his formative years, disdained drinking and drugs, viewing them as signs of indolence and artistic rot. Whereas Prince had recorded *For You* at the Record Plant in Sausalito under nearly monastic conditions, James created *Fire It Up!* at the same studio a year later while fueled by prodigious quantities of cocaine. The clash between the two artists was thus as much cultural as it was musical.

James expected to make short work of Prince in the competition between the two bands. He scoffed at Prince's androgynous image, which made him seem an unfit rival. What James was not aware of, however, was that Prince, as well as bassist Andre Cymone, had grown up amidst a daily battle of the bands on the Northside of Minneapolis, and reveled in the sort of combat that was about to unfold.

Prince's second album and James' *Fire It Up!* had been released within days of each other in October 1979. By the time Prince joined James' tour in January 1980, "I Wanna Be Your Lover" had been on the charts for several months and was slowly climbing; it would eventually reach number one on the Billboard R&B singles chart. The initial sales of *Fire It Up!*, meanwhile, were tepid.

Already feeling threatened, James lurched into erratic behavior from the tour's initial hours. At the first stop on February 22, 1980 at Fort Worth, Texas, he pointed what appeared to be a gun at Andre Cymone. It was in fact a stage prop that he used while performing his 1979 hit "Love Gun," but Andre nonetheless took James' "prank" as a dangerous and foolhardy transgression. Only with Prince's intervention was Andre dissuaded from a physical altercation with James. "Where I come from, if you pull a gun on somebody, then you better use it," Andre recalled later.[2]

In the coming nights, as the tour got into full swing, James settled down as he basked in the adulation of audiences that swelled to more than ten thousand on some stops. And it seemed he had little to worry about in terms of competition from Prince. Despite the strong chart performance of "Lover," audiences were reacting poorly to the opening act; most had come primarily to see James, and some were repulsed by the visual elements of Prince's act, which evoked homosexuality, transvestism, and a blurring of racial boundaries. That some of the tour's stops were deep in America's Bible Belt aggravated such reactions, and racist and anti-gay epithets were frequently hurled during Prince's first several songs. Seemingly oblivious to the innate moral conservatism of the landscape he was traversing, Prince often played in the nude other than the now-standard pair of black underwear.

Only after a number of dates did this dynamic began to shift. Gradually, by mid-set on many evenings, the band watched with surprise as catcalls turned into cheers.[3] The audiences above all wanted to party, and the energy of Prince's band was ebullient and infectious. And although Prince appeared effeminate on the surface, audiences quickly detected that his manic energy was in fact aggressively masculine. With his James Brown-inspired stage moves, assured falsetto vocals, and wailing guitar solos, the sheer diversity of his musical talents proved impossible to ignore.

Prince's compact set list, which never changed for the entire tour, included "Soft and Wet," "Why You Wanna Treat Me So Bad," "Still Waiting," "I Feel For You," "Sexy Dancer," "Just As Long As We're Together," and "I Wanna Be Your Lover." The rock and funk numbers blended perfectly, and James' sets seemed lumbering and bloated by comparison.

Prince's antipathy for his rival increased after James began making unwanted advances towards keyboardist Gayle Chapman. Prince's response to this threat, oddly, was to insist that Chapman's stage attire – which to date had consisted of a silk Olga brand nightgown – become even sexier. Chapman received a knock on her door late at night after a show in Jacksonville, Florida, and one of Prince's girlfriends handed over a bag of lingerie. "Prince says wear this or you're fired," the young woman said bluntly.[4]

After inspecting the items – which included a bra with cups that were several sizes larger than her petite breasts – an incredulous Chapman told the emissary to tell Prince that she would go shopping the next day, and that he could wait at least that long before firing her. Chapman visited a lingerie shop the next morning and selected a black corset. The entire exercise served in part as a way to further tweak James – not only could he not have Chapman, but she was becoming more sexually desirable by the day.

As the tour wore on, James and his entourage, lost in a haze of drugs and alcohol backstage, were largely oblivious to growing audience enthusiasm during Prince's opening sets. Prince, by contrast, watched James's performances from the side of the stage each night, pondering how to further upstage him.

One of James' set pieces was the song "Bustin' Out (On Funk)." As the band slogged through an instrumental introduction, James emerged from backstage wearing a striped jail suit, which he ripped off during the song's climax. While unimpressed with the gag itself, Prince was troubled by the similarity between James' outfit and the costume worn each night by his keyboardist, Matt Fink. The jailbird motif had been Fink's creation, and he expressed disappointment when Prince asked him to select another costume. Fink pointed out that James wore the jail suit for not even half of a single song – why did this justify a wholesale costume change?[5] Unmoved, the bandleader told Fink to chose a different persona.

Fink had previously considered a doctor's outfit complete with scrubs, and Prince quickly voiced his support for the idea. A wardrobe person was dispatched to a uniform shop and purchased a doctor's scrub suit and accoutrements such as a surgical mask and stethoscope.

Prince then directed Fink – henceforth to be known as "Dr. Fink" – to don not only the surgical mask but also a large pair of sunglasses, meaning that his entire face would be concealed. When Fink objected, Prince retorted that he should welcome the idea, which Prince insisted would give the keyboardist an air of mystery and intrigue.

After some grumbling, Fink agreed to don what had become an elaborate and cumbersome costume, more suited to the surgical suite than the stage. During sets he found himself sweating into the mask, which in turn caused his sunglasses to steam up. Unable to clearly see his keyboard and struggling even to breathe normally, Fink after several nights appealed to Prince for permission to at least discard the mask. Prince pondered the request for a moment, and then agreed to a point – Fink could remove the mask after one or two songs.[6]

Meanwhile, Prince concocted crueler forms of punishment for Rick James. After weeks of analyzing his rival's stage moves, Prince began to mimic them during his sets, right down to certain of James' hand gestures. He also began to lead the audience through some of the same chants that James used to engage his fans.

The goal was not to emulate but to embarrass, and the gambit was successful. Just as Prince had hoped, when James took the stage for his headlining slot, audiences assumed that he was imitating Prince, rather than vice versa. Simply by virtue of going on second, James looked foolish as he led the audiences through the same routines Prince had used an hour earlier.

Meanwhile, *Prince* continued to perform strongly on the charts, with *Fire It Up!* proving a commercial and critical disappointment relative to James' first two albums. Crowd reactions were also becoming more boisterous for Prince by the night, prompting his young band to play with even greater ferocity. "Sometimes I actually felt bad for Rick that he had to go on after us," Dickerson recalled.

By the time the tour reached his hometown of Buffalo, New York on April 2, 1980, it was clear to James that the tour had been for him a disaster. This night in particular was supposed to have been a triumphant homecoming, and James' mother and Buffalo's mayor were in attendance. But when James led the dignitaries to his dressing room, another humiliation ensued. A rendering of James had been drawn on a chalkboard in the room, complete with lengthy braids. Cologne had been sprayed on the image, and "Rick James" had been drawn in block letters at the bottom.[7]

The culprit was Andre Cymone, who later claimed that his intent had only been to draw a caricature of a television character called "Howdy Doody" on the board. Whether the braids and cologne had been added by a roadie – as Andre would later assert – or by the bassist himself, the result was the same: the embarrassment of James at the hands of an upstart band from Minneapolis, one led by a small, skinny man in a pair of black underwear, was now complete.

***

Between concerts, there were brief respites for sleep at roadside hotels, and seemingly little time for reflection. But Prince, who typically needed only several hours of sleep to refresh himself, used these quiet times to ponder his next steps and compose new songs on his guitar.

He had impressively bested James, but this meant little in the great scheme of things. He and James were fighting for a small slice of the overall pop music market; as he had insisted to

Warner Bros. from the beginning, Prince wanted to reach a larger and more diverse audience. And he wanted to greatly expand his artistic scope.

Prince began to explore material that was far removed from the R&B conventions that had characterized *For You* and, to a lesser extent, *Prince*. Various subcultures were percolating underneath the surface of popular music, and Prince was taking their measure. He had learned of developments in punk and New Wave through long conversations with Matt Fink and Dez Dickerson, both of whom were sophisticated consumers of musical trends. And he now began to incorporate these influences.

After a North Carolina concert, Prince composed a new song, "When You Were Mine," whose central guitar riff straddled pop and punk, evoking both the Beatles and New Wave artists like Elvis Costello. Lyrically, it described an unfaithful lover who failed even to change her dirty bed sheets before a sexual encounter with Prince.

As the tour arrived in Florida, Prince's bandmates elected to visit DisneyWorld during a rare day off before the next show. Fink, finding Prince strumming on a guitar on the balcony of his hotel room, invited him on the outing. Prince demurred but affably encouraged the keyboardist and the rest of the group to enjoy the time off. Fink paused for a moment to listen to the song Prince was playing; he would later learn that it had been "When You Were Mine."

Back in California, Prince's supporters at Warner Bros. felt a renewed confidence in his career. After the strong performance of *Prince* and the unqualified success of the tour, it appeared that their instincts in signing Prince – and their patience with his growing pains – had been vindicated, and that they had successfully identified a rising R&B star.

Had they been on the hotel balcony with him that afternoon, they might have realized that they also had on their hands a visionary.

12. ROUGH MIX

As he returned to Minnesota in late spring 1980 and prepared
to embark on his third album, Prince's greatest challenge
remained breaking out of a music industry paradigm that grouped
black and white artists into separate categories. For all of his pleas
to Warner Bros. that he not be constrained by this construct –
and for all of the company's promises that he would not – the
practical realities were far more complicated. The assurances
made by Mo Ostin and Lenny Waronker had not been insincere,
but Warners continued to operate under practices that had
calcified over generations, owing to failures of imagination, unfair
stereotyping, and sometimes outright racism. As a result, the task
of marketing a young African-American funk artist to a broad,
predominantly white audience was one for which no ready
template existed.

And there were other concerns. When Prince and his band
were travelling across America with Rick James, both his second
album and the single "I Wanna Be Your Lover" had enjoyed
chart success. But his impact had been limited to the R&B
market, and he had not necessarily built a loyal following. And
although *Prince* was a creative improvement over his first album,
it broke little stylistic ground. Continuing down these same paths
would not achieve Prince's much grander design.

Prince was now living in a rented home on Lake Minnetonka
in the community of Wayzata, Minnesota, where a 16-track studio
had been installed. He began developing rough drafts of songs to
be re-recorded later in a professional facility. The home studio
was a jury-rigged affair, with the drum booth frequently
becoming waterlogged as a result of seepage from an
abandoned cesspool near the house. The isolated setting
minimized distractions; most of the time, the only other person
present was an affable, unobtrusive engineer named Don Batts.

As he worked, Prince continued his analysis of new musical trends. "He had stacks and stacks of records in his house that he got free from Warner Bros.," recalled Matt Fink. "He was listening to just about everything." Prince quickly came to see that the edginess and minimalism of punk were creeping toward the mainstream. Bands like the Cars and Devo were incorporating elements of electronica, until recently a largely underground phenomenon.

His study of such developments was somewhat superficial – he was not inclined to immerse himself in any particular artist's work – but he rapidly absorbed ideas that intrigued him. On *Prince*, he had some success jumping from R&B to rock. Now, he began creating a genuine synthesis of styles, combining elements of rock, funk, punk, and New Wave.

The limited complement of equipment at the home studio left fewer instrumental choices – there was no room for a piano, for example – and he composed primarily on guitar. The new songs were rawer and more visceral than anything on his first two albums, and the galvanic sexual energy that he had discovered on tour also informed the new material. All told – and in part due to the production values of the home studio – Prince's new demos would not have sounded out of place on the college radio stations that were starting to play an outsized role in breaking new artists across the United States.

Despite his solitude during most of the sessions, Prince did collaborate actively with Matt Fink on the electronica-tinged "Dirty Mind," which emerged from a keyboard riff developed by Fink at a rehearsal. Prince added a bridge section during a lengthy session with Fink at the Lake Minnetonka home, and by midnight they had completed the instrumentation.

Prince then told Fink he was free to go, and the keyboardist went home to bed. Prince worked on the song throughout the night, arriving the next day at rehearsal with a rough mix, complete with vocals and other overdubs. He announced to the band that it would be the title track of the next album.

The lyrics of "Dirty Mind," which recount a carnal encounter in a car, reflected Prince's growing fascination with erotic themes. Whereas he had frequently sung of romantic heartbreak on his first two albums, this theme now became inverted; instead of being dumped, as on "Why You Wanna Treat Me So Bad?," he reemerged as a sexual aggressor for whom emotional intimacy was at best an afterthought. And the subject matter entered the realm of the perverse; the hard-rocking "Sister," for example, explored the taboo of incest. "Head," meanwhile, described Prince's encounter with a bride on the way to her wedding, one which ends with him ejaculating on her wedding gown.

Musically, the tracks covered a wide range of territory. "Sister," with its short duration and dissonant chords, was openly punkish. "Head" included New Wave elements but at root was a funk workout anchored by a taut bass-and-synthesizer motif. "When You Were Mine," the song he had composed in a North Carolina hotel room on tour, combined a strong melody and elements of surf-pop.

The immediacy of the songs was enhanced by the engineering techniques of Prince and Batts, which utilized negligible reverb on the drums and little distortion on guitars. Prince eschewed guitar soloing, and the most flamboyant instrumental flourish on any of the new numbers was provided by Matt Fink during a lengthy, frenetic synth solo on "Head" that sought to simulate a male orgasm.

In addition to his explorations of sexuality, Prince became more conversant in political and social issues, and these topics also found expression in his new songs. In the summer of 1980, the United States was experiencing political ferment, with Ronald Reagan – perceived by many as a reactionary and dangerous militarist – having seized the Republican presidential nomination. Protests against racism and nuclear proliferation were becoming widespread. Reacting in some measure to these developments, Prince recorded "Uptown," which depicted a utopian environment where members of different races were united by music and a shared ethos. (The song's title also referenced a hip Minneapolis neighborhood where he frequently visited, an indication of the continuing emotional importance of his hometown.) And Prince started to see himself as leader of such a community, someone who could unite disparate groups through his music.

Between sessions, Prince socialized with his band members, carrying forward the camaraderie that had emerged during the tour. One important change occurred, however: Gayle Chapman announced she was quitting. Her primary grievance was a lack of control; Prince's dictatorial tendencies, which included his directives concerning her clothing, irritated Chapman. This departure robbed the band of its only woman, a blow to Prince's desire for an inclusive ensemble.

He saw the remaining band members nearly every day at rehearsals. Prince, Matt Fink, and Andre Cymone also spent free time exercising together, lifting weights at Minneapolis gyms, swimming at a YMCA, and roller-skating around Lake Calhoun or Lake Harriet in the heart of Minneapolis. They sometimes visited a roller rink in the inner-ring suburb of St. Louis Park, Fink remembered, "to try to meet girls."

In such social settings, Prince was generally relaxed and unassuming. In fact, the group's playful interactions were not unlike those in his high school band Grand Central. Clowning around with band members, Prince enjoyed adopting various personas he had invented; one of his favorites was a bawdy, Richard Pryor-like character that reminded Fink of a stereotypical street-corner hustler. "When Prince was growing up in North Minneapolis, there was a lot of pimping, drug dealing, and underworldly stuff going on, and that's where this character emerged from," Matt Fink observed. "He had a fantasy of being someone outside the law."

But it was indeed a mere fantasy, and Prince never associated with the lowbrow types he caricatured; instead, he consciously chose as his associates people such as Fink, Bobby Z., and Dez Dickerson, who were ethical, low-key, and even a bit square. And the sensationalistic events of his new material were largely invented. The notorious "Sister," while inspired in part by his older half-sister Sharon Nelson, was an extremely backhanded homage to her sophisticated beauty as opposed to any real depiction of incest.

Prince's most complicated relationship in the band was with Andre Cymone, his former teenage roommate. Believing himself to be no less talented than Prince, the bassist carried the resentment of having to play a subordinate role to a close friend. This tension increased when Fink was singled out to contribute in the studio; Andre, despite his best efforts to remain cool, became increasingly jealous. "They shared the same bedroom, and then Prince starts becoming this big, huge star," noted Owen Husney, Prince's former manager. "That's got to affect you one way or the other."

Prince also perceived his friend on some level as a threat, which prompted him to hinder Andre's progress through various manipulations. When Andre expressed interest in setting up his own studio to work on songs, Prince insisted that this was unnecessary and that the bassist could use his equipment whenever he wished. This seemingly generous gesture, however, allowed Prince to keep physical custody of Andre's music. On one occasion, Andre came looking for demos, only to be told by Prince that he had "accidentally" erased a tape.

Ultimately, Prince seemed to believe that if Andre were also to succeed, this would somehow be to his detriment.

   ***

Another old neighborhood pal, former Grand Central drummer Morris Day, made his way back into Prince's orbit during the summer of 1980, albeit in an unglamorous capacity; he became a "runner" for Prince's band, picking up sandwiches and drinks during rehearsals.

During high school, Day's drum skills and knack for self-promotion secured him a place in Grand Central at the expense of Prince's cousin Chazz Smith. His mother, LaVonne Daugherty, had for a time been the band's manager. But following Prince's signing to Warner Bros., Day – like neighborhood friends other than Andre – found himself on the outside looking in.

Now, a potential change in fortunes arrived for Day. Prince, while attending a gig by Day's band Enterprise, had been enthralled by a saucy funk groove that Day had written. Deciding he wanted to use the riff, Prince offered Day financial compensation in the sum of $10,000. As an alternative, he offered to build a side project around Day at a later date. Day, preferring career advancement over modest financial gain, chose the latter option.

Prince adapted the drummer's riff by speeding up the tempo and then adding words. The song became "Partyup," Prince's most openly political work to date; its lyrics were inspired by opposition to draft registration in the United States, which was re-instituted over the summer of 1980 by President Jimmy Carter.

Prince also took steps to replace Gayle Chapman, and became impressed by a demo tape submitted by a 19-year-old, L.A.-based pianist named Lisa Coleman. Coleman had an ethereal, classical-influenced style that was far removed from that of either Chapman or Matt Fink, offering the possibility for a new dimension in the band's live sound.

Prince personally greeted Coleman at the airport when she arrived in Minneapolis, and their personal chemistry was immediate. This extended to their jamming together, resulting in a quick invitation for Lisa to join the band and move to

Minneapolis.

Lisa started out by living in Prince's spare bedroom. Their relationship remained platonic, and Lisa was in fact involved with a young woman named Wendy Melvoin, herself a guitarist, who remained in Los Angeles. Nonetheless, Prince took it upon himself to record a song called "Lisa" that described his new keyboardist as sexually kinky and offering to take her out "to get blasted." Not unlike "Sister," the song was a roundabout way of showing affection, albeit in this case with intimations of actual jealousy.

Work continued at the home studio, and Prince eventually accumulated about 10 songs. With demoing now complete, he had a realization: the songs had been enhanced, rather than hindered, by the imperfections of the home studio. Re-recording them in a professional facility would merely dilute their impact.

Prince selected the eight songs he felt were strongest and brought them to Warner Bros., declaring the material ready for release. The response throughout the company was shock and consternation. "He turned the record company into disarray," recalled Warners official Marylou Badeaux. "The promotions people would call me and say, 'I can't take this to radio! Is he crazy?'"

The concerns were many. The graphic lyrics threatened to hinder radio airplay, as did the unpolished sound. Other than "When You Were Mine," nothing suggested itself as a potential single.

Adding to the furor, Prince showed up for meetings at the company wearing the same bikini briefs and fishnet stockings that he wore onstage. One Warners staffer, encountering Prince in a hallway, berated him for the salacious lyrics he had been writing. Prince, undaunted, shot the staffer a withering look and stalked away.

It was clear that he would not be cowed by opposition to the album. But the fact remained that with only two albums under his belt, and still only 20 years old, Prince was courting conflict with his record label, with potentially perilous results. He was under contract with Warners for three albums only, meaning that if *Dirty Mind* tanked, his very career could be jeopardized. Warners had the right to reject an album it deemed insufficient, and he had seemingly given the company ample grounds to do just that.

Prince also continued to be a costly artist for Warners to maintain and promote. His large band created significant overhead, and he had squandered time and resources on two side projects – Sueann Carwell and the Rebels – that had been scrapped. Now, he was proving to be a mercurial and challenging partner, one with little regard for the norms of the music industry.

How Prince's broadside to the label was received – and whether his demands were accepted or rejected – had the potential to end his promising career almost as quickly as it had begun.

13. RAGGED EDGES

The task of overcoming Warner Bros.' opposition to *Dirty Mind*, as well as ensuring that Prince's career did not essentially spiral out of control, fell to managers Steve Fargnoli and Bob Cavallo. Fargnoli, who was named the third partner in Cavallo, Ruffalo & Fargnoli in recognition of his expanding role, continued to forge a personal bond with Prince. "Steve was one of a tiny handful of people that Prince really trusted," said Marylou Badeaux. "He had a sixth sense of what would work and what wouldn't."

Fargnoli immersed himself in virtually every detail of Prince's life, striving to match his client's energy and drive. But while he was more visible, behind the scenes it was senior partner Bob Cavallo who made many key strategic decisions and levelled out Fargnoli's occasional impulsiveness. As Howard Bloom, soon to become Prince's publicity agent, put it, "Cavallo was the mastermind – he was the general and Fargnoli was the troops."

Along with the complementary traits they brought to bear, both Cavallo and Fargnoli remained committed to overcoming Warners' concerns about *Dirty Mind*. After the initial shock had worn off at the company, Cavallo and Fargnoli presented arguments for the album that were cogent and forceful. *Dirty Mind*, they contended, would allow both Prince and Warners to capitalize on profound and rapid changes that were occurring within the music industry, examples of which abounded. The punk group the Clash had recently released a landmark album, *London Calling*, that had broken through to a broader audience. New Wave groups like The Knack and Blondie were scoring hits with lean, provocative songs that were a far cry from the sugary pop and bloated hard rock of the previous decade. *Dirty Mind* certainly fit within this paradigm.

Gradually, executives Mo Ostin and Lenny Waronker lined up behind the project. Russ Thyret, who had played an instrumental role in signing Prince, in turn exhorted the company's rank-and-file publicists and promoters, many of whom remained unconvinced. "Russ Thyret was a huge piece of the puzzle, and always saw Prince as an act for all formats," noted a Warners source.

Still, *Dirty Mind* would be one of the most sexually explicit albums released by a major label since the Rolling Stones' 1972 release *Exile on Main Street*, and pervasive doubts remained as to how the record would be received. The decision to release the album was ultimately a leap of faith; that the company made this leap owed much to the efforts of Cavallo and Fargnoli, but ultimately resulted from the iron will of the man who had created it.

***

Dirty Mind hit stores in October 1980. The black-and-white cover showed Prince in black bikini underwear, a trench coat, and a handkerchief around his neck. The "Rude Boy" pin on his coat had its origins in a punk-related style, England's "two-tone" ska movement, and *Rude Boy* was also the title of a 1980 film featuring the

Clash. The cover, like the music itself, was a declaration of rebellion by this young artist.

But just as some at Warner Bros. had feared, the album failed to carry forward the commercial momentum of Prince's second album. Many radio programmers were deterred by the lyrics and by stickers Warners placed on promo copies urging stations to "please audition before airing," resulting in minimal radio play. The first two singles, "Uptown" and "Dirty Mind," enjoyed some success on the Soul Singles Chart but failed to dent the Pop Singles Chart, and the album itself reached only No. 45 on the Pop Chart. The rock audience hadn't materialized, and, not surprisingly, some of the fans who had purchased his second album had defected. Prince's hybrid of R&B, New Wave, punk, funk, and rock was perhaps too far ahead of its time, and apparently more than a mainstream audience could digest.

Not willing to abandon the project prematurely, Warners decided to bankroll a U.S. tour of mid-sized clubs with Prince as the headliner. The band holed up in Minneapolis during the autumn of 1980, rehearsing intensely on the new material. Meanwhile, back in Los Angeles, his managers huddled to find a solution to the riddle of his career.

Cavallo and Fargnoli decided the support of the rock press was essential; they needed to convince the media, and through them the public, that Prince was not just a multi-talented curiosity, but a revolutionary figure, both musically and culturally. To execute this heady concept, Cavallo hit on the idea of hiring as a publicist the intriguing figure of Howard Bloom. A chatty man with an appearance and manner not far removed from that of the actor and comedian Woody Allen, Bloom was unique among his peers, an amateur scholar focusing on mass psychology and how music impacts social behavior. In working with artists, Bloom sought to identify what he called their "passion points," the unconscious psychological forces that, when unlocked, resulted in spontaneous and authentic creation.

Cavallo viewed Bloom's idiosyncrasies as perfectly matched for those of Prince. Another fortuitous element was Bloom's zeal for eliminating the music industry's artificial divide between black and white artists, one he deemed a form of apartheid. "The R&B chart was its own ghetto," Bloom recalled. "In the 1970s, it was incredibly unhip for any white person to work with any black artist. There was a wall, and it was segregation to the nth degree."

When Bloom received Cavallo's call, he was already familiar with Prince and had been impressed with his second album and its chart success. As a condition of his involvement, Bloom laid out several requirements. He wanted a month to study everything Prince had ever said and recorded, and then he needed at a minimum a full day alone with the artist. The goal was to burrow as far into Prince's psyche as possible and then translate his discoveries to the media.

Cavallo agreed, and several days before the *Dirty Mind* tour began, Bloom met with Prince after a rehearsal at the Shea Theater in Buffalo, New York, Bloom's hometown. But Bloom had by now become apprehensive about the assignment; word from various sources indicated that his new client was a withdrawn, arrogant figure who would never open up emotionally.

None of this proved to be true. During a session that lasted from 2 a.m. until 9 a.m., Prince free-associated about his tumultuous childhood, a formative visit at age five to see his father at a nightclub, teenage shenanigans in the Anderson basement, and more. Prince's passion points, not surprisingly, turned out to be a lust for fame, a conflicted relationship with both parents, and a voracious sexual appetite.

Bloom left the long session exhausted but fueled with excitement. Prince had a significant backstory that could be used to craft an intriguing and compelling public persona. He also had a quiet but unmistakable charisma that could translate well during interviews with sympathetic journalists.

As Bloom retreated to begin planning a media campaign, the *Dirty Mind* tour got under way. To help generate fan interest, Prince's managers wanted a strong opening act; a perfect opportunity arose when the R&B singer Teena Marie was dropped from Rick James' current tour in a cost-saving measure after weak grosses. Adding to the indignities James had earlier suffered at Prince's hands, she shifted over to the *Dirty Mind* bill.[1] Meanwhile, production and lighting designer Roy Bennett was hired to create Prince's stage show. "For an artist on their first tour, it was quite a big production for the time," noted Bennett, whose set design placed drummer Bobby Z. Rivkin and the two keyboardists, Matt Fink and Lisa Coleman, on risers behind Prince.

But despite the hours of planning and rehearsal that went into the tour, the poor performance of *Dirty Mind* proved to be a hindrance, one that Teena Marie's presence on the bill seemingly could not surmount. Pre-sales for the concerts were sluggish, leaving Warners potentially exposed to a major financial setback.

After kicking off in Buffalo on Dec. 4, 1980, the tour proceeded to Washington, D.C. and Raleigh, N.C., before reaching Manhattan's trendy East Village nightclub, the Ritz, on December 9, 1980. Opened by music impresario Jerry Brandt only nine months earlier, the Ritz was housed within New York City's historic Webster Hall, with a mission of showcasing new rock artists. Among these were the Irish rockers U2, who made their U.S. debut at the Ritz only three nights before Prince's scheduled performance.

The Ritz gig also brought into Prince's orbit Scotland-born Brenda Siobhan, an aspiring singer and the soon-to-be wife of set designer Roy Bennett. Brenda remained at home planning the couple's wedding while Roy was on tour and had not expected to see her fiancé for some time. But as the tour approached New York, Roy had premonitions about the upcoming gig. "I've got a feeling he's going to be really big," Roy told Brenda and urged her to attend the show.[2]

On the morning of December 9, 1980, Brenda and Roy left their hotel for the sound check at the Ritz. The mood abruptly changed when the couple learned that former Beatle John Lennon had been murdered the previous night outside his New York apartment building. Suddenly, a pall was cast on the event and the entire city.

By showtime the room was only about half-full, with Lennon's death seemingly having depressed turnout. But a number of New York cultural luminaries were in attendance, including Andy Warhol, funk producer Nile Rodgers, and singer Nona Hendryx. While *Dirty Mind* had yet to take hold among the general public, tastemakers and hipsters were clearly paying attention.

When Prince took the stage at about midnight, the crowd reacted boisterously to a show that took the album's explicit themes to a new level. The centerpiece was "Head," in which Prince simulated masturbation with his guitar during a lengthy instrumental break. Such performance art, while unlikely to play well in middle America, appealed perfectly to the assemblage at the Ritz.

For Brenda, her fiancé's prescience concerning the importance of the gig had been confirmed. "The whole vibe of that room was amazing," she recalled. "That was the point where we thought, this is happening."

But the sense of momentum dissipated as the tour departed Manhattan and reached into southern towns like Charleston, Chattanooga, and Baton Rouge, where crowds remained small. Warners cut the southern swing short, a demoralizing setback for Prince and the band.

Back in Minneapolis during a two-month break before the tour resumed, Prince himself began grappling with doubts. Had the Warners officials who had questioned the album's prospects been correct after all? For another perspective, Prince turned to the level-headed Dez Dickerson. The guitarist, while at root a loyal soldier, was never hesitant to give Prince unvarnished advice when asked.

Over dinner at an Indian restaurant, Prince candidly conveyed the concerns that were being voiced by Warners. In part to be reassuring, but also because he genuinely believed in the direction of *Dirty Mind*, the guitarist urged Prince not to worry. "I really thought we were onto something that hadn't been done before," Dickerson recalled.

Rehearsals resumed, with the tour scheduled to continue in March. Behind the scenes, Prince also began composing new music. Among the pieces he worked on was a dramatic ballad called "Do Me, Baby," a song with a fraught history. Former Grand Central percussionist Terry Jackson had first learned about the song years earlier when he saw its lyrics, written in Andre Cymone's handwriting, on a paper bag in Andre's bedroom. It had also been recorded by Prince and Andre in demo form in 1979 with Andre on lead vocals. In Jackson's mind, there was little question that Andre was the sole writer.

Now, without notice to Andre or anyone else, Prince began to plan the song as a focal point of his fourth album. Meanwhile, Andre was already chafing about Prince's failure to credit his contributions, such as those he had made to "Uptown." "The bass line of that song is based on something Andre came up with in a jam that we did at rehearsal," Dickerson recalled.[3]

When Andre arrived late to rehearsal one afternoon, he was stunned to hear the band playing a fully formed version of "Do Me, Baby." Prince had seized the song as his own, clearly with no intent of sharing credit, let alone acknowledging Andre as the exclusive writer.

"Why are you doing this, man?" Andre asked his friend in an anguished voice when the band stopped playing.

"Because I'm a star and you're not," Prince curtly responded, and turned away.[4]

For Andre, the incident was the breaking point, and the culmination of resentments that had been building for years. Not long thereafter, he told Prince that he was leaving to pursue a solo career. For other band members, the decision was unsurprising. "Andre was just not good at playing second fiddle, and would only take direction for so long," Bobby Z. observed. "He always saw himself as big as Prince someday."

The time for a major personnel change, however, could not have been worse. The second leg of the tour was being planned, and a short European swing was also in the works. And Cavallo and Fargnoli had achieved a booking on *Saturday Night Live*, a prestigious opportunity to raise the band's profile.

Hoping to delay Andre's departure, Prince appealed to Bernadette Anderson, insisting that Andre's abrupt departure would be potentially ruinous to his career. Anxious to avoid a rupture between her son and someone she still viewed as a kind of surrogate son, Bernadette urged Andre to postpone his exit. Andre relented, but he asked Prince to at least increase his anemic weekly salary for the remaining gigs. But even this request engendered opposition from the bandleader, prompting Andre to throw up his hands at his friend's intransigence. "I told him, 'You know what, I'll do it for free,'" he recalled.[5]

Prince had in fact for many months been evaluating potential replacements for Andre, conscious that the bassist's disgruntlement could prompt him to quit at any time. One of the musicians he scouted was 19-year-old Mark Brown, a member of the local band Fantasy. The band regularly performed at the club 7th Street Entry in downtown Minneapolis, and Prince attended their shows from time to time, creating a stir at the venue when he arrived.

Brown, a graduate of Washburn High School in the southwest part of the city, had been playing bass in one form or another since childhood; by the time he entered high school, he intended to pursue a career in music. To help make ends meet, he worked at the Town Crier Restaurant in Minneapolis, where he became friends with waitress Kim Upsher, Prince's sometime-girlfriend and high school classmate.

Brown was also friends with two other former schoolmates of Prince's, Terry Lewis and Jimmy Harris, who in recent months had coyly told him that his talent was being scouted by someone important. "They told me, 'Keep it up, someone's watching you,'" Brown recalled.[6]

After Prince invited him to a tryout, it became clear who the mystery suitor was. A few days later, Brown encountered Lewis and Harris and received their hearty congratulations about his new job. "They knew it before I did," Brown recalled. Brown then retreated to learn Prince's songbook, while the existing line-up prepared for the *Saturday Night Live* appearance and the continuation of the tour.

Howard Bloom, meanwhile, despite his successful meeting with Prince in Buffalo, felt the clock ticking as *Dirty Mind* and the tour faltered. The solution to these problems, Bloom felt, was to use Prince's tumultuous life story to attract the interest of influential journalists. Moreover, Prince's subversive, rebellious attributes needed to be highlighted.

Saturday Night Live offered a perfect forum for what Bloom hoped to achieve; it had a national audience, and was watched avidly by East and West Coast influencers who could spread the word about a new phenomenon. And as an ideal counterpoint to that appearance, Bloom landed Prince an interview with *Rolling Stone* magazine, the country's arbiter of cultural influence at the time. The article, entitled "Will the Little Girls Understand?", hit the streets just two days before the scheduled *SNL* appearance. As Bloom had hoped, the article portrayed Prince in a mysterious and intriguing light, and it was accompanied by a glowing, 4.5-out-of-5 star review of *Dirty Mind*. The review's content was tailor-made to Bloom's grand strategy, presenting Prince as a rebel. "At its best, *Dirty Mind* is absolutely filthy," wrote critic Ken Tucker. "Prince's sly wit – intentionally coarse – amounts to nothing less than an early, prescient call to arms against the elitist puritanism of the Reagan era." And indeed, the environment in the United States suddenly seemed perfect for *Dirty Mind*; the election of Ronald Reagan in November 1980 had left many people ready to embrace the very sort of anti-establishment figure that Prince now seemed to be.

The *SNL* performance and *Rolling Stone* article created a powerful one-two punch of publicity. On *SNL*, Prince and the band played a raw version of "Partyup," ending with the bandleader slamming his microphone to the floor for emphasis. In the coming weeks, the *Rolling Stone* article produced a domino effect of other publications wanting to interview Prince, including alternative magazines such as *New Musical Express* and *New York Rocker*.

The tour resumed on March 9, 1981 before a hometown Minneapolis crowd at First Avenue. From there, riding the Bloom-generated wave of positive publicity, ticket and album sales for the *Dirty Mind* tour improved. Prince's management focused on urban centers, seeking to consolidate an audience of artists, intellectuals, rebels, and students. Shows at clubs in Boston and Chicago sold out, and the tour returned to the Ritz in Manhattan on March 22, a show again attended by luminaries, including Mick Jagger.

With the mood around the tour now much lighter, Prince began a flirtatious friendship with Jill Jones, a back-up singer for opening act Teena Marie. Jones, 17, was no stranger to the music industry, having started with Marie at age 15, and was the daughter of a fashion model and a jazz drummer. Among the famous musicians she had known growing up was family friend Rick James, a frequent guest at Jones family barbecues. Despite her age, Jones was self-aware and underawed by fame, and her interactions with Prince had a saucy edge. This dynamic, as well as her hard-to-get approach, further piqued his interest. Jones was in turn mesmerized by Prince's musical talent. "Prince's shows were electric," she recalled. "People just went crazy."[7] Jones also became friends with Andre; Prince, to discourage him from making any advances, falsely told him that Jones was married.[8]

But even as the tour's fortunes improved, another dynamic began shifting within the band. During the hiatus, Dez Dickerson had experienced a life-changing epiphany in his living room in North St. Paul, becoming a born-again Christian as a result. While this did not radically change Dickerson's personality – he remained self-effacing and low-key – it increased concerns he had already been harboring over Prince's increasingly explicit lyrics.

Dickerson did not raise his misgivings with Prince, but shared with the bandleader the spiritual change he had undergone. "He was like, 'Oh, that's cool. I've got my relationship with God, and you've got yours,'" Dickerson remembered. But while the exchange was pleasant, it was clear that the guitarist's moral views were increasingly incompatible with the music the band was playing on a nightly basis.

***

After the conclusion of the *Dirty Mind* tour, the band prepared for a brief European swing. It was now apparent that the album had ultimately triumphed in a manner that transcended record sales or hit singles. Prince's instincts about releasing *Dirty Mind* in its demoed form had been vindicated; just as he, Fargnoli, and Cavallo had hoped, the album had helped mark the transition from the glossy, bombastic sounds of the 1970s to a tighter, more compact aesthetic.

During a triumphal interview with an alternative publication, Prince reveled in the album's stripped-down approach.

"It's not going to win any awards [for production]," he said in a manner that made clear his disdain for such accolades. "I used to be a perfectionist – too much of one. The ragged edges tend to be a bit truer."[9]

165

14. EXAGGERATIONS

As Prince and the band headed overseas in late May 1981 for three shows in Amsterdam, London, and Paris, and as media interest grew, one question was how much of Prince's true biography to reveal and how much to fictionalize. Both Prince and Howard Bloom wished to create an air of intrigue, raising the possibility of inflating the dramatic elements of his life story.

At the same time, Prince's history, even in an unadulterated form, contained enough pathos and pain to intrigue journalists. Thus, as he sat for interviews in Europe and the United States during the *Dirty Mind* campaign, elements of his childhood were conveyed accurately, such as his father leaving his family when Prince was seven. Other aspects of the story, however, were distorted or misrepresented. *Dirty Mind* was characterized as being wholly autobiographical, right down to the depiction of incest on "Sister." Meanwhile, he consistently misrepresented his ethnic heritage. In one interview, his father John L. Nelson was a mix of black and Italian and his mother was Italian and "something else." In another, his father became part Italian and part Filipino.

His misstatements were prompted in part by one thing that he did convey truthfully: he had become estranged from his family. This was hardly surprising in the case of his mother, given the traumatic circumstances that had caused him to leave home at age 12. But his father had supported his musical activities throughout his teen years, and their relations had been friendly. Somehow, however – and the reason was not made clear – that relationship too had foundered.

Even apart from his family relationships, Prince's sources of emotional intimacy had diminished. His long association with Andre Cymone was in its twilight, with the bassist about to depart the band for good following the European shows. His relationship with Dez

Dickerson had begun to cool somewhat following the guitarist's religious conversion. Prince's relationships with women, meanwhile, were characterized mainly by lust as opposed to emotional connection. It was primarily with the gay Lisa Coleman that he began developing something close to a friendship.

Still, the atmosphere around the band remained upbeat during the brief European swing. Prince explored the urban counterculture of Paris, Amsterdam, and London, and came away stimulated. Prince's show in London, however, drew only about 75 people, demonstrating that the media buzz around *Dirty Mind* was not translating into ticket sales. But Prince's demeanor remained relaxed and enthusiastic, including with the press. Although he scoffed to reporters that he didn't like interviews, he also discouraged one journalist from ending their conversation, offering to answer more questions.

During another interview, he criticized Warners for impeding his progress. "I was conned into thinking I only had to establish a black American audience, instead of what I really wanted to do," he said.[10]

In addition to sowing mystery about his ethnic origins, Prince knew that some fans and journalists assumed he was gay or bisexual. His attire certainly suggested this; that his lyrics were directed towards women was perhaps irrelevant, given the large number of gay artists who did the same.

A newly written song, "Jack U Off," was sure to create further debate on this score. Although band members were aware that he was straight, the sexual acts that Prince described himself performing in the song had strong homoerotic overtones, whether intended or not. "When you talk about street lingo, where I come from, guys don't jack girls off," Mark Brown noted. "But I don't think Prince knew that, he was just in his own world."

Prince, who as a result of Lisa's presence in the band was becoming more conversant with gay culture, did not seem uncomfortable with perceptions that he might be at least bisexual. If anything, this could generate media curiosity, as well as further establish him as a unifying, cross-cultural figure. "What I like most about my audience is there are blacks and whites, straights and gays, conservative and non-conservative, and they're all having a good time," he told one European journalist.

Religious themes were also on his mind, and he told one interviewer that themes of "sin and salvation" would populate his next record. And on a deeper level, Prince had gradually begun to think of himself as an instrument of God, someone put on earth to act out a destiny.

Two nights after the sparsely attended show in London, the band played a Paris nightclub, although their arrival was delayed for several hours by a customs issue. The show was viewed by a small, lethargic crowd, some fixed near the front of the stage like mannequins. Some band members also seemed tired after months of touring that had concluded with a long flight to Europe. Bobby Z. lagged behind the beat at times, Andre hit various wrong notes, and Dickerson's guitar occasionally fell out of tune.

But Prince, unconcerned by the tiny audience and unaffected by the tumult of the last six months, exuded as much energy as at any point of the tour, prancing in a manner that evoked Mick Jagger and coaxing feedback from his guitar like Hendrix. When Fink hit a sustained high keyboard chord during "Partyup," Prince threw his arms towards the heavens like a spellbound preacher. By the end of the show, he had stripped down to a black thong bikini, his sweaty body seeming to consist of nothing but muscle and sinew.

After the show, the band headed back to the United States, minus one – Andre Cymone remained in Europe for two weeks of sightseeing, an anticlimactic coda to the union between himself and Prince. The implications were far more than musical. Andre and his family had rescued Prince, providing him a home, a place to use his instruments, and a sense of community. Andre was also his most tangible connection to the Northside of Minneapolis where he had grown up. Bit by bit, Prince had shed the friends who had been part of that neighborhood, and with the departure of Andre, his most important connection to the Northside was ending.

Andre, despite his frustrations over songwriting credits and other matters, felt little rancor towards his friend as they went their separate ways. Whatever his future held, Andre remained confident that it would involve music.

As for Prince, any sentimental feelings quickly fell by the wayside as he left Europe, having been changed in some small but perceptible way by his visit, ready to go home and start recording again.

15. FRANKENSTEIN'S MONSTER

Mark Brown, Prince, and Dez Dickerson on the *Controversy* Tour

After returning to Minnesota in April 1981, Prince purchased a house on the shores of verdant Lake Riley in southwest suburban Chanhassen, not far from his previous rented home on Lake Minnetonka. He promptly had the house painted purple. The color had not previously seemed to hold any great significance for him; it had made an appearance only in the unreleased 1976 song "Leaving for New York," which contained the psychedelic image of a "purple lawn." But this unusual decorative choice showed that Prince saw the color as reflecting some part of his persona.

He also had Don Batts install a sixteen-track studio in the basement. The equipment was more advanced than at the Lake Minnetonka studio, allowing for a polished sound. The more expansive space also allowed Prince's piano – which hadn't been used at all on *Dirty Mind* – to be wired from the living room down to the studio.

Even before beginning work on his fourth album, Prince's first priority was making good on his bargain with Morris Day over

"Partyup" – to create a side project for Day. He approached the task not out of obligation but with gusto. His plan was for the project's live incarnation to be as much theatrical as musical; Day would be the drummer, and Alexander O'Neal, a talented Minneapolis soul singer, would be the singer and front man. O'Neal would act as a wisecracking hustler very much resembling Prince's "pimp" persona that he joked around with in social situations.

Unfortunately, Prince's courtship of O'Neal proved brief and rocky; the singer wanted more money and freer artistic rein than Prince was willing to allow. The project appeared stymied. Surprisingly, Prince then suggested that Day himself could be the vocalist and frontman.

The idea on its face was counter-intuitive; Day's talents were far better suited to the drum kit, and he considered himself a musician rather than an entertainer. Still, he gradually warmed to the idea and became intrigued by the character Prince was asking him to play, which was not entirely removed from Day's own flamboyant personality.

Work on the project began in April 1981. Recording on his own as usual, Prince created a foundation of funk grooves and then sang guide vocals for Day to later imitate. Prince adopted a raspy voice that reflected the pimp persona. The plan was to release an album by late summer and then have the band perform shows, all without Prince's involvement being revealed.

As Day learned the vocal parts, Prince recruited a group of talented Minneapolis musicians for the group's live lineup: Terry Lewis on bass, Jimmy "Jam" Harris and Monte Moir on keyboards, Jellybean Johnson on drums, and Illinois-born Jesse Johnson (no relation to Jellybean) on guitar. He named the band the Time, which was a derivation of the name of Flyte Tyme, a Northside group that had included Harris and Lewis during Prince's teen years. Prince planned for the band members to become integral to the project's

171

image, preening onstage in vintage suits as they played.

And the Time was only part of his plans for a roster of side projects that he would direct from behind the scenes. During the late spring and early summer of 1981, Prince began planning an all-female group called "The Hookers" whose members would sing explicit lyrics while wearing lingerie onstage. The concept was not dissimilar to the Rick James-created ensemble the Mary Jane Girls, and James would later grumble that Prince had stolen his idea. Several songs were recorded, and three women were selected, rather arbitrarily, for the live act: girlfriend Susan Moonsie, wardrobe assistant Brenda Bennett (the wife of set designer Roy), and Jamie Shoop, an employee of Cavallo, Ruffalo & Fargnoli. Prince recorded several songs for the project during the summer, including a potent funk groove called "Drive Me Wild," but it shifted to the back burner as Prince focused on the Time.

Musically, the Time reflected Prince's funk roots more than any of his projects to date. Whereas his first two albums featured mostly poppy R&B, and *Dirty Mind* showed movement toward rock and New Wave, the material he recorded for the Time included long-form grooves reminiscent of the iconic '70s funk group Parliament-Funkadelic, headed by George Clinton. "Get It Up" lasted more than nine minutes, and the stripped-down funk number "Cool" went on even longer, representing the two longest songs Prince had recorded.

Despite the strength of the material, the project became frustrating for Morris Day, who was anything but a natural singer. Prince pushed him relentlessly to imitate the guide vocals; when Lisa Coleman stopped by during one of the sessions, she found Day in tears.[1]

Other than Day, the band members played no role in the studio. But a grueling schedule of rehearsals in anticipation of live shows began, with Prince showing the members how to faithfully execute the songs he had recorded. After several weeks, feeling matters were under control, Prince retreated to focus on his fourth album. As the Time members continued rehearsing on their own, the band started to place its own stamp on the songs and developed a powerful chemistry. Prince's reaction was one of pride that his handpicked lineup had proved so effective. "He could see that we were getting pretty frightening, so he started to leave us alone," recalled Jellybean Johnson.

The group's first album, *The Time*, was released in July 1981 on Warner Bros. Records. No songwriting credits appeared on the front cover or inner sleeve, but production credit was split between Morris Day and one "Jamie Starr," who had also received an engineering credit on *Dirty Mind*. Speculation appeared in the Minneapolis press that Jamie Starr was a Prince alias, and that he had been deeply involved in the creation of the album. Prince, his managers, and Morris Day all issued denials that were nonetheless ambiguous enough to stoke this mystery.

The album became a surprise hit, eventually reaching No. 7 on the Billboard Soul Chart and No. 50 on the Pop Chart. In fact, the album outperformed the initial sales of *Dirty Mind*, which was in many ways a less accessible record than *The Time*. Prince had demonstrated his ability to create a successful side project out of whole cloth, which further fueled his confidence and ambition.

***

As Prince turned his attention to his fourth album, a pastiche of new influences emerged. Cold, electronic textures, a staple of New Wave bands like Kraftwerk and Devo, made their way into the songs. He began to use his lower vocal register on some songs, part of his repertoire rarely used on his first three albums.

Lyrically, the song "Controversy" explored the themes of gender identity and religion that he had been reflecting upon during the *Dirty Mind* tour. The song was structurally more complex than anything on his previous albums, and it combined synthesizer and guitar in a manner that few of Prince's contemporaries had explored.

Prince also explored a vocal scream technique like that pioneered by James Brown and also used occasionally by Stevie Wonder, notably on the song "Superstition." Few pop artists had used this method, owing to its strain on vocal chords and the difficulty in creating a sound that was dramatic rather than grating. On "Controversy," Prince issued a lengthy scream at the song's climactic point, adding a startling element to an already powerful composition.

Screams were also used liberally on the ballad "Do Me, Baby." The song was a straightforward soul ballad intended to appeal largely to female listeners, reflecting Prince's R&B roots and containing none of the avant-garde elements making their way into much of the new work.

While much of the new album was completed in his Lake Riley home, Prince also traveled to Los Angeles to work at two studios, Hollywood Sound and Sunset Sound. At the latter facility, he used a Linn LM-1 drum machine, a tool created by the California-based technician Roger Linn, on the song "Private Joy." This was the first drum machine on the market to incorporate samples from real drums, as opposed to electronically generated sounds. Linn had created a prototype for the machine in 1979, and Stevie Wonder began to use it by 1980. The group Heaven 17 used it prominently on the underground hit "(We Don't Need This) Fascist Groove Thang," which was getting significant airplay in Europe during Prince's 1981 visit.

Prince saw that the Linn would further diminish his need for musicians and studio technicians. Creating full-band recordings anywhere inspiration struck – in hotel rooms, at home, or anywhere in between – suddenly became possible. "When I heard 'Private Joy' for the first time, that was the moment I knew things were going to change," remembered Bobby Z. Rivkin. "Recording drums is an expensive and slow process; it takes a long time to get a good sound. The Linn gave him an instant good sound."

The lyrics to "Private Joy" were directed at Susan Moonsie, whom he began dating after the *Dirty Mind* tour. Prince had met her in high school and even spent some nights on her family's couch before the Anderson family took him in. When she emerged as a romantic interest in late 1980, his friends found her to be intelligent and grounded – perhaps the perfect complement to a mercurial artist with an outsized ego. "She was more of a girlfriend than any girlfriend he had ever had," observed Rivkin. Added Alan Leeds, soon to become Prince's tour manager and who would get to know Moonsie well in coming years: "She saw Prince as a hugely creative, but lonely young fellow who needed tons of support, tender loving care, and encouragement. And this was all during a critical time in his development."

But a basic problem also afflicted their relationship: Prince's increasing interest in casual sex. Over the course of the *Dirty Mind* tour, the attention of groupies had boosted his confidence, and these encounters dovetailed perfectly with his exploration of erotic themes in his songwriting. Meanwhile, other girlfriends seemed to be waiting in the wings, including Jill Jones. Amidst all of this, Moonsie was caught between her affection for Prince and her unwillingness to put up with his unfaithfulness. "Moonsie's boundaries were not negotiable," observed Leeds. "She wouldn't jump up and down or holler and scream, but Prince knew she would never tolerate any behavior that even bordered on disrespect."

***

After months of work at home and in Los Angeles, Prince presented his new material to Warners and his management. Unlike the disputes that developed over *Dirty Mind*, there was an almost unanimous consensus that it could establish Prince as even more of an underground phenomenon, and one with crossover potential. "I thought it was a brilliant album," recalled Warners' Marylou Badeaux. Like *Dirty Mind*, the album had no obvious hit single, and some of its more ambitious experiments, such as the abstruse spoken-word piece "Annie Christian," were not successful. But such audacity was exactly what alternative press journalists and cult fans were coming to love about Prince.

The album, entitled *Controversy*, was readied for release in October 1981. Visually, the cover carried forth the post-punk vibe of *Dirty Mind*: Prince in a lavender trench coat, again with the Rude Boy pin attached. Floating behind him and on the back cover were faux tabloid newspaper headlines that mocked society's fascination with sensationalism.

Somewhat to the surprise of Prince and Warners, some critics who received pre-release copies were put off by the hodge-podge of styles and his excursions into specific political issues such as disarmament (on "Ronnie, Talk to Russia") and gun violence ("Annie Christian.") The concern seemed to be that Prince's core message of sexual freedom, which rang through so clearly on *Dirty Mind*, had been diluted.

"Controversy," the album's lead single, had little impact on the Pop Singles Chart after being released in September in advance of the album, reaching only No. 70. Still, airplay was strong in urban markets and on alternative rock stations, and Prince's managers began planning a tour of mid-sized theaters in the United States.

The Time, meanwhile, played its first shows in Minneapolis clubs in fall 1981. Day had fully grown into the cartoonish character that Prince had created, and the band had become impeccably tight. But Prince's initial satisfaction gradually shifted in the direction of jealously over how good the band was; as Bobby Z. put it, Prince had begun to worry that he had created "a Frankenstein's monster" that he could no longer control.

Three members of the Time were most threatening to Prince: keyboardist Jimmy "Jam" Harris, bassist Terry Lewis, and guitarist Jesse Johnson. Johnson in particular was a terror on the guitar, playing leads with a ferocity that rivaled Prince's. "Prince frequently intimated that the only guitarist he's really afraid of is Jesse Johnson," recalled Alan Leeds.

But despite Prince's conflicted feelings, it was clear that the Time could help sell tickets for the upcoming tour as an opening act. For audiences, this could also offer a kind of entertaining competition between the groups, not unlike that between Prince and Rick James on the *Fire It Up!* tour. And indeed, right down to the personnel involved, the tour would have echoes of the fierce musical combat of Prince's teen years on the Northside. But with him this time being the maestro behind the entire pageant, the outcome was seemingly preordained.

***

"Do Me, Baby," a song that was in significant part Andre Cymone's creation, would eventually be released as *Controversy*'s third single. Its provenance would be debated for decades, and it would serve as a rallying point for those who questioned Prince's fair-mindedness in sharing songwriting credit.

At the time, the shock of hearing "Do Me, Baby" on the radio proved greater than Andre had expected. Upset, he called Pepe Willie to ask what his legal options were; at this point, however, they were nil. "I told Andre he should have copyrighted it, and that there was nothing I could do," said Willie.

For Andre – as well as certain other Prince associates – this was only the most egregious example of Prince using a friend's ideas without credit. And various other compositions, not just involving Andre, would work their way into this debate over the years.

Some associates, however, believed that such controversies were overblown. Bobby Z., for example, noted that while various band members offered up riffs at rehearsals, it was Prince who fashioned this raw clay into finished pieces. "There's a big misconception between a riff, a lick, and a songwriter," he argued. "The songwriter is the guy who conceptualizes the words and the music. Ninety-nine percent of the time, when Prince says he wrote the song, he wrote the song." Owen Husney struck a similar note. "When people are jamming, ideas float around," he said. "When Prince and Andre would jam, and something cool came out of it, Prince was the outlet to make it happen on record and on radio. Andre wasn't."

Poignantly, but in some respects fittingly as an unexpected farewell to his former best friend, "Do Me, Baby" made an appearance on the last night Prince ever performed, April 14, 2016.

16. SHOCK AND SATISFACTION

Among those who saw Prince perform at the Ritz in New York City during the *Dirty Mind* tour had been Rolling Stones front man Mick Jagger. The Stones, long conscious of the debt they owed to black musical forms, often offered opening slots to African-American artists like Stevie Wonder and Billy Preston. Now, as the band prepared for its first U.S. tour in many years in support of its Tattoo You album, Jagger invited Prince to join the Stones at the Los Angeles Coliseum, on Friday, October 9 and Sunday, October 11, 1981, and also at two more shows in Detroit. He and his managers readily accepted what was a tremendous promotional opportunity.

A sold-out crowd of more than 94,000 people was expected to attend the Los Angeles shows, and most would never have heard of Prince. It would be Mark Brown's second gig with the band, a staggering transition from the small nightclubs he had been playing during his very short musical career. In the weeks running up to the show, Dez Dickerson warned Prince that the reaction of a large, anonymous crowd of Stones fans would be entirely different from anything he had ever experienced.

October 9, 1981, turned out to be an unseasonably warm day in Los Angeles, and a capacity crowd packed the Los Angeles Memorial Coliseum to witness the greatest pure rock band of its generation. Some had arrived very early in the morning to secure places near the stage; many were inebriated by the time the music was to begin in the late afternoon. Those up close included hundreds of members of the notorious Hell's Angels Motorcycle Club, which had created violent altercations at the Stones' famed concert at Altamont in 1969, resulting in the death of an audience member.

Many fans had expected only two opening acts, the J. Geils

Band and George Thorogood and the Destroyers, blues bands very much in the Rolling Stones tradition. But when promoter Bill Graham, a legendary figure who had advanced the careers of many artists, took the stage and announced that Prince would be performing first, many in the audience shouted their displeasure.

Backstage, Prince and his bandmates felt a wave of dread. The dynamics quickly became clear – an impatient, predominately white crowd, fueled by masculine energy and pumped full of alcohol, was about to witness a small, scantily dressed African-American and his mixed-race, mixed-gender backing band. "We're set up to die," drummer Bobby Z. recalled thinking.[1]

Some attendees did take offense to Prince's attire, which consisted of a trench coat, leg warmers, and a leather thong. Still, reaction to the distortion-drenched "Bambi" was largely positive. The band segued immediately into "When You Were Mine," whose jaunty rhythms also produced a generally agreeable response. But the small army of bikers and boozers closer up was losing its patience; some began tossing trash, and in some cases, lighted cigarettes. An orange thrown at Mark Brown was impaled on the tuning pegs of his bass.[2]

Bill Graham, disgusted by the reaction and concerned about the band's safety, came out and stopped the set. As Prince and the members listened from backstage, the promoter grabbed a mic and shouted that anyone not enjoying the show should leave for a beer, prompting one fan to throw something at Graham. "You'll pay big money to see this guy someday," a defiant Graham shot back.

Prince and the band returned and launched into "Uptown." But the cascade of debris became heavier, forcing them to cut the song short and leave the stage. A wordless Prince immediately left the arena. The band quickly followed; they soon learned that he had gone straight to the airport and left town.

The next performance at the Coliseum was scheduled for two days later, but word quickly arrived that Prince did not intend to come back. Manager Steve Fargnoli, not ready to relinquish the opportunity that the concerts represented, urged him to return. The band leader emphatically refused.

Fargnoli turned to Mick Jagger for help. The Stones' leader, reaching Prince by phone, told stories of abuse heaped on the Stones during their early days, describing this as simply a hazard of being an uncompromising artist. Prince listened politely but refused to budge.

With the band members still hunkered down in Los Angeles, Fargnoli turned to Dez Dickerson as a last resort. Over the course of a nearly 45-minute call with Prince, Dickerson insisted that they could not allow themselves to be intimidated, particularly where racism was a factor. "I told Prince about playing in biker bars, where no black man had ever set foot before," Dickerson recalled. "I told him that you can't let them run you out of town."

Finally, the band leader relented and got on a plane for Los Angeles. When he arrived, his misgivings remained clear. "It was one of the only times I saw Prince visibly, physically have to do something against his will," Bobby Z. recalled.[3]

Still, by the time the band took the stage in the late afternoon, Prince had steeled himself. The band again launched into "Bambi," and before the song was a minute old Prince burst into a searing guitar solo. Mark Brown, showing immense resiliency under trying circumstances, stayed fully in sync with Bobby Z.'s drumming.

As had been the case on the first night, reaction from crowd members further from the stage was enthusiastic. But the events of Friday night had spread through word-of-mouth and newspaper reports; hundreds of people, intent on one-upsmanship, had come loaded for bear with rotting fruits and vegetables. One person brought a cooked ham to throw; another had soaked raw chicken in a bag of hot water, rendering it fetid and gray. By the second song, "When U Were Mine," these items were hurled at the band, along with racist and homophobic jeers.[4]

The band members dodged projectiles and sidestepped debris as it crash-landed. The noise in the stadium was deafening, adding to their disorientation. Still, no one missed a note or a beat. Matt Fink's high keyboard notes rang out above the din, Prince soloed, and Mark Brown defiantly shouted his back-up lines during the chorus.

Bobby Z. then kicked the band into the rockabilly-tinged "Jack U Off." As Prince began singing the explicit lyrics, the cascade of trash resumed. At the song's crescendo, all of the instruments dropped away, leaving Prince's voice naked and echoing across the cavernous arena.

"As a matter of fact," he snarled, "You can jack *me* off!"

And with that, the floodgates opened. Even more dangerous items were thrown, including an empty bottle of Jack Daniels. A bottle of orange juice narrowly missed Prince, smashing against the drum riser and cascading the liquid across the stage.

Bobby Z., refusing to give up, tore into "Uptown" as soon as "Jack U Off" ended. But Prince, now fearing for his safety, left the stage. Unaware, the band continued playing what became an instrumental version of the song. Mark Brown soon also retreated backstage, but Dickerson remained, insistently taking one guitar solo after another. But the keyboards soon dropped out, leaving only Dickerson and Bobby Z. playing, and the song seemed about to peter out.

Then, without warning, Brown's warm bass tone kicked back in, signaling his return. The distorted roar of Prince's guitar then also re-appeared. Reunited at full strength, the band pushed gamely through the end of "Uptown." They then completed "Why U Wanna Treat Me So Bad?" and left the stage.

Backstage, the band members felt a mixture of shock and satisfaction. Just as Dickerson had hoped in speaking to Prince the night before, they had refused to be intimidated. This was justly recognized by some as a victory. "He played the full 20 minutes, exactly what his contract permitted him to do," recalled Ken

Tucker, a *Rolling Stone* critic who witnessed the concert. "And he played magnificently, his small body leaning into the abuse and turning it into a triumph."

Nonetheless, Prince and his management agreed that the remaining shows with the Stones would be scrapped. And while the band's perseverance had been remarkable, the experience brought certain uncomfortable truths into focus. Prince remained largely an underground phenomenon, a critic's darling whose reputation far exceeded his record sales or concert receipts, and whose androgynous image suddenly seemed more of a liability than selling point. A mass audience – one composed not of intellectuals, urbanites, and journalists, but of everyday Americans, some with ingrained prejudices – might not be ready for Prince, now or perhaps ever. "I never thought we'd cross over after that," Bobby Z. said. "I just thought that this was it."

After the show, Prince consoled 19-year-old Mark Brown, fearing the bassist might quit the band after experiencing such trauma so early in his tenure. He assured Brown that the band had plenty of fans on their side, even if it was not the vast sea of people that had attended the Stones concerts. "Mark," he said, looking earnestly at the bassist, "this isn't our audience."

And indeed, as the band headed home, the notion that Prince and his band could ever reach an audience like that in Los Angeles Coliseum seemed as remote as the spring at the beginning of a long Minnesota winter.

17. BATTLE II

After returning home, Prince and his band, as well as the Time, resumed rehearsals for the upcoming *Controversy* tour, to start in November 1981 in Pittsburgh, Pennsylvania. The acts were booked into venues with capacities of about 2,000 to 8,000 people and were joined in some cities by the popular funk group Zapp (also on the Warner Bros. label), led by Roger Troutman. Sales were strong, fueled by the strong performance of both *Controversy* and *The Time*.

The second date of the tour, a two-set night at the Warner Theatre in Washington, D.C., drew a large and diverse audience. Opening with "Sexuality" from *Controversy*, the band ripped through a powerful set, demonstrating that the new unit had jelled. Mark Brown's bass playing, although far more workmanlike than spectacular, fit more comfortably in the band's sound than had Andre Cymone's busier work. The set also carried forth the sexualized energy of the *Dirty Mind* tour, including the lengthy guitar masturbation sequence on "Head." But this centerpiece became more musical and less sensationalistic as Prince took solos that combined elements of jazz, rock, and funk. Despite the relative absence of lead guitar on his two most recent albums, it was apparent that Prince had the potential to be a virtuoso on the instrument.

Offstage, Prince and his band at first continued to enjoy the camaraderie that had characterized the *Dirty Mind* tour. The entire group travelled on a single bus, where they socialized and watched videos of the previous shows.

For the African-American members of the band – Brown and Dickerson – life on the road was not without its awkward moments of being stared down by whites, particularly in southern cities. One morning before a show in Tampa, Florida, Dickerson was getting a cup of coffee in the hotel restaurant when he experienced a moment of terror: a huge man who looked like the quintessential redneck biker – long hair, muscles, tattoos – was striding toward him. "I thought I was about to die," the guitarist remembered. Fortunately, the hulking figure passed right by, and may have even grunted a hello.

About an hour later, Dickerson received a phone call summoning him to Prince's room for a band meeting. As he entered, he was shocked to see the same hulking figure from the restaurant. Seeking to quickly put the aghast guitarist at ease, Prince introduced Dickerson to Chick Huntsberry, his new bodyguard.

The next day, Huntsberry's presence proved intimidating to all, and the bodyguard spent most of the ride to Jacksonville surrounded by empty seats. Finally, Dickerson approached him and found the bodyguard to be a warm, friendly person who had lived a rough but fascinating life that had included working security at biker bars.

At six feet six inches and over 300 pounds, the bearded, tattooed Huntsberry really did look like a refugee from a motorcycle gang, and the contrast between him and Prince was stark to the point of absurdity. At first, Prince thought so too; although he agreed with his managers that more security was needed, he couldn't imagine having Huntsberry shadow him. A couple of days later, Prince mentioned to Dickerson that he was going to send the bodyguard home.

"Why?" Dickerson asked.

"He's just too big, he scares me," Prince responded. Dickerson related the conversation he had had with Huntsberry on the bus and urged Prince to keep him. "I think he's a good guy – you should give him a chance," Dickerson said.

Prince thought about it and decided to follow Dickerson's advice. And as the bodyguard began accompanying him almost everywhere, Prince came to feel comforted by having a human barricade against the world, not unlike the security provided by his athletic friends Duane Nelson and Paul Mitchell during high school. Soon, he and Huntsberry became inseparable.

For the rest of the entourage, there was a downside to this new arrangement, as suddenly their access to Prince was restricted. "It was a turning point for the closeness we used to have," noted set designer Bennett. The symbolism of Huntsberry's imposing presence at the dressing room door was clear to Prince's colleagues: they were no longer nearly as welcome.

***

As the tour continued, a more serious source of tension emerged: the Time was becoming a crack funk outfit capable of upstaging Prince. Guitarist Jesse Johnson and bassist Terry Lewis were more technically skilled than their counterparts in Prince's band, and Day had emerged as a charismatic frontman. Gradually, both bands became conscious of a growing rivalry. "To a point it was real positive," observed Time keyboardist Moir. "On our side it was, 'Let's kick his ass tonight!' But after a while, it became unhealthy."

As the tour went on, Prince began to feel upstaged, and the Time chafed at Prince's domineering tendencies. Members wanted to write their own music, which they doubted Prince would ever allow. Then there was the issue of money. The Time had taken off commercially, but the band members were living on a small weekly salary. "At one point, Jesse Johnson and those guys were eating peanut butter out of a jar in their hotel rooms so they could save what little money they got so they could have something when they got home," said Prince's cousin Chazz Smith. "And Morris didn't have any money, either."

***

During a break from the tour in January 1982, Prince attended the American Music Awards in Los Angeles. His old nemesis Rick James was performing, along with Stevie Wonder and other artists. Although Prince had trounced him on the *Fire*

It Up! tour, James had enjoyed a massive hit in 1981 with "Super Freak," a laurel that so far had eluded Prince.

The two men encountered each other at a party following the show. Prince was immediately drawn to the stunningly attractive woman on James' arm, 23-year-old Denise Matthews. Her copper skin, sexual magnetism, and overall appearance in many respects mirrored Prince's. "It's been said that when they met, they both stopped in their tracks; looking at each other, it was like seeing themselves, but of the opposite sex," said soon-to-be tour manager Alan Leeds.

Matthews' looks and surface confidence masked a difficult past. Born in Niagara Falls, Canada, she had suffered frequent physical abuse at the hands of her alcoholic father. After he died when Matthews was just 15, her mother also descended into alcoholism. Nonetheless, Matthews managed to graduate high school and left for Toronto to pursue a show business career. Despite having little native acting ability, she landed the lead part in the B-movie *Tanya's Island*, about a damsel pursued by an ape in a tropical paradise. But this did little to jumpstart her career. And so Matthews, like so many other young women from across North America pursuing the same dream, set her sights on Hollywood and moved to Los Angeles.

Upon encountering Matthews at the party, Prince made immediate advances, which she rebuffed; he again propositioned her with an early morning phone call to her hotel room, and she again demurred. But upon learning that she was also a singer, he hatched an idea: Matthews should join him in Minnesota after the tour to participate in the Hookers, his all-female side project.

With neither her romance with Rick James nor her faltering career offering any reason to stay in Los Angeles, she agreed, cognizant that his offer certainly came with romantic strings attached. And thus Matthews, at heart a vulnerable and volatile person, entered into a relationship that would be an ill-formed hybrid of professional, romantic, and sexual elements, one in which her agency and power would be limited at best. This dynamic would affect her in ways she could not have foreseen.

***

As the tour's second leg began in late January, the Time continued to upstage Prince on many evenings. At a show at the Capital Theatre in Passaic, New Jersey – the final night of three back-to-back shows – the Time's set was relaxed and confident. Prince's set was more wooden, and during the interlude of "Head," his guitar was out of tune both with itself and with Mark Brown's bass, prompting him to truncate the segment.

Tension continued to build as the tour neared its conclusion. On March 8, 1982, a show took place at Minneapolis' First Avenue club that was planned as a Prince-only gig. Prince played a rock-heavy set that included intriguing new material, including "All the Critics Love U in New York," featuring dueling solos by Prince and Dickerson.

At the end of the short set, Prince called the members of the Time onstage to perform a few songs, but he held on to his own microphone to interject comments. "This is my stage," he said tauntingly to Day. He also threatened to have Chick Huntsberry remove one of the Time's members – ostensibly a joke, but one whose underlying hostility was apparent.

At the end of the Time's mini-set, Prince brought his own personnel back for "Partyup," but unexpectedly kept Morris on the drum set. Suddenly, Day – and the audience – got a tantalizing taste of how things might have unfolded if Prince had chosen his hotheaded high school friend over the more restrained Bobby Z. Rivkin. Day coaxed "Partyup" along at a faster-than-usual tempo, masterfully shifting the dynamic range throughout. Then, mid-song, Prince let Day take a drum solo that showed off all of his pyrotechnic skills. This, far more than the smarmy caricature that fronted the Time, was the true Morris Day – a savvy and skilled musician capable of essentially leading a band from behind the drum kit.

As the Time's set – having ultimately been co-opted by Prince – concluded, the audience and participants alike felt dizzied. The evening had been a strange admixture of elements, with Prince's behavior running the gamut from beneficence to hostility. He had allowed Day to shine on "Partyup," and had also called Sueann Carwell to the stage to take a brief vocal solo on "Still Waiting." But he had also flaunted his authority one way or another throughout the night, creating an undercurrent of unease.

As the tour resumed for its final dates, four nights in a row in the South and Midwest, the competitive resentments between Prince and the Time began to boil over beyond the stage. After one show, a Time member hurled a nasty comment at Bobby Z.; another night, Jesse Johnson said something that Prince interpreted as an insult to his mother.

The hostility burst to the surface during the last show of the tour at Riverfront Stadium in Cincinnati. During their opening set, the Time found themselves being pelted by eggs from offstage. Gradually, they realized that Prince and some of his band members were the culprits. Towards the end of the set, Prince and his accomplices abducted dancer Jerome Benton from the stage and poured honey over him. Then they pelted him with garbage. "They tarred and feathered him, basically," recalled Fink, who did not participate and insisted to the band members that he wanted no part of the battle.

Then, as the Time's set ended, Chick Huntsberry grabbed Jesse Johnson and hauled him to Prince's dressing room. There, Huntsberry handcuffed Johnson to a horizontal coat rack bolted into a brick wall. Prince came in and began taunting Johnson and tossing Doritos chips and other pieces of food at him.

The various members of Prince's band and crew in the room looked on with horror as the episode continued. "It was a cruel thing to do," observed Roy Bennett. Fink recalled, "I just sat there and said to myself, this is getting out of hand."

Johnson writhed furiously in his cuffs. Finally, to the amazement of the onlookers, he managed to rip the entire twelve-foot-long coat rack out of the wall. His hands were still cuffed to the rack, which he began swinging wildly. "Jesse was uncontrollable," Fink said. "He just lost it. Chick had to contain the situation before someone got hurt."

Huntsberry restrained Johnson and then released him. A furious Johnson fled the dressing room and breathlessly told the rest of the Time what had happened. They immediately began gathering food to use in retaliation. Prince's managers, upon learning what was afoot, issued the Time a stern admonition: nothing must be thrown during Prince's set. The Time interpreted this as narrowly as possible, and as Prince and the band left the stage at the end of their set, the Time hurled eggs at them. Prince's team responded by throwing yet more food as the fight spilled into the backstage area.

The road managers, foreseeing possible trouble and wanting to forestall actual violence, sought to preserve some element of playfulness by ordering dozens of cream pies to be used by the combatants. The Time now had the advantage, having donned plastic bags to avoid having their clothes ruined. "They turned into warriors, literally," remembered Fink. The battle continued back at the hotel, where the ensembles threw whatever edibles they could find at each other.

In the end, there was significant damage to hotel rooms; Prince insisted that Morris Day pay for most of it, arguing falsely that the Time had initiated the fight. Thus, what might have produced a catharsis instead generated another grievance for the Time to nurse. And Johnson, in particular, remained bitter both about the dressing room incident and Prince's stifling domination over the Time. "Jesse's hostility toward Prince was really bad, it was scary," said Fink. "Jesse had a major ego problem, and issues occur when people with an ego problem are in a subordinate position."

For Day, as the Time's leader, the situation presented myriad dilemmas. He had achieved a measure of personal notoriety, but was financially broke. The Time had the talent to succeed on its own, but without the support of Warner Bros. and Prince's management, this momentum could disappear overnight. As for Prince, he saw the group as entirely his creation; he had written the songs, developed the concept, and provided the necessary resources. The group was a tangible expression of part of his psyche, and its independence was something that he could not help seeing as a threat.

As a result of these dynamics, the Time's survival turned on the extent to which its members were willing to remain subservient, and how much Prince could loosen even slightly his desire for control.

18. SMORGASBORD OF ATTITUDE AND VIBE

Denise Matthews, aka Vanity, on the *1999* Tour

Withdrawing to his hotel room in Cincinnati on March 14, 1982 following the epic food fight, Prince telephoned Los Angeles-based Jill Jones, with whom he had stayed in touch following the *Dirty Mind* tour. He told her that he intended to record much of his fifth album in Los Angeles, and invited her to contribute backing vocals and to work on a potential Jones solo project. Now 18 years old, Jones imagined that all signs were pointing towards a serious romance. What Jones didn't know was that a very similar set of invitations had been proffered to Denise Matthews in January in Los Angeles, thus setting up a potential conflict between side projects and lovers.

With these multiple wheels in motion, Prince prepared to work on three simultaneous projects: his fifth album, the Time's second, and the debut effort of the all-female group he was planning to build around Matthews. Prince proposed a stage name to Matthews: she would be called "Vagina," a name that would certainly draw all sorts of attention, wanted or unwanted. Understandably, Matthews rejected the idea, and they compromised on "Vanity." A new entry in the growing constellation of Prince-authored personas was thus born.

As he juggled these multiple projects, Prince's pace in the studio became more rapid than ever before. His efficiency was improved by pervasive use of the Linn LM-1 drum machine, which he had explored first on *Controversy*'s "Private Joy." He began using a feature relatively unexplored by the LM-1's early adopters: each of its sound samples had a dedicated output, allowing them to be individually routed through external effects. Prince started running the samples through his Boss guitar pedals, allowing for an unusual palette of sounds. Although Roger Linn's original intent had been to create a more naturalistic drum machine, in Prince's hands the tool became almost another kind of instrument altogether. "He always wanted to keep people guessing," noted engineer Don Batts. "Clavets were tuned to the point where they sounded like tin cans."

Prince also used the innovative technique of overdubbing synthesizer parts repeatedly to create a thick slather. Among the new tracks using these methods was "Nasty Girl," recorded for the Vanity project, which used a complex Linn pattern and many layers of Oberheim synth.

Between recording sessions, Prince corralled members of his entourage for yet another project: a film to be based on concert footage shot during the *Controversy* tour interspersed with dramatic vignettes. Dubbed *The Second Coming*, the film's director was Chuck Statler, a music video veteran who had previously shot a clip for the Time song "Cool."[1]

The dramatic scenes, such as they were, were shot in Prince's purple-painted home and focused around Prince's interactions with several women in lingerie, including Susan Moonsie. Little about the production went according to plan;

among other things, the heavy use of film equipment in a residential neighborhood blew out a transformer on a utility pole. Prince insisted on countless takes of each scene, an exercise that soon became excruciating.[2]

Between shoots, Statler began to edit together concert footage with the dramatic sequences, which were largely incoherent. Eventually Prince stopped by to see the results. Without warning or explanation, he told Statler the project was being abandoned. None of it would be formally released during Prince's career.[3]

Soon thereafter, Prince left Minnesota for Los Angeles and began a series of studio sessions at Sunset Sound over the late spring and early summer of 1982. He began living in Studio City, a community in the San Fernando Valley, and his primary love interest became Jill Jones. "We were together 24-7," she recalled.[4] Much of their time was spent at recording studios, followed by occasional visits to obscure Los Angeles eateries in the early morning hours.

Peggy McCreary, a staff engineer at Sunset Sound assigned to Prince's project, felt a sense of dread when she learned of his impending arrival. A former waitress and gofer at Hollywood's legendary Roxy club, McCreary had landed her coveted slot at Sunset after taking night classes in engineering. Knowing little about Prince other than that he sang about fellatio and incest, she envisioned him as boorish and inappropriate, perhaps a crasser version of Barry White, the soul singer known for his vivid evocations of sex.

When Prince entered the studio, her first surprise was his size; he was slight and delicate, more china doll than prowling wolf. He was also shy and hardly spoke. When McCreary asked a question, Prince mumbled unintelligibly while avoiding eye contact.

"Look," she said bluntly as the session continued, "I'm not going to be able to do this unless you talk to me."

Seemingly appreciating her directness, he began to open up. Soon enough, between recording tasks, Prince was chatting amiably about girlfriends, plans for the future, and even his childhood.

During this first session Prince and McCreary worked on "Let's Pretend We're Married," which was based around a descending, minor-key line floating over another keyboard riff that chugged away like a freight train. The vocal melody followed the same melody as the lead synth line, and an LM-1 pattern anchored the groove.

The song was haunting and disconcerting, with its lyrics alternating between humor and profanity. In asking his partner whether or not she is busy for "the next seven years," Prince makes oblique reference to the Marilyn Monroe film *The Seven Year Itch*, about the point where marital monogamy supposedly becomes a bore.

In the control booth between takes, Prince's behavior remained nothing but respectful towards McCreary. But in weeks to come, although she continued to see occasional flashes of Prince's sociable side, his workaholic tendencies dominated. Often alone with him in the studio, the demands on McCreary became brutal, with sessions often dragging on for as long as twenty-four hours. Basic needs were seen as distractions; when McCreary would suggest getting something to eat, Prince responded that food made him sleepy and that he preferred to go hungry. When he saw her yawning, Prince would offer a brief respite, telling her to step outside while he recorded a vocal. Even after sessions, McCreary was expected to remain and create rough mixes of the songs he had finished. "He had no tolerance for human weakness," she remembered.

Prince was also unpredictable and arbitrary in his scheduling. Not infrequently, McCreary was awakened by late-night or early-morning phone calls ordering her to the studio. Other times he would fail to show up for previously booked sessions, leaving her waiting anxiously. She would knit sweaters to pass the time, only to learn, late in the day, that Prince had packed his things and returned to Minneapolis. On yet other occasions, he would show up at the studio in a stretch limousine, insisting that they drive to nearby Santa Monica and catch an obscure art film.

The pace of recording was just as rapid during return stints to Minnesota, where he continued to work with Don Batts. In very short order, Prince had recorded dozens of songs for the new projects.

After Prince completed tracking for the Vanity record, he reshuffled the band's line-up. Jamie Shoop – who was more interested in the business side of the music industry and continued to work with Prince's management team – bowed out, leaving a trio of Matthews, Moonsie, and Bennett. Prince dubbed the group Vanity 6, a reference to the number of breasts in the ensemble.

Meanwhile, the romance between Prince and Matthews, which began amid a glow of sexual chemistry, soon became combustible. As usual, Prince continued to see other women, including Jill Jones and Vanity bandmate Susan Moonsie, and Matthews' fits of jealousy left him, in turn, feeling cornered. "His relationship with Vanity wasn't as close as with Susan," said Roy Bennett. "There was no way to have a close relationship with her; she wasn't that kind of person." Indeed, as Prince got to know Matthews, he enjoyed her company less; he found her abrasive and insufficiently demure. But he became outraged whenever Matthews showed signs of independence, either romantically or professionally. Because her family background of abuse and alcoholism left her at risk for similar behaviors, these volatile circumstances were fraught with peril.

Whatever his ambivalence about Matthews, Prince treated the Vanity 6 project with almost grave seriousness. Unfortunately, the material was dragged down by the lack of vocal talent among its members. Matthews, who handled most of the lead duties, exhibited neither range nor emotional depth, and while Bennett did display some vocal chops, neither she nor Moonsie could be mistaken for seasoned professional singers.

Despite these problems, *Vanity 6*, released in August 1982, further demonstrated Prince's ability to turn side projects into commercial successes. The album reached No. 6 on the Black Chart and No. 45 on the Pop Chart, selling nearly 500,000 units during its initial run. Prince's team again issued a party line that Vanity 6 was an independent group and that he had not been involved, although enough hints were dropped with journalists to keep the mystery alive.

Meanwhile, the Time's second album, *What Time Is It?*, was another success. It reached No. 2 on the Black Chart and went gold in the process. The single "777-9311" became a modest hit, creating a hassle for Dez Dickerson, who had not known that his phone number was going to be used as the title of the song; when calls from strangers poured in at all hours of the night, he was forced to have it changed.

With two side projects now well established, Prince turned his attention to his own fifth album. On *Controversy*, Prince had let the title track stretch out to over seven minutes. With his new material, he continued to push long-form grooves, which became the rule rather than the exception. Songs like "D.M.S.R" and "Automatic" led the listener through a labyrinth of popping bass solos, short guitar solos, impulsive screams, and esoteric sound effects. The lyrics continued to mine dark sexual themes; "Automatic" explored domination and submission, while "Lady Cab Driver" contained explicitly violent imagery.

The material was more experimental than almost anything on the pop charts, suggesting that Prince was treating artistic considerations as paramount. And he was also stocking his own album with more challenging and less commercially accessible material than was being used for the Time and Vanity 6 projects. At the same time, he wrote an impassioned mid-tempo ballad called "Little Red Corvette" that was easily the most fully integrated pop song of his career. In an unusual display of inclusiveness in the studio, Prince asked Dez Dickerson to add a guitar solo to the song.

When Prince presented the completed album to Bob Cavallo and Steve Fargnoli in Los Angeles, they were pleased with the material and delighted to hear an apparent hit single in "Little Red Corvette." After digesting the work, though, the managers felt something was missing: an over-arching, thematic song in the vein of "Controversy," which had provided a conceptual and musical foundation for that album.

Prince, while not pleased to hear he had created anything less than a masterpiece, took their views as a personal challenge. "He yelled at us, and then he went back to Minneapolis and kept recording," remembered Cavallo. What emerged from these efforts was "1999," which became the title track of the album. He made a crucial decision during the mixing process. The verse vocals had been recorded as a three-part harmony featuring himself, Dickerson, and Lisa Coleman, but in the final mix, he dropped out two of the voices on each line so that each singer became a lead vocalist – Lisa on the first line, Dickerson on the second, and Prince on the third. The result evoked Sly & the Family Stone classics that used a similar baton-passing technique, including "Sing A Simple Song" and "Hot Fun In The Summertime."

The album was now complete. The length of the songs, however, necessitated a double album. Warner Bros. was initially resistant to this, believing it would be difficult to market. But Fargnoli was once again persuasive in presenting Prince's arguments to the label, and Mo Ostin threw his pivotal support behind the project.

1999, released in October 1982, was greeted with fervor by music critics, who found it a much fuller realization of the ideas Prince had explored on his previous two albums. *Rolling Stone* commended Prince for "keeping the songs constantly kinetic with an inventive series of shocks and surprises." In the eyes of the critical establishment, *1999* graduated him into a full-fledged creative force, an iconoclastic figure certainly in a league with revered artists such as the Clash and Lou Reed.

To promote *1999*, Cavallo and Fargnoli organized a major concert tour to begin in November, just weeks after the album's release. The tour featured opening sets by the Time and Vanity 6, making it an extravaganza that revealed Prince's various artistic personae. The Roy Bennett-designed stage set featured props such as motorized Venetian blinds (which served as a backdrop for the entire tableau), an elevated catwalk, and a brass bed. The song list emphasized *Controversy* and *1999*, while also including the more obscure "How Come U Don't Call Me Anymore?," a piano ballad released as a B-side to the single of "1999." Prince's confidence as a performer was in full bloom, and the audiences at the venues, which had capacities ranging from 7,500 to 10,000, were enraptured.

Less pleasant were the offstage dynamics. Prince's bandmates felt increasingly distanced from their leader, as Chick Huntsberry's presence again proved intimidating. Prince traveled on a separate bus during much of the tour, accompanied usually by Huntsberry, Fargnoli, and a member of his growing complement of girlfriends. The vehicle became Prince's hermetic universe; even after arriving in a city, he often remained cloistered in the bus until going onstage, returning afterward to record musical ideas on a portable machine or to have sex.

Of Prince's bandmates, Dickerson was the most disgruntled, in significant part due to his discomfort in playing Prince's explicit songs. During the *1999* swing, Dickerson voiced his concerns directly to Prince, appealing to his own sense of spirituality. The band leader seemed sympathetic, but only to a point. "There were a few times where I really felt his heart was open, that he was seriously weighing the things I was saying," Dickerson remembered. "But he had consciously built his notoriety on being controversial; there was a conflict between what he knew to be right and what was working in his career."

The guitarist seemed certain to depart after the tour. An heir apparent quickly emerged: nineteen-year-old Wendy Melvoin, Lisa's girlfriend. She had grown up with Lisa in the San Fernando Valley, and they had known each other since childhood. Wendy was Lisa's companion on the tour, and upon learning she played guitar, Prince invited her to sit in with the band during sound checks. Prince immediately liked her sound, which was more emotionally expressive than Dickerson's. She was a negligible soloist, but Prince at this point was happy to be the band's sole lead guitarist. Wendy's tough, mildly masculine image would add to the band's already intriguing appearance.

Prince's relationship with the members of the Time, meanwhile, had not healed much since the epic food fight. The band wanted to participate in the group's second album, and being excluded from the creative process had created immense frustration. The success of an album that bore their name, but which they had in fact had no hand in, only underscored that they were essentially puppets.

The dynamic worsened when Prince began complaining, without any basis at all, that the Time was performing weakly in concert. "He would come in and get all over their case," remembered Roy Bennett. "He would ride them heavily, and, obviously, when you're doing a great job and someone's telling you you're screwing up, you wonder, 'What is this guy? What does he want?' It caused major tension."

Unbeknownst to Prince, Lewis and Harris had started doing production work for other groups on the side, and their patience with Prince's insistence on control was wearing thin. "I'm sure they felt that at some point he would loosen up the reins, but he never did," Bennett observed. "They're two very talented guys, and the last thing they wanted was to be told what to do all the time."

Fargnoli and Cavallo, not wanting another tour to devolve into open conflict between the bands, began seeking an experienced road manager to bring order to the swing. Among the candidates was Alan Leeds, a thirty-three-year-old music industry veteran who had worked extensively with James Brown and was an expert in funk and jazz history. Prince, when presented by Fargnoli with the names of several applicants and learning about their backgrounds, said simply, "Get the James Brown guy."

After quitting college at the age of twenty-two to do tour promotion for the Godfather of Soul, Leeds had become Brown's tour manager and a confidant during a critical stretch of his career in the early 1970s. A deep thinker with a melancholy handsomeness, Leeds was indefatigable in handling the complex logistics of running tours. Perhaps even more importantly, he was adroit and gracious in dealing with larger-than-life personalities like James Brown and his new client.

When he joined up with the *1999* tour, Leeds was at first roundly ignored by Prince and had to communicate through Huntsberry. But Prince soon opened up, interested in learning more about Leeds' years with James Brown. Leeds joined Huntsberry in shadowing Prince virtually everywhere he went.

Another important arrival on the scene was the duo of Vaughn Terry Jelks and Louis Wells, two experienced and imaginative clothing designers who had worked with Earth, Wind & Fire and others. At first, they received the same wordless treatment as Leeds had, and it was unclear whether their presence was welcome. But one evening hanging out backstage, Jelks noticed that his jacket had gone missing. "I looked around, and there was Prince wearing it," he recalled. "That's when I knew he liked what we were doing."

From there, Prince began to exchange ideas with the duo,

and they began to formulate visual ideas for his next project. But a degree of tension quickly emerged between Prince and Jelks, primarily because Jelks' mellow charisma and flamboyant attire caught the attention of many women within the entourage, including some Prince also fancied. "I was like, 'You can have any woman in the world, can't I at least have one?'" Jelks recalled.

Such jealousies aside, the arrival of the Jelks/Wells team, along with Leeds, brought a greater sense of professionalism to the tour. Yet, the rivalry between Prince's band and the Time persisted, with the opening act again upstaging Prince in some cities. Finally, Prince showed his insecurities by booting the band from the bill during appearances in important cities such as New York and Los Angeles. But this tactic essentially backfired, as crowds thinned out somewhat when fans learned that the Time, who had become extremely popular in urban communities, would not be on the bill.

Money remained another point of contention. Morris Day, believing that his stage presence was key to the group's success, frequently had heated discussions with Prince about compensation. The response was always the same: since he wrote all of the music, neither Day nor anyone else in the band deserved anything extra. Adding to the unfairness was the fact that the Time's instrumental members also served as the backing band for Vanity 6, performing behind a pink curtain; they received no compensation for these sets.

Vanity 6's sets were enhanced by the Time's shrouded presence as its three members soldiered through the songs Prince had written for them. Brenda Bennett, a tough-minded Bostonian, gamely handled her ill-suited role as a damsel in lingerie, and Moonsie clearly enjoyed being onstage, dancing with abandon and flaunting her white teddy. But for the supposed bandleader, Denise Matthews, the entire exercise was strained and inorganic; her thin vocals failed to cut through the mix and her charisma failed to translate to the stage.

The morass of pressures that Matthews found herself stuck in – an uncomfortable role as a front person, her romantic competition with Moonsie and Jill Jones, and the intoxicating whiff of fame around the tour – proved overwhelming, and she began to drink to dull her emotions. While fans thought of her as Prince's leading lady, he had given up on this idea rather quickly; she remained a sexual option for him, but only one of many. "He juggled the affairs on a day-to-day basis – some nights Vanity would disappear with Prince, then some nights Jill Jones would end up on the Prince bus, leaving Vanity in the hotel stewing," said tour manager Leeds. "He seemed unfazed by the resultant drama, but it clearly affected everyone else."

Matthews' bandmate Moonsie, who for several years had been the closest thing to Prince's true girlfriend, refused to tolerate these shenanigans and withdrew from the romantic sweepstakes. "She was never frantic about him," said Roy Bennett. "She knew who he was, what he was up to, and she wouldn't take his shit." And rather than playing the wounded ex-lover, Moonsie forged a friendship with Matthews and sought to comfort her during what was nearing a public meltdown.

All told, despite the quality of the music emanating from the stage each night, the *1999* tour was a chaotic and unpredictable affair, involving many outsized personalities and multiple conflict points. Prince and the Time were again locked in combat; Prince's girlfriends were stepping on each other's toes; and Prince was engaged in jealous rivalries even with his own clothing designer. As Vaughn Terry Jelks put it, "The whole thing was one big smorgasbord of attitude and vibe."

***

Despite his incessant erotic encounters with women, it was a physical, albeit non-sexual, encounter with two other men during the tour that had perhaps as much lasting impact. One evening backstage, clothing designer Louis Wells, a strong and athletic individual, encountered Prince's bodyguard Chick Huntsberry and struck up a conversation about professional wrestling. They soon began playfully wrestling against each other, quickly drawing a crowd from others backstage. Surprisingly, Wells managed to pin down Huntsberry and lock up his arms, drawing cheers from the onlookers.

Out of nowhere, Prince emerged from his private dressing room and made a beeline for the fight. He jumped on Wells, joining in the boyish fun. Wells now found himself improbably sandwiched between the massive Huntsberry and the diminuitive Prince. Flexing his powerful frame, Wells easily cast Prince off; he then picked up the bandleader and threw him on a nearby couch.

This defeat provoked not anger but cackling laughter from Prince, who seemed to have enjoyed the experience as much as anything else that happened on the tour. "For a week after that, he talked about nothing besides our free-for-all," Wells recalled.

Wells had stumbled upon a spontaneous, authentically joyful side of Prince that rarely showed itself. The encounter resembled the fantasy renditions of pro wrestlers Mad Dog Vachon and Verne Gagne that Prince had enjoyed with his friend Paul Mitchell during high school, when he had felt free to engage in childlike play. For this brief moment with Wells and Huntsberry, Prince was no longer an aloof rock star, but just another one of the guys.

***

In late 1982 and early 1983, as the tour marched on across the country, Prince achieved several commercial breakthroughs. MTV, the cable television channel that played exclusively music videos, began airing the video for "1999," making Prince one of the few black artists in rotation on a channel that dominated the music industry. The racial divides that had characterized pop music throughout the seventies and into the early eighties were finally coming down, and Prince became one of the pioneers in introducing African-American styles to vast numbers of white consumers.

In February 1983, the release of "Little Red Corvette" brought Prince his first big hit, shooting to No. 6 on the Pop Singles Chart. The melodic pop song demonstrated conclusively that he was not simply a funk musician with a cult following, but a budding songwriter capable of working in different styles. These developments all boosted *1999*, which would sell three million copies in its first year. Additional tour dates were booked, this time into arenas with capacities of over 10,000 people.

After the tour wrapped in Chicago in April 1983, a calm of sorts settled over the Prince camp. Dez Dickerson quit and was replaced by Wendy Melvoin, a shift that eliminated a source of tension within the band but also robbed it of a major talent. Wendy moved in with Lisa at the Residence Inn in Eden Prairie, a complex that provided long-term housing mainly for corporate clients. Alan Leeds also relocated to the Minneapolis area, maintaining close contact with Cavallo and Fargnoli in Los Angeles as he handled Prince's day-to-day affairs.

Prince worked to rebuild the atmosphere of community within his team that had been eroded by the arrival of Huntsberry and the struggles with the Time. Bandmates and associates were invited over for cookouts and to watch videos. He gathered everyone for bowling nights, basketball games, and afternoons of softball. While these activities were generally pleasant and diverting, Prince's hyper-competitiveness sometimes reared its head. "In softball, someone would obviously be out, and Prince would say 'No, he was safe!'" Leeds said. "Well, what are you going to do? If you protested, he was gonna take his bats and gloves and go home."

When not acting as an umpire, Prince worked on new material. Bob Cavallo, during his visits to the purple house in

Chanhassen, was enthralled when Prince would spontaneously sit down at a piano and begin singing. "It was as if he had a direct line to the heavens," the manager recalled. Similarly, Alan Leeds had concluded that in terms of pure songwriting ability, Prince was the most talented figure he had encountered. "The music was just pouring out of him," Leeds recalled.

Indeed, Prince was so prolific that, at the age of 24, he had created a small music empire consisting of himself and two alter-ego acts. *1999* had been a commercial breakthrough and also an artistic achievement, one of the most adventurous albums by a rising pop artist in years. And after a successful tour, as well as ample radio and television exposure, he had become an internationally known star.

But this rise had also left a degree of carnage in its wake. The nominal heads of the Time and Vanity 6 felt frustrated and humiliated, with Day considering his exit and Matthews' stability beginning to crumble. His treatment of his expanding cadre of lovers had become cavalier and sometimes callous, causing hurt feelings and making it unlikely that Prince would receive genuine emotional support from any of them. And despite the softball games and movie nights, there was an air of contrivance around such events; everyone knew that once the next tour began, Prince would again draw a curtain – or perhaps even erect a wall – between himself and his entourage.

Still, Prince's aloofness served his purpose of having maximum time and energy to lay down the new musical ideas that were forming so quickly in his mind. His successes so far had occurred not despite his self-isolating tendencies, but in many respects because of them.

Indeed, all told, the goals he had articulated for himself many years ago had been almost fully achieved. He was nearly as successful as pop's leading hit makers but more authentically cool than any of them. He had not only innovated African-American musical forms, but was now bringing them to a broad audience. His admonition to Warners' Lenny Waronker after being signed to that label – "don't make me black" – had proved prophetic, to the point where he was now transcending race without repudiating any aspect of his heritage.

It was at this moment in his career, with his star ascending, that Prince ceased giving interviews to the media. Media fascination about his story was reaching new heights – and now, suddenly, journalists would be left to their own devices in figuring out how to tell it. This would surely generate even more speculation about who exactly this brilliant and inscrutable figure was.

Still, one thing was clear to everyone – Prince, more than any pop star in recent memory, had achieved almost all of this on his own. There was collaboration, but on his terms only; there was cooperation, but it typically ran in only one direction. In the studio, he was more of an auteur than even Stevie Wonder; as a band leader, he was nearly as iron-handed as James Brown. Few pop artists, let alone one so young, had ever sought such pervasive control over every phase of their activities; fewer still had exercised it so rigidly.

The benefits to this approach were almost too many to number. Prince had ensured that no lover, friend, or family member had any meaningful claim upon his time or attention; he had almost unlimited financial resources; and his accountability to his record company and managers was minimal.

That there were also downsides and inherent dangers to this mode of operation was not something that Prince would acknowledge, neither now nor at any point during a career that was poised to enter the stratosphere.

19. DREAMS COME TRUE

Prince on the *1999* Tour

The idea of starring in a music film remained of acute interest to Prince even after he discarded *The Second Coming* project that had been started after the *Controversy* tour. Ultimately, that project had amounted to little more than friends goofing around inside of a purple-painted house in their underwear, and to move beyond this required financing. "There's a point where you've got to deal with a film company, or you're just an amateur making a very expensive home movie," noted tour manager Alan Leeds.

Leeds himself frequently attended movies with Prince, typically flanking the artist with a bodyguard as they sat in theatres. Prince, although not an extremely sophisticated student of cinema, enjoyed films ranging from the Sylvester Stallone film *Rambo* to David Lynch's *Eraserhead*.

For his own potential film, Prince had an amorphous concept called "The Dawn" that he had been pondering during the *1999* tour. He now wanted access to an experienced screenwriter to develop the idea.[1] Financing presented another immediate obstacle; Warner Bros. Pictures, the filmmaking arm of the company that released his albums, showed no interest when first approached by manager Steve Fargnoli. Disgusted and blaming this failure on his managers, he used a key piece of leverage against them. With their contractual relationship with him about to expire, Prince indicated that securing a movie deal was a prerequisite to keeping him as a client.

The unflappable Bob Cavallo approached Mo Ostin, the chairman of Warner Bros. Records, in early 1983 and explained the dilemma. Ostin, who felt comfortable enough with Prince's career progress to support the idea, in turn approached Mark Canton, the head of production at Warner Bros. Pictures. After a successful meeting between Canton and Prince, a series of interlocking transactions was negotiated. Prince and his managers both agreed to put up about $1 million collectively toward the project. Warners Pictures agreed to provide additional funding for production costs, and Warner Bros. Records committed to covering cost overruns.[2]

On its face, the notion that a young artist well below the level of superstardom could be a mass box office draw seemed implausible. But the support of Warners officials for the project was no accident. These powerful executives understood Prince's talents, but were also well acquainted with his relentless work ethic and discipline. And Prince cultivated entertainment czars with poise and charm. "He never said an unkind word to me during the ten years I worked with him," remembered Cavallo. "And he knew exactly how to articulate what he wanted, even if it wasn't in a whole lot of words."

Prince now had the funding to set the production into motion. Developing a film would be an immensely complex process, and Prince had to function essentially as the chief executive officer of a mid-sized company. Above him sat a *de facto* board of directors that included Ostin, Canton, and to some extent his own manager Cavallo, all of whom needed to remain personally invested in the project. Any failures of execution could jeopardize that support in a moment.

Below Prince in the organization structure would be several mid-level officials with diverse portfolios. These included Alan Leeds, and two important players to be named later – the film's screenwriter and director.

Leeds, who had relocated his family to Minneapolis, took over day-to-day operations, establishing a base in a cavernous warehouse in the Minneapolis suburb of St. Louis Park where rehearsals and acting classes would take place. As the manager with the most day-to-day contact with Prince, Leeds found his job at once exhilarating and jarring. Appreciating Leeds' knowledge of R&B music, Prince sometimes treated him as almost a mentor, and on a few occasions, the bandleader even opened up emotionally to Leeds. But in the end, the tour manager, like everyone else, was expected to fulfill whatever need emerged in the moment. "It was as if he were saying to me, 'Okay, now I want Alan the big brother,'" Leeds recalled. "Then it might be, 'Now I want Alan the best friend.' Then it might be 'Now I want Alan the gofer.' I'd better not confuse the three roles, because if he sends me on a mission and I come into rehearsal empty-handed, and I start laughing and joking like we did in front of the TV last night, I'm not going to last very long."

Back in Los Angeles, Cavallo and Fargnoli searched for a screenwriter and director, eventually handing both roles to experienced television director William Blinn. Prince envisioned a tale of a struggling musician who overcomes the odds to achieve stardom. Blinn, while comfortable with this concept, initially had great difficulty communicating with Prince, finding him at best cryptic and at worst completely unresponsive. When they went to a movie together in an effort to warm things up, Prince left without a word after twenty minutes.

But the relationship gradually improved, and an outline of a script called "Dreams" emerged from their discussions. Prince would play the tortured performer known as "the Kid," a nickname coined by Cavallo. Morris Day, leader of the Time, would be the Kid's professional and romantic rival; they would quarrel over the beautiful Vanity, played by Denise Matthews. Another key element was the Kid's troubled family life, particularly his relationship with an abusive father. All of this would take place against the backdrop of an incestuous, highly competitive music scene not unlike the one Prince had known during his teen years in Minneapolis.

As Blinn fleshed out his screenplay, Prince composed new songs and taught them to his band, a unit he now formally dubbed the Revolution. The band personnel from the *1999* tour remained intact, except for the replacement of Dez Dickerson with Wendy Melvoin, which significantly changed both the sound and social dynamics of the band. Melvoin, just nineteen, had never even played in a band before, but this lack of context had a freeing effect. She joked with Prince and treated him with little deference, something he found refreshing, and they quickly developed a close friendship. "Everyone else was more or less intimidated by him, but Wendy came the furthest of anyone I've ever seen at pulling Prince out of his shell," remembered studio engineer Susan Rogers.

Seeing Wendy as a potential star, Prince made her a focal point of the Revolution. Her guitar work was distinctive in its use of dense, ethereal chords. Her vaguely masculine appearance – she had an asymmetrical haircut and a kind of toughness – created an intriguing counterpoint to Prince's more feminine androgyny.

As the band immersed itself in rehearsals and acting classes, Prince constantly reminded everyone how important the movie was to all of their fortunes. "Do you have what it takes to be a star?" Prince asked Matt Fink one day at rehearsal. Fink, taken aback by the blunt query, said that he did, but Prince responded with a sarcastic smirk, indicating that he found the response unconvincing. But gradually, through a combination of cajolery, flattery, and intimidation, Prince persuaded his comrades that the film would rocket their careers into the stratosphere. "Prince would say to me all the time, 'Mark, after this, you're never going to have to work again,'" recalled bassist Brown.

These promises were ultimately a form of psychological motivation; seeing wonderful things ahead, the Revolution remained focused through exhausting preparations for the movie. "He convinced them they were a self-contained band, and he played that to the hilt to get whatever he needed out of them," said Leeds.

Even as the new band took shape, the production hit a snag; William Blinn's television series *Fame* was renewed for a third season, leaving him without time to complete the script. Cavallo and Fargnoli began a hasty search for another writer-director that led them to thirty-year-old Albert Magnoli, previously an editor for the renowned director James Foley, and whom Foley had recommended. At first, Magnoli was uninspired by Blinn's script and said he would pass. But a brainstorming session with Cavallo left him much more optimistic, and Magnoli agreed to meet with Prince. They connected with surprising ease, and Magnoli took the job.

Meanwhile, with Prince having succeeded in turning his five-piece band into a powerhouse, the Revolution's debut took place on the sweltering night of August 3, 1983 at First Avenue, Prince's favorite hometown club. The club was packed with admirers for a show that would raise money for the Minnesota Dance Theatre, a facility where Prince and the band were tutored for the movie. An extensive last-minute guest list submitted by Warners and Prince meant an overcapacity crowd, leading to concerns that fire marshals might shut the event down before it even started.[3]

Outside the club, engineer David Rivkin captured the show on tape from a mobile studio. The band was unaware that anything was out of the ordinary, as Prince typically recorded every show. But Prince, hoping that some of the live recordings would be used for the movie's soundtrack, planned in advance to wring every ounce of emotion from the performance. The night would also include the live debut of a swelling rock ballad called "Purple Rain."

In the balcony, taking in the band's nine-song set, Albert Magnoli watched intently as Wendy took the stage for the encore, and struck the opening chord of "Purple Rain." She ran through the chord progression once, and then was joined by the rest of the Revolution, who backed her. After playing the progression nine complete times, in a moment of 19-year-old awkwardness, she smiled anxiously and seemed ready to break character. Prince finally appeared, prompting Wendy to right herself. Wearing a purple brocade jacket and hoop earring, Prince was soaked in sweat after an already long night. He joined Wendy on guitar briefly, then flung his guitar behind his back and approached the mic stand. Seemingly overcome with emotion, Prince backed away again before starting to sing.

The first performance of "Purple Rain" lasted more than thirteen minutes. The crowd was silent until the end as it took in the new song. Magnoli, from the balcony, wondered if this vulnerable rock ballad might provide the emotional climax for a movie that was essentially a story of the Kid's search for redemption. After the show, Magnoli shared his idea with Prince, venturing that "Purple Rain" might be the missing puzzle piece that would make the movie whole. Prince initially objected, saying the song was unfinished. Undeterred, Magnoli continued to argue forcefully for the song's inclusion. Prince, his resistance softening, then asked whether "Purple Rain" could also be used as the title of the film.[4] And with that, a major building block of the film – and indeed, Prince's entire career – was in place.

Among the guests Wendy Melvoin invited to Minneapolis for her debut with Prince's band in August 1983 was her twin sister Susannah, who greatly resembled Wendy but had a more feminine style. Prince was delighted to discover that his favorite new band member had a beautiful double, and an instant mutual attraction developed. Well-educated and stylish, Susannah stimulated Prince intellectually as well as physically. But she had a boyfriend in California and was not immediately available for a romance, which infuriated Prince.

This jealously helped to inspire the stunning ballad "The Beautiful Ones," which he recorded in September. The song, which explodes into a torrent of jealous screams in its climax, was a brilliant amalgam of emotions. It was designed for the axial moment of the movie's plot, as the Kid furiously insists that Apollonia choose between him and his rival Morris.

Prince also planned to include music in the film by the Time and Vanity 6. But both groups would in truth be, as had been the case on their earlier albums, essentially fictions; Prince would write, perform, and record most of the songs, with vocals being the only major contribution of the groups' supposed captains, Morris Day and Denise Matthews.

Among the songs recorded over the summer of 1983 for the second Vanity 6 album was "Vibrator," in which Denise Matthews sings about a sex toy whose batteries run out. The song then recounts her visit to a convenience store run by her romantic rival, Jill Jones, who offers to take the device downstairs to install new batteries, and presumably to use it as well. Matthews then encounters a clerk at a second store, played by Prince, who both provides batteries and hurries Matthews home to bed; the song then concludes with a torrent of Matthews' moans.

Such absurdities provided little actual relief for Matthews, whose excitement about being in a motion picture was sapped by her ongoing frustration at being a puppet band leader and having to complete for Prince's attention with a bevy of other women. Morris Day felt equally frustrated by his role, and Prince underscored his powerlessness by firing Jimmy Harris and Terry Lewis after they missed a show as a result of their work on a side project. This move effectively tore the group apart, as original members Monte Moir and Jellybean Johnson quit, unwilling to continue without Harris and Lewis. Prince restocked the lineup with relatively unknown Minneapolis musicians, leaving Day and Jesse Johnson with a dramatically different Time.

To make matters worse, Day developed a cocaine problem, making him even more moody and confrontational.[5] As recording of the Time's third record began, and Day again went through the tedious exercise of mimicking Prince's guide vocals note for note, it was apparent the end was near for the Time. "It was a very tense situation," recalled Susan Rogers. "Morris was very unhappy and basically non-participating. He was going to get the movie over with, and then it was obvious that he was out of there."

This left Jesse Johnson – who felt underpaid and overworked, and who remained angry about the coat rack incident – as the group's leader. Like Harris and Lewis before him, the talented Johnson wanted badly to express his own ideas and succeed on his own merits; realizing Prince would never allow this, he also began to consider going solo.

Initially, much of the public and media were fooled into thinking that both the Time and Vanity 6 were freestanding groups that created their own music. But when Prince finally started dropping public hints that he was in fact Jamie Starr, the alleged producer of these acts, being unmasked added to the humiliations of Day and Vanity. "When you realized that Vanity 6 was really all his concept, from the lingerie they wore, to the songs they sang, to the music that was played behind them, it wasn't the same," Leeds remembered. Furious about these issues and her disintegrating romance with Prince, Matthews started to numb her feelings through heavy drinking and cocaine use, starting her down a road that would eventually leave her health in ruins.

Partly as a retort to Prince for his womanizing, Matthews flaunted affairs she was having with both men and women. She also developed a close friendship with Alan Leeds, who found Matthews lonely and increasingly upset about Prince's treatment of her. "It didn't take long to realize she was a competitive pistol that hungered for companionship and wasn't about to let Prince's desire for control sentence her to the confines of her hotel room," he remembered.

A turning point in the relationship came when Vanity had an affair with Albert Magnoli, enraging Prince. Despite production being only about two months away, the transgression was intolerable and Prince fired Matthews from the production. He made no effort to correct the record when she claimed to the media that she had left over money issues; the point was that she was gone.

Prince and his team now scrambled to fill this key vacancy on short notice. Hundreds of obscure and would-be actresses answered a call to audition for the vacant role. Prince quickly settled on 22-year-old Patricia Kotero of Santa Monica, California, who had starred in the miniseries *Mystic Warriors*. The reason for the selection was obvious to everyone: Kotero looked very much like Matthews, just as Matthews had resembled Prince's previous girlfriend Susan Moonsie. Prince inauspiciously dubbed her Apollonia, after a character in the first *Godfather* film who is killed by a car bomb.

Shortly after recruiting Kotero, he took her to a Los Angeles nightclub where he had heard that Denise Matthews would be partying. As he had hoped, Matthews was aghast to see Prince with a woman who looked almost like a mirror image of herself. The message was clear: replacing her had not been difficult.

Few of Prince's associates had been impressed with Matthews' musical talents, although there was some hope that her charisma would translate to the silver screen. But Patricia Kotero was something else altogether. Although her sultry appearance was almost indistinguishable from that of her predecessor, her personal magnetism paled in comparison. Plucked from obscurity to star in a film and to front a singing group, she was immediately in over her head, displaying little talent in either area. She lacked Matthews' edge; all that remained of the character Prince had created was physical beauty. "I don't think she was creative or clever enough to hold Prince's interest," said one frequent visitor to the set. Nonetheless, she became the front person of Apollonia 6, with Susan Moonsie and Brenda Bennett reprising their Vanity 6 roles.

Although Prince believed that Apollonia could probably skate through her thin role in *Purple Rain*, he concluded her vocal talents were not worth expending any of his better songs on. A bounty of strong material was considered for her *Apollonia 6* album, only to be reclaimed for other uses, leaving mainly filler. "He was not optimistic about Apollonia 6, so he wasn't going to be really critical about those songs," Rogers noted.

Nonetheless, some of Prince's associates were troubled that even subpar material would be used for such a dubious project. With Matthews and now Kotero, a pattern was emerging: Prince would squander time, energy, and music on women simply because their beauty fascinated him. "The Vanities and the Apollonias bothered me," said Matt Fink. "I thought he could be producing extremely talented people, not people who were there for their looks rather than their singing."

While Apollonia denied in the press that she and Prince became romantically involved, rumors to the contrary flew on the set of *Purple Rain*. "She and Prince did have a brief fling," confirmed one knowledgeable source. "But I don't think he ever had a genuine flame for her. And there's no doubt that part of his attraction to Apollonia was a desire to get Vanity's goat."

    ***

With all elements of the film finally in place, shooting began in November 1983 in Minneapolis. The pace was rapid, as Magnoli struggled to complete work before the arrival of winter made outdoor scenes impossible. But the young director also tried to keep the atmosphere loose and informal; scenes were shot in as few takes as possible, creating a playful energy between Prince and his associates. Shooting of the musical numbers took place at First Avenue, where hundreds of extras cheered and danced as Prince and the Revolution, as well as The Time, lip-synched to previously recorded material.

A major surprise was the on-screen magnetism of Morris Day, who channeled his frustrations into a bravura performance despite a growing drug problem. "During the making of the movie, more than once he had to be physically dragged out of his house and driven to the set, between the paranoia and exhaustion from all-night freebase binges," said an insider who was sometimes sent to roust Day. Still, Day managed to play his character, a slick, sleazy, self-absorbed womanizer, with the perfect degree of camp. Some observers credited Day with stealing his scenes with Prince, whose onscreen presence during non-musical sequences proved to be relatively thin and weak.

With the Minneapolis scenes complete, the next step was to decamp to Los Angeles to complete outdoor shooting in warmer weather. But the initial funding from Mo Ostin had run out, placing an obstacle in front of the production. Cavallo and Fargnoli entered another intense round of negotiations with Warner Bros. Pictures as Prince and his team of actors and musicians anxiously waited. Word eventually came that the company had agreed to provide additional financing and also to distribute the film. *Purple Rain* was going to make it to cinemas, representing the realization of one of Prince's lifelong dreams. "We were on a pretty exciting ride at that point, and we knew where it was going," said Roy Bennett. "There was something big out there for us; we just never knew how big."

***

The emotional lift of the film being greenlighted sent Prince into a frenzy of recording. He continued to insist that even complicated songs be completed in a single session, meaning that engineers were required to work as long as 24 hours straight. From late January through March of 1984, Prince completed the remainder of the *Purple Rain* soundtrack; the backbone of what would be his follow-up to *Purple Rain*; the third Time album; the Apollonia 6 album; an album built around the percussionist and singer Sheila Escovedo, whom he dubbed Sheila E.; and various single B-sides and unreleased songs.

Various innovative recording approaches were used. "Erotic City," which would emerge as a single B-side from *Purple Rain*, utilized the technique of changing the tape speed while recording vocals and guitars, creating unusual effects when the song was mixed down at normal speed. During the mixing process for "When Doves Cry," conceived as a centerpiece of the film soundtrack, he dropped out the bass line, giving the song a minimalistic feel that was contrary to just about anything on the pop charts. As Marylou Badeaux recalled, the reaction from one official at Warners was, "What kind of fucking record is this, with a bunch of strange sounds?" But Prince was adamant that it be the first single from the album.

"When Doves Cry," released in May 1984, vindicated his instincts and took Prince's commercial success to a new level. It shot to No. 1 on the Pop Singles Chart and sold a million units, becoming the best-selling song of the year. This immediately created an atmosphere of excitement in Prince's camp as the film was readied for a mid-summer release.

Meanwhile, Prince had developed strong feelings for Susannah Melvoin, who put her relationship on hold and moved to Minnesota to be with him. Her hopes of being his only love interest were quickly dashed, as he had also started a significant romance with Sheila Escovedo. For both Sheila and Susannah, two strangers now linked by their pursuit of the same man, what at first seemed like a storybook romance with a powerful pop star became tumultuous and painful. Howard Bloom, Prince's press agent, became close with Escovedo and found her often distraught about her relationship with Prince. "Sheila E. wanted to live with him for the rest of her life, and it wasn't going to happen; it was awful for her," Bloom said.

Jill Jones also remained an on-again, off-again girlfriend, and Prince was generally ready to sleep with virtually any woman who grabbed his attention. Bloom recalls, for example, dispatching a publicist from his company to meet with Prince and getting a call that afternoon asking him to send the woman back for carnal purposes. "He was sexually omnivorous," remembers Bloom, who refused to fulfill Prince's request. "Life for him was a sexual hors d'oeuvres tray."

***

On June 7, 1984 – Prince's 26th birthday – a party for friends, family, and others took place at First Avenue, just weeks before the release of the *Purple Rain* album. In addition to his large entourage, Prince invited old friends from the neighborhood. His ties to the Northside had frayed considerably over the years, and the event offered an opportunity for Prince to reconnect with aspects of his formative years.

Among the old friends who attended was Terry Jackson, the former percussionist for Prince's high school band Grand Central. Prince had long held a disproportionate grudge against Jackson over a high school spat over Prince stealing food from the Jackson family kitchen. The repercussions of that incident, which had devolved into Prince throwing a rake comb and then Jackson hoisting a golf club, had reverberated through the years. When Prince was forming his first professional band, in 1978, at first it had seemed that the scars might have healed and Jackson might have a space in the ensemble. But that possibility vanished when Prince had haughtily told the percussionist to pack up his equipment and leave the rehearsal space. Timbales, Prince told Jackson, would not be part of the future of R&B music.

Tonight, Jackson felt proud of his friend and hopeful that the hatchet had finally been buried. Happily, he found himself dancing with the belle of the ball, Apollonia, as dozens of friends and other onlookers watched. But when Prince saw them, he stalked over and made his anger apparent. As Jackson backed off, Prince then pointed up at the ceiling as a new song began playing over the speakers. "Listen," Prince said. "This is what I meant about timbales!"

The song was "The Glamorous Life," which Prince had written and recorded for Sheila E. Among its key elements was Escovedo's frenetic percussion, which included a very prominent use of timbales.

Jackson, stunned that Prince even remembered their interaction of nearly six years earlier, walked away in dismay. Even tonight, Jackson, for one, needed to be reminded that Prince's victories in some measure had come at someone else's expense.

***

Not long after the party, the various elements of the *Purple Rain* campaign were finally unspooled, and their success was of a magnitude that no one had thought to anticipate. Soon after being released in June 1984, the *Purple Rain* soundtrack displaced Bruce Springsteen's *Born In the USA* from the No. 1 position on Billboard's Album Chart. Prince's album would go on to hold the top slot for 12 weeks, and it sold 16.3 million records worldwide.

This success did nothing to alienate hip rock journalists, who largely felt that *Purple Rain* had satisfied all of their great expectations for Prince. Here was an album that ranged from iconoclastic funk ("When Doves Cry") to blistering guitar rock ("Let's Go Crazy") to stirring R&B ballads ("The Beautiful

Ones"). It was difficult to find songs on the album that were not candidates for Prince classics.

The film itself grossed $70 million and was among the top moneymakers of 1984, making Prince one of the most visible entertainers in the entire world. Reaction from film critics was largely strong, and the entire project became a significant cultural phenomenon.

Not much more than a year earlier, Prince had remained an up-and-coming artist with a sizeable following and a modest entourage. Now, he was an international superstar, and also widely recognized as a consequential artist. Every hunch he followed, and every idiosyncratic decision he made had panned out. He had succeeded at creating a grand synthesis of rock, R&B, and funk that was already influencing other artists.

But for all of his foresight, the pressures that came with these victories would prove to be greater than even Prince himself could have imagined.

20. TYPECAST

Prince on the 1985 *Purple Rain* Tour

To satisfy all of the hype that had formed around Prince, the *Purple Rain* tour had to be an extravaganza. The stage set, designed by Roy Bennett, was the most elaborate of Prince's career, costing $300,000 and featuring props such as a purple bathtub that rose from below the stage. Hours of preparation were required to integrate these complicated elements. It was the tub – perched on a platform and propelled by a hydraulic lift that would make it rise from the stage – that proved most problematic, particularly when it fell with Prince in it during a rehearsal. Although his injuries were not grave, Prince did suffer significant bruising.[1]

More consequentially, the set featured risers that were stacked on top of each other to achieve great height. Prince jumped from them multiple times during each show while wearing four-inch heels. This would occur night after night for the duration of the tour, which lasted an entire year, placing an immense muscular and orthopedic strain on Prince's body. Over the course of this tour, Prince began using prescription painkillers to cope with the pain caused by these injuries.[2]

***

The compressed tour schedule included ninety concerts in thirty-two cities across the United States. To pull off the complicated logistics of the swing, Prince's organization had to attain a new level of discipline and efficiency. With Steve Fargnoli continuing to spend most of his time in Los Angeles, the key player on the scene in Minneapolis remained tour manager Alan Leeds. He was joined by Karen Krattinger, an attractive, tough-minded Georgian who had been road manager for the S.O.S. Band. Temperamentally, Leeds and Krattinger were near opposites and complemented each other perfectly; he was a strategic, sometimes lofty thinker with a passion for R&B music, while she was a meticulously organized administrator with almost no interest in artistic issues. Together, they became the linchpins of Prince's team and also served as close personal aides to Prince. With the help of numerous others within Prince's organization, they orchestrated one of the most elaborate pop tours of 1984-85.

The opening night, at Joe Louis Arena in the Prince stronghold of Detroit, demonstrated how thoroughly *Purple Rain* had captured the public's attention. The 20,000 fans went into a frenzy the moment the spoken words that begin "Let's Go Crazy" crackled over the speakers. The crowd-pleasing show focused on *Purple Rain* (eight of its nine tracks were played) and *1999*. Although certain vaudevillian touches – the bathtub and other props, as well as Prince's five costume changes – drew objections from some critics, who would have preferred more spontaneity, fans seemed enraptured.

The tour packed arenas everywhere it went, with shows selling out mere hours after being announced. The crowds were not only much larger than any Prince had experienced as a headlining performer, but had a very different flavor; suburban parents brought children who had begged for concert tickets, whites greatly outnumbered blacks. It was, in short, the generic mass audience that gravitates toward any artist of the moment. The days of Prince as an underground phenomenon were gone forever.

Along with casual fans checking out the next big thing, the crowds contained large numbers of zealots who identified, in many cases excessively, with the Prince and the Revolution of *Purple Rain*. Largely as a result of the film, each band member became highly recognizable. "They all had their own very vocal pockets of fans at shows," Leeds recalled. "Wendy and Lisa in particular were instant role models for every aspiring young female musician in the country." The wild desire of fans and groupies to meet and touch their new heroes kept the atmosphere charged with emotion and expectation. "It became a circus," noted drummer Bobby Z. Rivkin. "There were people dressed up in costumes, people dressed up as you. It was extremely exciting, but you had to be careful – it was very powerful."

To satisfy the expectations of new admirers, Prince had created a show in which the visual elements were just as important as the music. But in the process, something was lost: the subversive energy of earlier tours was stifled by the props and choreographed routines that Prince felt were integral to a major-market production. Dez Dickerson, watching from the sidelines, felt vaguely nauseated by the spectacle. "It was a big part of why I had left – he wanted the shows to become more and more structured and would often say, 'I want it to be like a Broadway play,'" Dickerson recalled. "For me, it was going in an entirely different direction from what I felt was the heart of what we do as a craft. I didn't want to become Wayne Newton in high heels."

Among the show's stranger elements was an interlude during which Prince had an anguished "conversation with God" against swirls of synthesizers. While largely incomprehensible, this dialogue seemed to reflect Prince's struggle to reconcile his lustful side with more traditional morality. With the largest crowds of his career looking on, Prince seemed intent on showing that he recognized a higher authority and was, at heart, a God-fearing man.

As he watched the show, publicist Bloom saw that an important, and in many respects unfortunate, transition was occurring in Prince's career and his psyche. From *Dirty Mind* through *1999*, he had been a rebel who rejected prevailing social norms. Now, having achieved the heights of fame, Prince felt an obligation to curtail the more outlandish elements of his character. With so many young people around the world fixated on him, perhaps he even felt the need to become something of a role model. "Prince had been rebelling against God and morality, and now God and morality were taking him over," Bloom observed. "His emphasis was not on sexuality any more, but on God."

Still, the sexual elements of Prince's music and persona, now that he was a household name, gave pause to social conservatives and moralists. In late 1984, for example, thirty-six-year-old Tipper Gore, wife of the handsome young senator Albert Gore, discovered her daughter listening to *Purple Rain* and was shocked in particular by the lyrics of "Darling Nikki," which refer to a woman masturbating with magazines. Four months later, Gore and several other well-connected women in Washington started the "Parents' Music Resource Center" to advocate for commercial restrictions on prurient lyrics. This eventually resulted in the placement of warning labels on certain "explicit" albums, with Prince's music having been a driving impetus for the campaign.

While Prince was hardly unaware of the publicity value of Gore's attacks on him, the charge that his music corrupted the minds of children stung. In many respects, his bedrock value system was conservative and hierarchical, and it was becoming even more so. While working on the Family project in 1984, Prince pulled a song called "Feline" from the project because group member Paul Peterson felt it offended his religious sensibilities and, even more importantly, his mother. "Prince is gonna be the first one to listen when someone says 'My religion doesn't allow me to do this,'" recalled engineer Susan Rogers. "Those words carry a lot of weight for him. He also respects mothers and respects family life even though he didn't have such a good one of his own." While Prince had previously been more reluctant to accommodate band members' concerns – witness his refusal to drop "Head" from the live set at Dez Dickerson's request during the *Controversy* tour – by the mid-1980s, with his fame broadening, he now felt some pressure to dial back such elements.

The downside of all this was that Prince's music and persona gradually became less subversive and arguably less interesting. He became a modern pop icon, but to do so was forced to give up some of his edge and distinctiveness. "First you rebel against something," noted publicist Bloom, "and then you turn into it."

***

The crushing fame brought on by *Purple Rain* brought on another transition: Prince became even more cloistered and remote from many of his own associates. He moved everywhere with a phalanx of bodyguards led by Chick Huntsberry. "It was ridiculous; you felt like you were going to be frisked every time you walked backstage," said Marylou Badeaux, now a Warner Bros. president, who had previously enjoyed easy access to Prince. Gradually, it became difficult even to discuss important issues. "He just kind of shut himself off; he became a different person at that point," recalled production designer Roy Bennett. "Between Prince and everybody else, a wall came up."

Upon leaving the stage each night, Prince was flanked by bodyguards and whisked away in a limousine, sometimes leaving band members unsure even whether there would be an encore.

"There were two or three times where the band felt the response was so amazing that certainly he would come back, but meanwhile he was already in his car halfway back to the hotel," remembered Badeaux. Ensconced in his room, he usually studied a videotape of the previous night's performance or played piano, rarely entertaining guests other than female companions.

One of the few former colleagues who stayed in touch, Dez Dickerson, felt a dramatically different atmosphere when Prince invited him and his wife Becky back to his hotel after a show in Washington, D.C. The large suite housed a grand piano that was trucked from city to city, and various handlers, including a private chef, buzzed about.

As Dickerson and Prince became immersed in a jocular conversation, the rock star pretenses melted away; for a moment it was if they were back in Minneapolis, goofing around after rehearsal. "He was starting to kind of come back to life again, like in the old days," the guitarist recalled. As he and Becky left, Dickerson remarked that they should all get together and go shopping in Georgetown, as they had on previous tours. Prince's eyes lit up with expectation, but then just as quickly a sad look crossed his face. "Nah, I can't do stuff like that anymore," he said. "I can't go out." Dickerson realized things had changed irrevocably. He said goodbye and left, and although the two men would remain in sporadic contact over the years, their communications usually ran through Prince's intermediaries. "We never really had any quality time together after that," Dickerson said.

Dickerson was hardly alone in feeling a drastic change. Each member of the band had at some point during recent years considered Prince a friend, but now felt they were being treated more as employees. "Prince wanted to keep it all business," Matt Fink remembered. While Prince's friendships with Wendy and Lisa would rekindle once the pressures of the tour abated, the closeness that Fink, drummer Rivkin, and bassist Mark Brown had once enjoyed with him would never quite return.

***

Well before the circus-like *Purple Rain* tour lurched to a close, the man at the center of this extravaganza was in some respects ready for it all to be over. That part of Prince that craved stardom was, of course, elated by the public frenzy over the film, album, and tour. He had achieved the sort of fame that turns a name into a household word. And to a large extent, this was just what he had sought since starting his professional music career at age eighteen. But another, equally important part of Prince longed for artistic respect, the sort that he worried might be incompatible with indiscriminate public adoration. "I think he really had fears of being typecast as Mr. *Purple Rain*," observed Alan Leeds. "By the time that tour was over, he was so sick of that music and that whole concept." Add in to the mix the fact that Prince was at this point in his career no great fan of being on the road for long periods of time, and it created a situation that only exacerbated his tendency to cloister himself during off hours. "Six months was his limit; he burned out after that," noted Matt Fink. While some band members wanted to cash in on *Purple Rain* by taking the tour to Europe, Prince's goal was to finish the U.S. swing and get back into the studio.

Mark Brown, only in his early twenties and experiencing a heady rush of fame he never could have anticipated, began drinking heavily. "For me, the whole thing was a little too much at a young age," he said. "When life comes to you that easy, you start abusing it, it doesn't matter who you are. If you don't take it in perspective, you will start to burn out, and I believe that's what happened to all of us."

Light recreational use of marijuana and cocaine among some band members and other members of Prince's circle was not unheard of, but never became rampant. Prince himself, despite using painkillers behind the scenes for legitimate medical reasons, never participated in recreational drug use. But among members of the crew, the men and women who erected stage sets and transported the heavy equipment in trucks, cocaine use became commonplace. Always the first to arrive in a city on the day of the show, the crew undertook the Herculean task of setting up for the band's afternoon sound check. When the show finally concluded late at night, they packed up and drove on to the next city to begin the same cycle again; under such conditions, the use of stimulants became perhaps the only means of staying awake. "There were serious amounts of drugs going on within the crew," said Roy Bennett. "It was ridiculous, people wouldn't sleep for days." Added another knowledgeable source: "Almost everyone outside of Prince and the band were using coke. I sometimes think coke kept the buses and trucks afloat for those six or seven months."

Secluded in his hotel room or his private dressing room, Prince remained oblivious to all of this. Reports of the crew's activities finally reached him near the end of the tour, but by this time it was too late to become outraged; the exhausted crew members would do whatever was necessary to complete the grueling swing and return home.

    ***

With the triumph of *Purple Rain*, Prince had become, unquestionably, part of pop music's elite, the handful of stars that define any given decade. His main competitors, in terms of both record sales and sheer visibility, were Michael Jackson, Madonna, and Bruce Springsteen.

Prince's new fame, however, would not come without a price. Some of his associates felt that he became far too identified with *Purple Rain*. So many stars before him, having achieved similar prominence, were soon reduced to cartoon-like status. Could a similar fate befall Prince?

"The tour was the closest thing to 'Beatlemania' for Prince and his group," said Eric Leeds. "It was really a phenomenon that was greater than Prince; the vast majority of the fans were enthralled with *Purple Rain* more than with what Prince was about in totality. One of the biggest mistakes he made was to think that *Purple Rain* was going to be the norm rather than the exception."

And just as the characters of *Purple Rain* represented divisions in his psyche, the external Prince was split over how to proceed after having become one of the most successful pop stars of his time.

21. BACKLASH

Even before *Purple Rain* was released, Prince had started to plan his subsequent projects and to consider new directions. *Purple Rain* in many respects constituted the apotheosis of techniques Prince had been exploring for years, including the use of the Oberheim synth for horn lines and the LM-1 in place of drums. But he now began to contemplate a return to analogue drum textures and also something that had long been unthinkable for Prince – the use of actual horns, a staple of R&B music that he had deliberately eschewed.

Over the spring months of 1984, Prince had been discussing the potential use of horns with Alan Leeds, who happened to have a brother, Eric, who was a skilled saxophonist. Prince readily agreed to have Eric flown in to Minneapolis for a meeting and to hear some of the music Prince potentially wanted him to play on. Those songs were slated for a new side project to replace the Time; one of the first was "Mutiny," whose vengeful lyrics were directed towards Morris Day and Jesse Johnson for having left the Time.[1] Prince planned to call the new side project "the

Family," which had been the name of a Northside band that Prince's Grand Central competed with during his high school years.

Like the Time, the group would be nominally independent from Prince, although he planned to record the bulk of the Family's music on his own and then piece together a band from his friends and associates. Three former Time members were recruited, including sideman Paul Peterson as the lead singer, and Prince's girlfriend Susannah Melvoin was added as the second vocalist.

In a significant departure from his previous work, Prince asked an outsider to add strings to his music. Prince learned from Wendy and Lisa about the respected orchestral composer Clare Fischer, who had worked with R&B artists such as Rufus. Intrigued, Prince sent him several of the Family tracks for his input even before meeting him. "Prince said, 'I want movie music,'" noted engineer David Z. Rivkin, who contacted Fischer. "Fischer's arrangements cut across the track like there was a movie going on, and that's what Prince wanted. Something dissonant, something weird – the guy just sliced across the tracks sideways, independent of the music almost." Delighted with the outcome, Prince became superstitious about the relationship and insisted upon never seeing Fischer in person, preferring to simply forward him tapes.

Consistent with these explorations, Prince resolved that his next albums would demonstrate musical growth and travel in a radically different direction. To help achieve this goal, he convened a school of sorts – an informal but intensive survey of important rock and jazz musicians of the twentieth century. As a youth, Prince had been exposed only to Minneapolis' very limited menu of radio stations, and by the time he reached his late teen years, he was too immersed in his own music to make learning about other artists a priority. To make up for this gap in his education, Prince began encouraging members of his inner circle to share with him their extensive knowledge of various musical forms.

His friends were well suited to the task. Bandmates Wendy and Lisa, and his girlfriend Susannah Melvoin, all steeped in the music of the sixties and seventies, played him records by the Beatles, Rolling Stones, Led Zeppelin, and others. Saxophonist Eric Leeds and his brother Alan, both jazz aficionados, exposed Prince to the canons of Miles Davis, Duke Ellington, and Charles Mingus. And percussionist and drummer Sheila E. introduced him to contemporary jazz-fusion artists like Weather Report. "I always enjoyed eavesdropping on whatever Prince might be listening to in his dressing room," recalled Alan Leeds, who would hear everything from classic Al Green to Miles Davis' *Sketches Of Spain* to early Little Richard.

Prince's inner circle was beginning to resemble a salon, as he found himself surrounded by stimulating, creative, and sophisticated people who were themselves bound together by musical affinities, friendship, and family ties. Both of the Leeds brothers at times served as mentor or older-brother figures to him, and twins Susannah and Wendy, so similar in temperament and appearance, also enjoyed deep personal bonds with Prince. The creative synergy among Prince, Wendy, and Lisa strengthened almost by the day. Lisa's brother, David Coleman, and Wendy and Susannah's brother, Jonathan Melvoin, both talented musicians, occasionally passed through the creative circuit as well and played on various songs.

Prince absorbed voraciously the information offered by his friends, and immediately applied this knowledge in the studio. Still, his innate impatience gave his studies a rushed quality, as he rarely focused on any subject in detail. During conversations with friends, Prince would not hesitate to abruptly and rudely cut someone off the moment he began to lose interest. "There was a certain submission to the friendship, even when you were sitting around talking about Duke Ellington or Miles Davis," recalled

Alan Leeds. "He wanted to hear what you had to say, but he wanted to hear it in response to his specific questions. He didn't want a lot of editorializing."

Prince's approach to songwriting became at least marginally more collaborative, as he sometimes let his bandmates, especially Wendy and Lisa, add their voices to the composing process. A turning point in this respect was the song "Around The World In A Day," the first draft of which was written and recorded not by Prince, but by David Coleman, Lisa's brother. For a birthday present in June 1984, Coleman received from Prince three days of "lock-out" recording at Hollywood's Sunset Sound, giving him exclusive access to the expensive facility for this seventy-two-hour period.

Coleman was himself a sophisticated musician with an unusual palette of influences. Like his sister, he was impacted by his musical parents, and when he was just ten he formed a band with Lisa (called Waldorf Salad) that was signed to A&M Records. After being trained in cello, he taught himself a variety of instruments, including guitar. Through a close friendship during high school with a young woman from Beirut, he became fascinated with Middle Eastern culture, studying Arabic and learning a variety of international instruments. This influence emerged during his Sunset Sound sessions, where Coleman recorded a song using a fretless Arabic guitar called an oud, an Arabic drum known as a darbouka, and finger cymbals.

Coleman circulated the song, entitled "Around The World In A Day," among family members and friends, and via Lisa the song soon made its way to Prince. Both its sing-song melody and exotic instrumentation intrigued him, and the song's psychedelic feel echoed the 1960s music he had discovered through Wendy, Lisa, and Susannah. When Coleman bumped into him at a concert in Los Angeles, Prince effused about the song and said this was exactly the sort of thing he was interested in exploring – not on the next album, but the one after that.

The timetable quickly accelerated. Coleman had expected little more to come of Prince's interest, but shortly after the Los Angeles encounter he received a phone call from Steve Fargnoli's office asking him to bring tapes of the song and all of his Middle Eastern instruments to Minneapolis. In mid-September 1984, Coleman and his musical partner Jonathan Melvoin (who would tragically die of a heroin overdose in 1996 at age 34) met Prince at a Minneapolis warehouse to rerecord the song. As Prince explored the array of exotic instruments Coleman and Melvoin had on hand, the session quickly took on a playful energy. When Coleman broke out Saudi Arabian "fireman cymbals," Prince got into the spirit by exuberantly banging on them while blowing a police whistle. Coleman recalled Prince, who had over that same summer become one of the biggest stars in the world, as an engaging, unpretentious collaborator with an almost boyish enthusiasm. "He was just so charming and unassuming," Coleman remembered.

The finished song did not differ greatly in feel or sound from Coleman's original demo, save for Prince's singing and the LM-1 pattern he added. Prince altered Coleman's lyrics but retained the title and chorus phrase. "Around The World In A Day" set the tone for Prince's next project: it would have a decidedly experimental tinge and would showcase new influences, particularly sixties oriented psychedelic rock. It would seemingly also make some allowance for collaborative songwriting.

Exactly how group-oriented the project would be, however, remained an issue of contention. As Prince focused his energies on his own songwriting, an undercurrent of tension developed between him and the rest of the Revolution, who had a number of simmering grievances. In one sense, it was the headiest of times for Wendy and Lisa, Matt Fink, Mark Brown, and Bobby Z. Rivkin, who remained awash in popular adoration as a result of *Purple Rain*. Seeing themselves on movie screens and televisions was the stuff of childhood fantasies come true. Still, less pleasant realities also intruded. First, there was money: Prince had become a multi-millionaire almost overnight, and they had not. Mark Brown recalls that he and the others were making about $2,200 a week, and that at the end of the tour, each Revolution member received a mere $15,000 bonus. "It was a slap in the face. We had grossed him over $80 million," said Brown, who nonetheless says he blames Prince's accountants and managers more than the bandleader himself. (Prince would later give band members a much larger bonus, said to have been in the range of $1 million each, as a thank you for *Purple Rain*, but by that point Brown had left the group).

The band members also felt that Prince, by stealing away to recording studios without them (as he often did during the tour), slighted their contributions. The one thing they had to hang onto was that they were part of the Revolution – an entity that Prince, throughout the making of *Purple Rain*, had insisted was an integral part of his identity. The band members considered themselves part of perhaps the most distinctive and influential pop group of their time. "They pretty much felt they were the second coming of the Beatles as a band," said Alan Leeds. "They had an enormously inflated sense of their importance to the project."

But to Prince, regardless of what he had told his bandmates to motivate them during preparations for the film, the Revolution was ultimately a backing group whose membership he could change at will. This was underscored when midway through the *Purple Rain* tour, Eric Leeds showed up backstage. On the second evening of a three-night stand in Greenville, South Carolina, Prince asked Eric if he had brought along his saxophone. Having rarely played anywhere larger than a nightclub, Eric jumped onstage for the climactic "Baby, I'm A Star." At one point during the lengthy jam, Prince cut off the band and let Eric solo in front of the 15,000-person crowd.

Prince liked what he heard, and invited Eric to join the tour. He began taking prominent solos, which diluted other members' time in the spotlight. The affable saxophonist was hard to dislike on a personal level, but other band members resented his intrusion into their private fraternity.

Eric's time in the spotlight was particularly difficult to swallow for Wendy, who throughout the tour had felt her star rising as female fans, in particular, reacted wildly to her presence onstage. Wendy's time to shine was "Purple Rain"; she began the song with shimmering guitar chords and, after the rest of the band joined in, was usually given several minutes to solo before Prince began singing. But at a show in Santa Monica, California, just before the band came out for an encore, Prince gathered them and issued a last-minute change; this time, Eric would play the solo. In an instant, Wendy's signature moment had been stolen from her, and it showed in her eyes the moment she left stage. "Wendy was whiter and paler than I've ever seen her before," said Alan Leeds. "Just crushed."

Prince was hardly unaware of his band members' frustrations and their desire for more stability and creative input, but his focus remained on his personal creative vision. And he was sending a clear message: adding new members and deciding who took solos remained his prerogative.

Prince recorded several other songs for his next project in 1984, again emphasizing an entirely different style from the guitar and rock-oriented sound of *Purple Rain*. "Pop Life," with Sheila E. on drums, was a languid, agreeable funk number with an overlay of psychedelia, including sampled crowd noise reminiscent of the Beatles' "A Day In The Life." Another new number, "Paisley Park," also relied on a slow tempo and utopian lyrics recalling songs like Jimi Hendrix's "Electric Ladyland." Even before the tour reached its peak, a grueling stretch of sixty-seven shows between December 26, 1984, and April 7, 1985, he managed to complete his new album, entitled *Around The World In A Day*, by flying to studios in Minneapolis and Los Angeles during breaks, and also by relying on mobile trucks that contained full recording setups.

The final song for the project, a ballad called "The Ladder," was created in a typical frenzy of activity. During a five-night stand of concerts at Minnesota's St. Paul Civic Center, Prince taught the band the tune during a sound check and recorded it with them the next day at a Minneapolis warehouse. And as the homecoming concerts continued, Prince used every free moment to complete the album.

On Christmas Eve 1984, he and the band played an emotional matinee show in St. Paul. Afterwards, engineer Susan Rogers gathered all of the tapes for the new album and drove a mobile truck to Prince's purple house on Kiowa Trail. She waited in the driveway until he arrived after the concert, when he recorded a final vocal and then sequenced the album with Rogers' help. They finished work after 4 a.m. on Christmas morning, with this constituting the full extent of Prince's holiday festivities. Rogers said, "He had nobody over there for Christmas – he was mainly interested in getting his record cut together."

***

The American Music Awards on January 28, 1985 at the Shrine Auditorium in Los Angeles served as yet another commemoration of Prince's remarkable 1984. Surrounded by his peers and competitors in the music industry, from Michael Jackson to Bruce Springsteen, Prince performed "Purple Rain" with his band and collected three awards: Favorite Album for *Purple Rain* in the black music category and the pop music category (for which the award was presented by Denise Matthews) and Favorite Single for "When Doves Cry." He was, in many respects, the very center of attention at this key music industry fete. The only sour note was Prince's strange obsession with security; many eyebrows were raised when, each time he was called to the podium, he brought along bodyguard Chick Huntsberry.

After the show, Prince, along with more than forty other pop stars, had been invited to A&M studios to participate in the recording of the song "We Are The World" for a charitable relief effort called USA for Africa. The main creative forces behind the song were its producer, the legendary bandleader Quincy Jones, and Michael Jackson, who wrote the music with Lionel Richie. The session was planned for the night of the American Music Awards to maximize the number of participants. Bruce Springsteen, Ray Charles, Stevie Wonder, Bob Dylan, Tina Turner, Diana Ross, Cindy Lauper all made their way to the studio.

A line of the song had been written for Prince to sing and a space in the studio blocked out for him to stand next to Michael Jackson. But at some point during the course of the evening, he decided not to show up, and instead took a limousine to the restaurant Carlos & Charlie's on Sunset Boulevard with Jill Jones and several bodyguards. (Primary bodyguard Huntsberry was not present). As Prince and his entourage exited the Mexican restaurant at about 2 a.m., several paparazzi descended on him, and one audacious photographer jumped into his limousine. Prince and his friends were justifiably frightened and outraged, and the bodyguards reacted by seizing the photographer's camera and forcefully ejecting him from the car. The police were summoned, and one bodyguard, six-foot-nine-inch, 300-pound Lawrence Gibson, was arrested for battery, and the other, Prince's friend Wally Safford, for robbery.

Predictably, the confluence of these back-to-back events – Prince's no-show at a high-profile charitable event, and a violent incident involving his security staff – brought down a hail of negative publicity. Any nuances in either story were blurred, and Prince came off as self-centered, security-obsessed, and, most damningly, unwilling to drop his rock star pretenses for a charitable cause.

***

Warner Bros. had in early 1985 agreed to give Prince his own record label under the Warners umbrella, which he dubbed Paisley Park Records. *Around the World in a Day* would be the label's first release. Prince previewed the finished album for Warner Bros. during a ceremonious "listening party" for about twenty company officials in early February 1985 in Los Angeles. Joni Mitchell and Prince's father, John L. Nelson, were among the special guests present. Attendees were seated on the floor of a large conference room, and as the high-pitched flute that begins "Around The World In A Day" lilted from the speakers, Prince and Lisa walked in holding flowers; the whole scene was, according to one attendee, "very Haight-Ashbury."

After each song, the assembled executives applauded heartily. But in truth, many were surprised by the subdued, languorous feel of the disc's first three songs: "Around The World In A Day," "Paisley Park," and the protracted ballad "Condition Of The Heart." Not until the fourth cut, the infectiously melodic "Raspberry Beret" (featuring a very Beatles-like string section composed by Wendy and Lisa) did anything resembling a Top 40 hit emerge. All told, it was a strange follow-up to the hyper-kinetic *Purple Rain*. "He told me he could see on the faces of the Warner Bros. people that it wasn't really working," remembered Eric Leeds.

Prince's associates realized this rather downbeat album was unlikely to sell nearly as many copies as *Purple Rain*. Having reached the pinnacle of fame, his strategy seemingly was to trade in some of that success for enhanced artistic credibility. And, to his friends and bandmates, he seemed at peace with that decision, even if not everyone agreed with it. "I felt it was a mistake timing-wise to put something else out soon after *Purple Rain*," keyboardist Matt Fink said, a view shared by many officials at Warner Bros., who believed that Prince was saturating the market with his music. But Prince, who saw *Around The World In A Day* as reaffirming his commitment to artistry, was relatively unconcerned with marketing issues. For at least the moment (and his feelings would certainly change in coming years) he had accepted that there would never be another year like 1984 for him. He had attained a level of fame that was neither possible to perpetuate nor, in the end, particularly worth saving.

    ***

Among the many celebrities who handed trophies to Prince at the American Music Awards show in January was Madonna, one of his rivals for mid-1980s fame. The parallels between the lives and careers of the two stars were notable. Madonna Louise Ciccone was born just two months later than Prince, and both grew up in the Midwest (Prince in Minneapolis, Madonna in Bay City, Michigan). Both suffered difficult childhoods, with Madonna losing her mother at age five, and Prince enduring his parents' separation at age seven. Both sang unabashedly and graphically about sex and thrived on creating controversy to advance their careers.

In the several months following the awards show, a romance between them unfolded. While both were involved in other, more serious relationships – Prince with Susannah Melvoin, Sheila E., and Jill Jones, and Madonna with the mercurial actor Sean Penn – this celebrity coupling generated ample publicity. They were seen at restaurants and clubs in Los Angeles and also turned up at each other's concerts, sometimes briefly performing together, such as during a February 1985 show at the Los Angeles Forum, where Madonna banged a tambourine during "Baby, I'm A Star."

But while the tabloids spoke breathlessly of a red-hot romance, their personal chemistry was at best awkward. While Madonna was mesmerized by Prince's pure musical talent, something about his personality was too fey, delicate, and self-conscious for her – a man's man like Sean Penn was more likely to stir her passions. "They were like oil and water," recalled Alan Leeds. Where Prince was demure and cryptic, she was boisterous and rowdy; where he was mystical, she was concrete; and where he was sometimes remote and haughty, she was generally down-to-earth and relaxed. Prince's road manager Karen Krattinger was startled to learn that Madonna treated her own staff in essence as friends. "She would say to her assistant, 'Hey, I'm hungry, should we get some food?'" Krattinger remembered. Prince, by contrast, would simply issue orders.

With their incompatibilities clear, the romance between Prince and Madonna would peter out in late 1985. For now, the dalliance for both was a perk of fame and means of generating even more publicity.

***

Even as he reached the pinnacle of fame, Prince engaged in various charitable efforts that were unjustly obscured by his absence from the "We Are the World" session. During the Purple Rain tour he held various benefit concerts and food drives, including concerts for the hearing-impaired. And he offered to contribute a song to the *We Are The World* album in lieu of having participated in the recording of the title song. He cut the song, "4 The Tears In Your Eyes," during a rare day off from the tour; the exhausted duo of Prince and Susan Rogers worked in the vast, empty Louisiana Superdome, which the day before had been filled with 70,000 screaming fans. Unable to find any food, Rogers finally scrounged up some warm cokes and stale salami sandwiches that served as their only sustenance during a long day of recording. "He put in his time for the cause in a very noble and gracious way although no one was there to see it," Rogers said.

Yet the incident involving his bodyguards, along with the aloof, ultra-cool image he presented through the media, solidified public perceptions of him as an eccentric egomaniac. And matters were not helped when the *National Enquirer* published an article, based on an interview with Huntsberry (who had recently quit his post) entitled "The Real Prince: He's Trapped in a Bizarre Secret World of Terror." It described Prince as (among

243

other things) a cloistered weirdo with an obsession for Marilyn Monroe.

Prince poured some of his frustration about these developments into a pair of brilliant songs, "Hello" and "Old Friends 4 Sale," recorded in the spring of 1985. "Hello" was essentially a blow-by-blow description of the evening of the "We Are the World" session. Musically, the song pulsated with energy and featured touches such as a sped-up guitar solo and a harpsichord-like keyboard riff. "Old Friends 4 Sale" straddled the border of blues and jazz and incorporated strings by Clare Fischer. The song's title seemed a direct reference to Huntsberry's selling of his story to the *National Enquirer*, and the lyrics also addressed the cocaine problem that prompted the bodyguard to sell his account to the tabloid. The unusually personal words also mentioned Prince's manager, Steve Fargnoli, by name and alluded to the angst of the post-*Purple Rain* period. These two strong songs, however, were deemed too personal for prominent release: "Hello" would become a B-side to "Pop Life," the second single from *Around The World In A Day*, and "Old Friends" would end up far off the public's radar screen for a long time. A version of the song would finally be released in 1999 on *The Vault . . . Old Friends 4 Sale*, but by that time Prince had changed many of the lyrics, making them far less revealing.

Recording these songs seemed to help Prince put his recent media imbroglios behind him, at least from an emotional standpoint. Still, he recognized that the controversies over "We Are The World," the bodyguard incident, and the *National Enquirer* article threatened to detract from the release of *Around The World In A Day*. Facing the media scrutiny and sensationalism that accompanies superstardom, Prince redoubled his efforts to recast himself as an artist, rather than a celebrity to be packaged, sold, and exposed.

As the new album was readied for distribution in spring 1985, Prince handed Warner Bros.' publicity department a series

244

of directives that left label officials perplexed about how to market the album. Intent on the project being viewed as an integrated artistic statement, he ordered that neither singles nor videos accompany the release. Nor did Prince want a high-octane publicity campaign; in fact, he forbade the label even from running advertisements in leading trade publications. Warners officials, unable to say no after *Purple Rain,* reluctantly acceded to every demand and simply hoped for the best. "Everybody was having a heart attack,'" observed Marylou Badeaux. "But we ended up doing it his way."

***

Despite Prince's unorthodox approach to publicity, his new album debuted at No. 1 on the Billboard Pop Chart after its release in April 1985, displacing the *We Are The World* album from this position. Yet this magnificent start was in essence an aftershock from *Purple Rain;* just as Warners had feared, sales of the album tapered off quickly, and *Around The World In A Day* exited the No. 1 slot after just three weeks.

Although it had seemed that Prince was prepared for a return to a more modest level of fame, the reality of seeing *Around The World In A Day* fade so quickly proved disconcerting. Suddenly ambivalent about his minimalist promotional strategy, he agreed to rush out a single and video of "Raspberry Beret," both of which performed strongly on their own but failed to turn *Around The World In A Day* into any sort of blockbuster. (The single's B-side, the blistering rock cut "She's Always In My Hair," written about Jill Jones, had more sheer power than anything on the album itself.) With the album stalling, Warners searched the album in vain for an instantly accessible pop hook that might turn things around; the second single, "Pop Life," reached No. 7 but failed to boost album sales significantly.

Adding to Prince's frustration was that the album was not universally greeted as a masterpiece by music critics. While some applauded his efforts to incorporate new influences into his sound, many in the same breath concluded that he had fallen somewhat short of the mark. In comments that must have seemed particularly biting, some critics ridiculed his efforts to emulate the spirit and style of the 1960s, finding these excursions strained and overly literal; Jim Miller of *Newsweek*, for example, called the record "an eerie attempt to recapture the utopian whimsy that characterized the Beatles' *Sgt. Pepper.*"

Prince, who had not given an interview since 1983, undertook efforts to repair his image. An extensive conversation with him appeared in the September 1985 issue of *Rolling Stone*, and his image graced the cover with the headline "Prince Talks." He used this platform to defend *Around The World In A Day* and to argue that he had made a conscious choice to target the album at serious fans, rather than the millions who casually purchased *Purple Rain*. "You know how easy it would have been to open *Around The World In A Day* with the guitar solo that's on the end of "Let's Go Crazy?" he said. "That would have shut everybody up who said the album wasn't half as powerful." He also denied that the music or styles of the 1960s had swayed him. "The influence wasn't the Beatles," he asserted. "They were great for what they did, but I don't know how that would hang today."

Prince also made a deliberate effort to soften and demystify his persona, inviting *Rolling Stone* into his purple house. The story portrayed his digs as surprisingly modest, and issued an almost point-by-point rebuttal of the *National Enquirer* article: "No," reporter Neal Karlen wrote, "The man does not live in an armed fortress with only a food taster and wall-to-wall, life-size murals of Marilyn Monroe to talk to."

Notwithstanding Prince's belated publicity campaign, which also included broadcast interviews with MTV and a Detroit radio station, the commercial fortunes of *Around The World In A Day* did not improve. The multi-platinum album was not a failure (it sold three million copies in the United States alone), but it almost seemed like one next to the unrealistic benchmark of *Purple Rain*, which moved more than 11 million units in the States during its initial run. Something fundamental had changed; Prince could no longer claim the mantle as the most commercially successful artist in popular music.

In many respects, however, this was beside the point. *Around The World In A Day* if anything increased Prince's stature as an artistic figure; although some critics were dissatisfied with the album as a whole, they also applauded him for trying to challenge himself and his audience. And as he prepared for his next project, Prince was prepared to continue – and indeed, to accelerate – his artistic growth.

The *Purple Rain* Tour (Paul Natkin)

Clothing designers Terry Wells and Vaughn Terry Jelks with Prince's bodyguard Chick Huntsberry (courtesy Vaughn Terry Jelks)

Terrance Jackson, percussionist for Prince's first band, Grand Central (courtesy Terry Jackson)

Purple Rain tour (Paul Natkin)

Birthday party, 1984 (Paul Natkin)

At a Sheila E. concert, the Ritz, New York (Paul Natkin)

22. PRINCE AND THE COUNTERREVOLUTION

While the Beatles and other sixties rock bands were the primary influence on *Around The World In A Day*, Prince soon began exploring other genres, including the jazz fusion compositions of Miles Davis and others. Influenced by Miles' rich textures and by the ethnic allusions in the music of Duke Ellington, Prince continued to move in new stylistic directions, for the first time in his career integrating saxophone and trumpet into his music.

Eric Leeds, with his sophisticated knowledge of jazz and vast record collection, also contributed significantly to Prince's ongoing musical education. "I talked up Miles a lot to Prince," Leeds noted. And Prince recruited Leeds' friend Matt "Atlanta Bliss" Blistan on trumpet, creating a full horn section.

Prince also began work on a new album (ultimately titled *Parade*) that melded the various sounds and styles he had been exploring – psychedelia, string arrangements, and the jazzier textures made possible by Leeds' presence.

Just ten days after the conclusion of the exhausting Purple Rain tour, Prince decamped to Sunset Sound studios in Los Angeles and commenced a series of prolific and adventurous sessions. For the next several months, each of Sunset Sound's three studios was typically in use by either Prince or his associates. The atmosphere was festive, as musicians popped from one studio to another to check on each other's progress, also playing Ping-Pong in the recreation room and shooting baskets on a court that sat between Studios 2 and 3. Prince was among the most competitive and skilled at both games. When he needed privacy, Studio 3, a self-contained building with a bathroom and kitchen, provided him a hermetic work environment, which he decorated with scarves, Christmas lights, candles, and a queen-sized bed with purple sheets, where he would lie and write lyrics.

Along with the planned use of horns (which were overdubbed by Leeds after Prince recorded basic tracks), the *Parade* sessions found other changes afoot. Rather than programming patterns on his Linn LM-1 drum machine, which had been a signature of his sound on *1999*, *Purple Rain*, and *Around The World In A Day*, Prince returned to the use of live drums that marked his earlier albums. As the session got underway, he settled in behind the drum kit, taped lyrics to a music stand in front of him, and signaled engineer Susan Rogers to start the tape. He instructed her not to stop it if he stopped playing, and then ripped off four songs in a row, with brief pauses between them. Each composition was fully mapped out in his head, and he used the taped-up lyric sheets as a guide to the structures.

After finishing, Prince returned to the control booth, bristling with energy and enthusiasm. "Alright, here we go! Where's my bass?" he said to Rogers. Following the same process, he laid down bass guitar parts on each of the songs. Whereas many musicians can spend days on a single piece, Prince was sketching the better part of an album's side in an afternoon. When *Parade* was released, these four songs – "Christopher Tracy's Parade," "New Position," "I Wonder U," and "Under The Cherry Moon" – would appear in the same sequence Prince recorded them.

The manic pace continued as Prince stayed in Studio 3 virtually around the clock, catching brief respites of sleep at a rented home in nearby Beverly Hills. In short order, nine new songs were recorded. The chaotic "Life Can Be So Nice," with Sheila E. adding cowbells, was recorded at the tail end of a twenty-four-hour marathon session. Just as the exhausted engineers began to clean up, Prince barked out, "Fresh tapes!"

Although Prince often worked alone, Wendy and Lisa were frequent visitors to Sunset Sound, adding their own instrumental ideas to songs he had already recorded. Rapidly, the personal and creative chemistry of the troika of Prince, Wendy, and Lisa developed to the point where they virtually became a band within a band. "He was more comfortable with giving them a tape and saying, 'Put whatever you want on it and give it back to me,'" noted Rogers.

But inevitably, the ascendancy of Wendy and Lisa as Prince's closest friends and musical partners left the other members of the Revolution feeling excluded, and the band's tight chemistry began to erode. Matt Fink, who had been Prince's keyboardist since 1978 and had made modest contributions to *Dirty Mind* and *Purple Rain*, now felt a growing chill in the air. "I got married, and you kind of get cut out of the picture by Prince when that happens," he recalled. Bobby Z. also felt underutilized; Prince was now playing live drums in the studio and also jamming more and more often with Sheila E. And Mark Brown, dissatisfied with his role as a sideman, on several occasions almost quit before being dissuaded by Chick Huntsberry, with whom he developed a tight friendship.

In truth, the sense of common mission that the Revolution members had felt during the recording of Purple Rain and the shooting of the movie had all but dissipated by the time the tour ended. The addition of Eric Leeds as a virtual member on the tour served as fair warning to other members: Prince's plans and visions might not always include them in prominent roles – or include them at all.

Following the tour, Prince began spending more time both socially and in the studio with Wendy and Lisa. Not only lovers but lifelong friends, the two women had been composing together for years and in combination created a sound that struck listeners as unusually emotionally expressive. Lisa, with her classical training, was the superior musician, but their artistic symbiosis went far beyond instrumental chops. Their ideas proved a perfect complement to Prince's work; in places where his music threatened to become sterile or harshly minimalistic, the women would lend lushness and feeling. New songs like

"Our Destiny" and "Roadhouse Garden," both composed with Wendy and Lisa, demonstrated the melodic sophistication and pop-rock flavor that they brought to his sound.

Given Prince's resistance to surrendering creative space, his relationship with Wendy and Lisa would have had potential for instability even if strictly professional in nature. But there were other flashpoints as well – notably, his tumultuous and passionate relationship with Susannah Melvoin. When Susannah emerged as Prince's primary (though hardly only) girlfriend, Wendy suddenly found herself again sharing a large part of her life with the same person with whom she had shared a womb. Moreover, Susannah was a skilled vocalist, and Prince added her as a kind of adjunct member of the Revolution, making her part of the musical equation as well. Prince frequently socialized with Susannah, Wendy, and Lisa as a group. He enjoyed their company, and reveled in the ritual of entering restaurants and nightclubs with three beautiful women in tow. At times, though, the lack of privacy in his romantic life became frustrating. "He soon realized that dating Susannah was like dating all three, because Susannah shared things with her sister and Lisa that Prince was unaccustomed to his band being privy to – his private life," said a confidant who watched the relationship unfold.

The purely musical part of the Prince-Wendy-Lisa relationship was also marked by rapidly shifting dynamics. For the moment, Wendy and Lisa found themselves contributing more to Prince's music than ever before. They added musical embellishments to most of the new tracks he recorded at Sunset, and Wendy even took the lead vocal on the psychedelic oddity "I Wonder U." At the same time, from *For You* through *1999*, absolute self-sufficiency had defined Prince's career, and he was not about to surrender this lightly. As such, Wendy and Lisa could never be sure when Prince would reclaim his territory. What Wendy and Lisa wanted most – some definitive measure of equality and stability – was unlikely to come without a fight.

256

***

Of all of Prince's band members, the one who seemed ripe for defection was Mark Brown, a prospect that troubled Prince. He appreciated what Brown's unique, percussive style of playing brought to the Revolution's live sound and even asserted, in an interview with *Rolling Stone*, that if Brown were not in the band, he would not even use bass in his music. But Brown's true ambition, like that of Andre Cymone before him, was to become a figure not unlike Prince himself, a respected songwriter and producer of other bands. In 1984, unbeknownst to Prince, Brown took under his wing a seven piece rock funk outfit called Mazarati that he had discovered in the Minneapolis clubs. Soon he became essentially a member of the group, regularly jamming with them onstage. Because he worried that Prince would frown upon such extracurricular activities, Brown performed wearing a mask and identified himself onstage as "The Shadow." "I thought he was going to be pissed at me because I had kept it a secret from him," Brown recalled. But as this double life became more stressful, Mazarati guitarist Tony Christian urged Brown to let Prince know about the project. "Just tell him," Christian advised one evening as the two musicians were driving around Los Angeles. "The worst he can do is want a piece of it or tell you to stop."

Brown did approach Prince, who was more curious than angry. After taking in a Mazarati concert, Prince realized he might even have a new side project on his hands. He urged Brown not to take the group to another label, but to release its first album on Paisley Park Records. Brown agreed, despite his concerns about retaining creative control over the project. And as rehearsals for the album proceeded, Prince sometimes arrived unannounced, with his presence proving distracting and inhibiting. At gigs, he often jumped onstage to jam with Mazarati, and soon he even began telling group members how to dress. Gradually, the group lost its sense of identity.

When Mazarati began recording at Sunset Sound, Prince gave the group two songs for possible inclusion on its album. The group used "100 MPH" but passed on a number called "Jerk Out" because some members were offended by its explicit lyrics. Brown functioned as the producer of the sessions, but Prince, too busy with Parade to oversee the sessions himself, wanted a more veteran presence in the studio, and placed a call to engineer David Z. Rivkin in Minneapolis.

"Can you come out to L.A. for the weekend?" Prince asked. "I've got some stuff for you to do." Rivkin agreed, packed two pairs of pants, and booked a flight. When he arrived the next day, Prince greeted him boisterously. "Oh, by the way, you've got to be here for a couple of months!" he exclaimed. "We have a Mazarati album to do."

A few days after Rivkin's arrival, Prince took a break from his own work and poked his head into Studio 2, where Mazarati was working. When one of the band members asked off-handedly if he had any more songs for them, Prince paged Susan Rogers over a studio loudspeaker; when she arrived a few moments later, they disappeared into a room with an acoustic guitar and a four-track cassette recorder.

As he waited for Rogers to prepare the equipment, Prince tapped impatiently on the body of the acoustic guitar. "Rolling?" he asked. She quickly responded affirmatively, and Prince began briskly strumming a basic twelve-bar blues pattern and singing mournfully in his lower register. The song, "Kiss," was completed in just minutes, and Prince emerged with the tape. "Here, finish this off," he said to Rivkin and Brown. "Do what you want with this song!"

After Prince left, the group caucused. Tony Christian, Mazarati's rhythm guitarist, was not impressed. "Nobody liked the song," he recalled. Rivkin wasn't enthralled by "Kiss" either, but the song's blues orientation triggered ideas in his mind. He and Brown began reconstructing it, first creating a foundation of drums that made the piece peppier and more danceable. Rivkin added an infectious piano riff borrowed from an obscure Bo Diddley song called "Hey Man." He and Coke Johnson, another engineer present, used a studio trick that linked the acoustic guitar part to the hi-hat cymbal, making it follow the same jagged rhythm. Singer Terry Casey then added his own rendition of Prince's words, and Rivkin came up with an idea for a backing vocal part based on the song "Sweet Nothings" by pop singer Brenda Lee.

Working through the night, they completed the song by about nine a.m., when the band members went home as Rivkin and Johnson prepared a mix. When Prince stopped by around noon, Rivkin gave him a cassette. Intrigued, he took a portable boom box out to the basketball court in the center of the complex and blasted it. "He went ballistic," remembered Johnson. Prince could not believe that his languid blues number had been changed into something so funky and energetic. "This is too good for you guys!" Prince shouted. "I'm taking it back."

But after this initial reaction, Prince felt guilty about poaching the band's work. Huddling with engineers Rogers and Peggy McCreary, he asked their opinions. Although McCreary felt Mazarati should keep the song, Rogers cast the tie-breaking vote in favor of Prince because she felt "Kiss" would get more exposure on his album. With this resolved, Prince took the master tape and cut his own vocal (this time using his falsetto), replacing Terry Casey's. He also added a James Brown-style guitar lick at the beginning of the song and during pauses that recurred at the end of each chorus. Finally, he tweaked the mix, dropping out the bass guitar. He was finished in a little over an hour; "Kiss" had completed its transformation from a Prince song, to a Mazarati song, and back to a Prince song. It would eventually reach No. 1 on Billboard's Pop Singles Chart as the first single from *Parade*.

Not surprisingly, given its genesis, credit for the song was contested. Although Prince gave David Z. Rivkin an "arrangement" credit for the song, the rest of the credit states that "Kiss" was "produced, composed and written by Prince and the Revolution." In an apologetic call to Rivkin, Prince said that Warner Bros. would not allow him to give anyone other than himself a producer's billing. While Rivkin certainly didn't accept this flimsy explanation, he remained philosophical about the episode and concluded, in the end, that Prince's modest additions to the piece made it much better.

Mark Brown also claimed that he was in essence the producer of "Kiss," and remained chagrined that Rivkin, rather than he, received the arrangement credit. Brown said he gave Prince and his managers numerous opportunities to compensate him for his contributions to the song, but no action was ever taken.

***

Even as he worked on *Parade*, Prince was planning *Under The Cherry Moon*, his follow-up film project to *Purple Rain*. Success in the world of film remained a priority for him, and of all the laurels he had received for *Purple Rain*, the most meaningful had been his Academy Award for Best Original Song Score. At the ceremony, when he reached his backstage dressing room he handed his award to bodyguard Chick Huntsberry and bear-hugged with Steve Fargnoli. This was surprising and uncharacteristic. "I never found Prince to be a touchy-feely person who easily expressed any kind of physical affection, particularly towards men," noted Alan Leeds, who witnessed the embrace. "Even his handshake was wishy-washy, soft, and seemingly reluctant; this was the one-and-only exception I saw." The moment reflected Prince's spontaneous, heartfelt joy over receiving Hollywood's highest honor.

The stunning success of *Purple Rain* virtually guaranteed Prince the right to make whatever sort of film he wanted, within certain budgetary constraints. Just as he sought to enhance his status as a songwriter through the more challenging music of *Around The World In A Day*, Prince now wanted to create a movie that would be taken more seriously by critics than the melodramatic *Purple Rain*. He had a tentative idea for a wry comedy that would be shot in black and white. Prince also proved receptive to Fargnoli's idea of filming in France.

As a means of selecting locations for the film and exposing Prince to European culture, Fargnoli took him (along with Alan Leeds) to Paris in June 1985; they stayed at the Nova Park Hotel near the Champs-Elysees. Hoping that Prince would share his passion for Paris, Fargnoli proposed a variety of outings. But on the second day of the visit, Prince ducked into a music store and became enamored with several new pieces of equipment, including several cutting-edge synthesizers. He asked Leeds to arrange for a line of credit through Warner Bros.' local office, and, by that evening, Prince had a makeshift studio running in his hotel. "At that point we lost our mate to the gear," Leeds recalled. "Getting Prince away from his new toys was like pulling teeth." While Prince later agreed to visit the Louvre, he backed out at the last minute. And an evening drive past the Arc de Triomphe and the Eiffel Tower found Prince with no inclination to get out of the car to view these historic monuments.

Prince did show some willingness to visit restaurants and nightclubs, but in a curious reversal of rock star stereotypes, it was Fargnoli and Leeds who more often prowled the town. One night at a club, the men ended up so inebriated that they failed to recognize two women who joined their table as prostitutes, resulting in a bill of over $1,000 even though no physical contact occurred. A drunken Fargnoli shouted obscenities on the street as he and Leeds reached their hotel at about six a.m. As Fargnoli tried to steady himself using a street sign, Leeds heard a familiar sarcastic voice calling from a balcony above the street. "Look, Paris! That down there is my management!" shouted Prince, who was still fiddling with his new equipment. "Hey, down there on the street, can you bums quiet down and let a rock star get some work done?" Leeds, who was almost as drunk as Fargnoli, could do nothing but sit down on the sidewalk and start laughing.

Yet despite his resistance to sightseeing or partying, Prince was sold on the idea of filming overseas; he decided to shoot *Under The Cherry Moon* in Nice on the French Riviera, which he had visited on a side trip from Paris. A writer named Becky Johnson was commissioned to write the screenplay from Prince's basic idea about a poor piano player who meets a rich socialite.

Although Warners' film division in essence green-lighted Prince's next picture without even seeing a script, objections were raised when it was learned that he wanted to film in black and white. Prince held firm, and a compromise of sorts was reached; it would be shot in color, but transferred to black and white (which presumably kept alive the possibility of reversing Prince's decision). Michael Balhaus, who had worked with Martin Scorsese on several movies, was recruited as the cinematographer.

For *Purple Rain*, Prince had relied on friends and associates as the principal cast members, and he planned to do the same in *Under The Cherry Moon*. But the Revolution, after being a focal point of the previous movie, would not play a major role this time; instead, he cast friend Jerome Benton (also a member of the Family) as his comic foil and sidekick. Prince initially wanted Susannah Melvoin to play the female lead, but the studio prevailed on him to accept the casting of Kristin Scott Thomas. Selected as director was Mary Lambert, who had helmed various MTV videos.

A modest budget was approved, and Prince's team got the go-ahead to begin filming in Nice in fall 1985. Warner Bros.' film division had doubts about the project from the very beginning, but the die was cast – Prince was going to get an opportunity to build upon the tremendous success of *Purple Rain*.

***

Among Prince and his entourage, optimism reigned about *Under The Cherry Moon*. As he and several close advisors flew to Nice to start the project, Prince's recent setbacks – the "We Are the World" controversy and the rapid fall-off in sales of *Around The World In A Day* – seemed far away. And there was apparently another reason for cheer: Among those accompanying Prince on the flight was Susannah Melvoin, wearing something that looked very much like an engagement ring. Shortly before the team had left Minneapolis, an article appeared in *USA Today* reporting that Prince, one of the entertainment industry's most eligible bachelors, had proposed to Susannah.

In truth, he hadn't, exactly; Prince had given Susannah the ring, and she had chosen to interpret this as a marriage proposal, which perhaps it was. The *USA Today* article's origins were unclear – it was based upon anonymous sources – but Prince was incensed over this intrusion into his personal life. In truth, he remained deeply ambivalent about committing to Susannah, and now the whole matter was spilled out before the public.

The group cleared immigration and customs and arrived at the Beach Regency Hotel to a beautiful day – eighty degrees and sunny with a relaxing sea breeze. The penthouse suite, where Prince, Susannah, and bodyguard Gilbert Davison would be staying, occupied the majority of the top floor and had a wraparound balcony that afforded startling views of the ocean to the front, and the towering hills of Saint Paul de Vence to the rear.

Moments after being escorted to the penthouse, Prince silently steered Alan Leeds into the bedroom and out of earshot of the rest of the group. He ordered Leeds to immediately take Susannah home. More specifically, he wanted her brought to his residence in Minnesota. "I don't want her going to L.A. and crying on Wendy and Lisa's shoulders," Prince insisted.

Reluctantly, realizing that his job would be in jeopardy if he refused, Leeds agreed. But his wife, Gwen, upset with Prince's treatment of both Susannah and Alan, had to be restrained from going upstairs to confront Prince when she learned the news. Gwen was left alone for two days as Leeds flew Susannah home to Minneapolis and then immediately turned around and jumped on his third transatlantic flight in a week back to Nice.

With Susannah removed from the scene, Nice became a sexual playground for Prince. He met women at local nightclubs, and during the two-month shoot, he would enjoy visits from girlfriends Sheila E. and Jill Jones. He also had an affair with Scott Thomas, according to a knowledgeable source. "Prince and Kristin were definitely an item during the making of the film," the source said. "It was hardly an enduring relationship, but they spent an awful lot of private time together in Nice while filming."

The production itself, though, was far less of a lark. Director Lambert quickly alienated much of Prince's team with what they perceived as a haughty attitude, and the decision was made to dump her. Then, the inevitable happened: Prince himself took the helm, just four days into shooting. This action ratcheted up the pressure on Prince and immediately led to predictions in the media that *Under The Cherry Moon* was a doomed vanity project.

The initial fallout from Prince's takeover was mixed. It certainly created resentment within the larger Hollywood film community. Veteran actor Terrence Stamp quit the movie, unhappy with what he perceived as Prince's imperious manner. But Stamp's replacement, Steven Berkoff, developed a grudging respect for his novice director, and everyone seemed to agree that Prince, in contrast to Lambert, brought a highly disciplined and focused atmosphere to the set.

Yet there were more fundamental problems with *Under The Cherry Moon*, most notably its script, a confused, tone-deaf mixture of slapstick comedy and preening. The movie would obviously rise or fall on the acting ability of Prince and Jerome Benton — a dubious proposition at best, since it had been Morris

Day, not Prince, who carried much of *Purple Rain*. And with his very limited experience in directing (he had previously helmed only the "Raspberry Beret" video), the project ultimately proved too much even for Prince. By the time the filming was halfway completed, everyone involved, including Prince, seemed to realize that the wheels were coming off. "What it came down to, I think, was a case of the idea being more ambitious than the skills," observed Leeds. "There were some casting problems, scripting problems, and directing problems. You ain't gonna fix them with a night of conversation around the fireplace."

Other signs were mounting that Prince, for all his energy and ideas, had finally spread himself too thin. Shortly before he departed Minneapolis for Nice, his Paisley Park Records released the eponymous debut by the Family. Initially, enthusiasm was high that the Family would be a worthy successor to the Time, Prince's most successful side project to date. But while the Time was oriented principally toward black R&B listeners, the Family was tailored to white New Wave and pop fans. "We've got to go after some of that Duran Duran money," Prince exclaimed to engineer David Z. Rivkin during the sessions, referring to one of the slickest and most successful synth-pop groups of the 1980s.

While Prince recorded all of the basic tracks in a matter of days, including guide vocals for singer Paul Peterson, the next step proved much more difficult. Listening to the guides, Peterson struggled to imitate every nuance of Prince's vocals as ordered; Rivkin recalled one session where twelve hours were required to complete three lines. By the time Peterson finally finished the album, his enthusiasm for the project had all but disappeared.

Much of the material on the album was strong, showing the focus and experimental flare Prince brought to his music in the mid-eighties. Most of the instruments were played by Prince himself, with Eric Leeds' saxophone and Clare Fischer's strings prominent on several tracks. "I consider it as much a Prince album as anything else he's done," noted Eric.

The lead single, "The Screams Of Passion," generated some interest from radio, but the project as a whole faced a fundamental problem: no one was available to promote it. Band members Jerome Benton and Susannah Melvoin were in Nice (Susannah having been summoned back from Minneapolis by this point), meaning that the band could not play concerts. At Prince's Paisley Park Records, which released *The Family*, no one was really in charge, and in truth there was little to be in charge of, as the vanity label was lightly staffed and poorly organized. "Paisley certainly was an unfocused label in its very gestation at that time, and didn't even have a single employee, really," recalled Leeds. And although the label was a subsidiary of Warner Bros., its relationship with the parent company was too poorly defined to make a difference in terms of promotional muscle.

Further, like so many of Prince's satellite projects, the Family represented another awkward attempt to have someone else imitate his singing style. Paul Peterson's uncomfortable vocals undermined otherwise strong songs like "The Screams Of Passion" and "High Fashion."

Ultimately, the Family existed only as a front; the album would have been more successful if released (and sung) by Prince himself, rather than through a fictional band. "You cannot put somebody in a certain costume and automatically have them assume that role," said engineer Susan Rogers regarding Paul Peterson's failure to emerge as a credible front man. "It was an impossible task."

As *The Family* quickly faltered, failing to crack the Top 50 of the Pop Chart, a frustrated Paul Peterson called Prince in Nice and announced he was quitting the group. "If you're gonna be in charge of this band, you can't do four million other things at the same time," Peterson shouted. "Yes, I can!" Prince shot back. "I did it with the Time, didn't I? I did it with Sheila E.! I did it with Vanity 6!"

Although Prince and other members of the Family still believed that the project held promise, Peterson could not be convinced to stay. The group came to a quick end with the exit of its designated star. Soon after, a frustrated Prince complained to David Z. Rivkin, "I shouldn't have let him go so far away from me and out of my control."

***

Back in France, the shooting of *Under The Cherry Moon* limped to a close during November 1985. Even as it became apparent from dailies that the film was not working, Prince composed music for the soundtrack. He involved Wendy and Lisa in this process, renting them an apartment across the English Channel in London, where they recorded frequently at Advision Studios. The duo developed, among other things, an instrumental piece that would become the song "Mountains" on *Parade*. On weekends, Prince frequently joined them for recording sessions, socializing, and clothes-shopping sprees.

On the set in Nice, Prince seemed conflicted about Christopher Tracy, the character he had created for himself to play in the film. This charismatic, sexy, and somewhat snide piano player was hardly a sympathetic figure, and Prince's plan all along had been for Tracy to die at the end of the film, representing his own symbolic transcendence of these character flaws. But Warners, preferring a happy ending, pushed him to conclude with Tracy reforming and heading off into the sunset with love interest Mary.

The alternative ending was shot, and publicist Howard Bloom, viewing a cut of the film where Tracy survives, found himself believing in the character's redemptive journey. "Warner Bros. insisted on him getting the girl at the end, and it really worked," Bloom remembered. "This little asshole character that was so hard to identify with, you bonded with by the end."

But Prince favored the original ending. In the final cut, Tracy died (the victim of an assassination) with the result, in Bloom's view, that any meaning in the film was also destroyed. From the publicist's perspective, this was another powerful indication that Prince could no longer tolerate his own dark side, the part of his persona most responsible for making him a musical and cultural rebel. "His instincts were with God now," Bloom recalled. "He had created this character who was such a scamp, and he had to kill him."

As work on *Under The Cherry Moon* concluded, Prince also made a fateful decision about the future of his band. At a November wrap party, Susannah Melvoin and Eric Leeds again joined him in Nice, accompanied by guitarist Miko Weaver and bodyguards/dancers Greg Brooks and Wally Safford. All of these associates had been slated for the live lineup of the Family and after the band's demise had nothing to do. Eric had lunch with Prince and Susannah at the film studio commissary to discuss plans. "Well, what do we do now?" Eric asked Prince.

"Why don't you just come on with us?" he responded, which Eric took to be a formal invitation to join the Revolution. "Sounds good to me!" he said quickly.

Prince's overture, it turned out, extended to all of the ex-Family members, representing a dramatic expansion of the band. Weaver became the third guitarist, joining Prince and Wendy; Susannah was added as a backing vocalist; and Brooks, Safford, and Jerome Benton signed on as dancers. Finally, Leeds' friend Matt Blistan was drafted on trumpet, completing the Revolution's transition from a lean rock outfit into a full scale, eleven-member R&B ensemble.

Wendy, Lisa, and the other members of the Revolution learned of these changes when they arrived in Nice to shoot a video for "Girls & Boys," a song for *Parade* and the movie. Wendy and Lisa in particular were stunned by this further dilution of their own roles. The Revolution, which they viewed as their band almost as much as Prince's, had been commandeered by outside forces and transformed into something radically different than the group that had captured the public's imagination in *Purple Rain.*

During a break in choreography rehearsals for the video, Wendy's emotions bubbled forth in a tirade in the commissary. Sitting at a table with Bobby Z. Rivkin, Matt Fink, Eric Leeds, and Matt Blistan and with Brooks, Safford, and Benton within easy earshot, she began attacking her boss and, by extension, her new comrades. "Prince is out of his mind, he's ruined everything," she said. Looking at Leeds and Blistan, she said, "At least you guys are musicians, but now we're just an everyday funk band. We look like a circus. Doesn't he know what an ass his fans will think he is?"

Wendy's verbal slaps were clearly directed at the three dancers, who avoided a direct confrontation by ignoring her, but went on ogling female extras in the commissary, behavior that Wendy doubtlessly saw as symbolic of what had changed in the Revolution. Wendy and Lisa's arrival in Nice also led to another troubling discovery: Sheila E., Susannah's principal rival for Prince's affections, was there for a romantic visit. Wendy and Lisa resented her presence, especially in light of the way Susannah had earlier been sent home from Nice, and they worried that Sheila E. also coveted Rivkin's position as drummer in the band.

Numerous factors influenced Prince's restructuring of his band. According to Susan Rogers, he had a nebulous concept that the expanded Revolution would embody various groups of "twin" or "triplet" figures – Wendy and Susannah; himself and Miko Weaver; Eric Leeds and Matt Blistan; and the dancers. More concretely, Prince wanted to make productive use of the personnel he had recruited for the Family. Finally, he felt some obligation to reconnect with his R&B roots; after two rock-oriented albums, there were whispers in the media and among fans that Prince had become too "white" in his approach. The presence of dancers and a full horn section made Prince's group reminiscent of classic funk outfits like James Brown's Fabulous

Flames.

But whatever the rationale behind his decisions, the swelling of the Revolution changed things irrevocably and placed additional emotional stresses on his core band members. The new arrivals, by contrast, felt they represented the wave of the future. "I started calling the band the counter-Revolution," remembered Eric Leeds. "The name 'Revolution' did not have the same meaning to Prince after he expanded the band." The unit that had been so tightly knit during *Purple Rain* was now separated into feuding camps, and even more disturbingly, these factions were to a significant extent broken down along racial lines.

As *Parade* and *Under The Cherry Moon* were completed, matters were proceeding on two tracks – one toward collaboration, the other toward confrontation. Wendy and Lisa, just as they seemed to be making progress towards being accepted as true songwriting partners, found their roles in the live band diminished by the expansion of the Revolution. There were also indications that Prince, even as he stretched his songwriting in intriguing new directions, had become unfocused. *Parade* was in danger of being overshadowed by the boondoggle of *Under The Cherry Moon*, and the implosion of the Family destabilized the Revolution. Plus, he had more girlfriends than he could keep track of and was pitting them against each other. Surrounded by an increasingly large group of band members, lovers, and confidants, Prince was, in many respects, choosing to mentally and emotionally isolate himself by ignoring mounting signs of trouble and insistently keeping his own counsel – whatever the cost.

23. THE END

Prince loved being in the Minneapolis area during the springtime, and in 1986 there was something special to celebrate: he was moving into his new home on a property in the southwest suburb of Chanhassen. (He gave his previous residence, the famous purple house on Kiowa Trail, to his father, John L. Nelson.) Only a mile and a half away, construction began on Prince's Paisley Park studio complex, envisioned as the seat of an expanding musical empire.

His new three-level home (including a basement) sat on a verdant lot that afforded plenty of privacy. A long, circuitous driveway led from a security booth to the home, and the property was surrounded with a black fence. The residence itself sat about 200 yards back from rural Galpin Boulevard; trees masking the home added another layer of protection from the outside world. The exterior was painted yellow with purple balconies and window trim. Inside, the living room extended two stories up to a loft-like roof with exposed wooden beams. His master bedroom included a sitting area overlooking the living room. The rear of the house opened onto a small lake surrounded by woods, and the backyard sported a tennis court, basketball court, and swimming pool.

With its exposed wood, lack of high-tech amenities, and a square footage that was modest in comparison to what people might have expected from a global superstar, Prince's new abode felt perhaps more like an upscale ski lodge than a haven for the rich and famous. Indeed, far more money was poured into Paisley Park than his residence. "When I first visited the house, he saw my reaction and said 'I know, it's kind of small, isn't it'?" remembered Mark Brown. "I said I had expected some marble pillars or something, but he said he didn't go in for that gaudy stuff."

Susannah Melvoin was planning to move in, representing Prince's first real attempt at cohabitation. She and her close friend Karen Krattinger, now general manager of Prince's organization, took charge of decorating and organizing. Susannah added artsy touches throughout the residence, such as hanging large nude canvasses she had painted. The two women were also given free rein to shop for furnishings. And in what had been designed as a wine cellar, Krattinger meticulously organized thousands of videotapes Prince had made of shows and rehearsals. "It became this amazing history of his entire career," she noted.

Prince enjoyed hosting barbecues, sports, and video nights at his home. Among the frequent guests were Wendy and Lisa; Alan Leeds, along with his wife, Gwen, and son Tristan; Eric Leeds; and bodyguard/friend Gilbert Davison. During the spring and summer, Prince also gathered friends for softball games and bowling nights throughout Minneapolis. "It was nice for him to be able to incorporate his social life into his home," said Susan Rogers. "He had what he'd always wanted: people around him. They would go upstairs and watch TV or sit in the kitchen for hours telling jokes."

Although $10 million was being poured into the construction of Paisley Park, scheduled for completion in 1987, Prince also had a costly, state-of-the-art studio built in his home and insisted that it be large enough to accommodate group performances, something that had been impossible in his previous homes. In the studio control room, Susannah installed stained-glass windows that were illuminated by the morning sun, giving the studio a church-like serenity. Completion of the studio's technical elements fell to Rogers. Working with Westlake Audio of Los Angeles, the contractor designing the facility, she divided the basement of the Chanhassen home into a warren of "isolation" rooms where band members would set up during sessions. Prince's purple piano, too large for the basement, sat upstairs in the living room and was wired downstairs.

By mid-March, with Rogers still working out the studio's kinks, Prince without warning informed her that his bandmates were on the way over for a recording session. They planned to record "Power Fantastic," a song based on a composition by Lisa Coleman called "Carousel." She had been reluctant to share the idea; according to Rogers, she and Wendy may have been considering it for a solo project but after weeks of Prince's cajoling, she had finally let him work with it. Using her chordal melody, he arranged a jazz-like piece full of somber majesty that evoked Miles Davis' *Kind Of Blue*.

As the session began, Rogers discovered that the studio was one pair of headphones short and concluded that the only person who could spare them was herself. Since Prince was singing in the control room, the main speakers had to be shut off so that the playback would not be picked up by his microphone. Prince almost always vocalized alone, but he allowed Rogers to remain so she could monitor the song's progress. He sang in a corner of the room, his back turned away from her. As the band played, Rogers could hear nothing but Prince's falsetto vocal. It was one of the most intimate experiences of her career, and Rogers felt at the very center of artistic creation.

The band nailed "Power Fantastic" in one take. Eric Leeds,

who played a lilting flute solo, walked out of the studio feeling goosebumps. "That's one of the greatest things we ever did," he remarked; no one disagreed.

"Power Fantastic" was to be one of the cornerstones of Prince's next project, *The Dream Factory*. As work began, he let everyone stretch out a bit. He composed the lullaby-like ballad "A Place In Heaven" for Lisa to sing and took a day off while she completed the vocals on her own. When Lisa composed a solo piano piece, entitled "Visions," Prince surprised everyone by slotting it as the opening cut of *The Dream Factory*. "Teacher, Teacher" and "It's A Wonderful Day" included prominent vocal and songwriting contributions by Wendy and Lisa. "In A Large Room With No Light," a dense and busy jazz-fusion piece, featured live playing by most of the Revolution and drumming by Sheila E., whom Prince favored over Rivkin for such complex numbers. Susannah was put in charge of the album's cover art, which had a homemade look and included contributions from everyone in the band, with each member scrawling pictures and words that would appear on the front or back cover.

The collaborative ethos carried over to rehearsals, which included long improvisational sessions. One jam lasted so long that Mark Brown prepared and ate a sandwich even as he kept thwacking away at his bass to keep the groove going. No one could seem to get enough of playing. "I think that my greatest memories of my musical career are of rehearsals that were spectacular, not shows," Rivkin recalled. "It was an exciting, exciting time."

For Wendy and Lisa, this was just what they had hoped for. Prince's expansion of the band hadn't diminished their roles in the recording studio; in fact, they were given more latitude than ever before. While Eric Leeds had become an important and respected contributor, Prince made Wendy the second-in-command, letting her run rehearsals on days he did not attend.

274

"Her musical discipline, articulate assertiveness, and work ethic clearly made her the logical and most effective candidate, and deep down the whole band knew that," noted Alan Leeds.

Prince's openness to the influence of others also extended to his continued study of jazz. Eric, who often lent Prince albums, found him fascinated with John Coltrane's *Love Supreme* and classics from Duke Ellington's *Live At Newport*, such as "Diminuendo And Crescendo In Blue." Miles Davis remained a growing inspiration; when Eric mentioned that he had complimented Prince in a recent interview, Prince was deeply touched. "You know, Eric, that's what makes it worthwhile, when someone like that says something," he said.

Given the apparent mutual admiration, associates of both Prince and Miles were hopeful that a collaboration might materialize. When Miles moved from Columbia to Warner Bros. Records in 1985, the idea seemed even more possible. Prince recorded a song called "Can I Play With U?," which he sent to Miles along with a note urging him to add whatever he liked. Miles cut a horn part but didn't seem particularly inspired by the pedestrian song; after receiving it back, Prince decided not to release it. Still, their respect for each other remained strong. "Prince does so many things, it's almost like he can do it all," Miles would write in his 1989 autobiography, *Miles*. "For me, he can be the new Duke Ellington of our time if he just keeps at it."

They would appear together onstage once, in a performance at Paisley Park in 1987, and Prince would continue to send Miles tracks from time to time. According to Alan Leeds, who helped arrange the initial meeting between the two musicians, Miles would have preferred a face-to-face collaboration to Prince's favored practice of sending tapes through the mail. "Up until his illness and death, Miles continued romancing the idea of an eventual album collaboration with Prince – an idea Prince never rejected but never brought himself to take seriously enough to commence writing or recording together," Leeds said. "Instead,

Prince made periodic offers of various tracks. Miles held out, wishing for the opportunity to actually work together. Alas, it never happened."

A few days after recording "Can I Play With U?," Prince undertook a series of jazz-like jams at Sunset Sound with Eric Leeds, Sheila E. on drums, and Levi Seacer, Jr. (a member of Sheila's own band), on bass. These sessions represented one of the most genuinely democratic collaborations in Prince's career, as he, and everyone else present, threw out ideas that straddled the border of jazz and funk. "He was dealing with musicians of a very high caliber," recalled Eric. "Water seeks its own level, and I think he was finding the better quality of water." Various instrumental numbers were recorded, and Prince seriously considered releasing some of them under the anonymous banner of a group called the Flesh.

This interesting project was tabled, and Prince's jazz excursions became more solitary. Playing all the basic instruments by himself, he recorded an album of instrumentals and had Eric Leeds overdub saxophone parts. Eric, while pleased to be involved in the new project, had found the Flesh sessions much more galvanizing. "What had been a dialogue between musicians now became a script," he remarked later.

The album, released under the name of the fictional group Madhouse and called simply *8* (it contained eight songs, with each identified by a number rather than a name), was released in January 1987 without any credits. While Prince's involvement was at first denied by his management, eventually word leaked out that he and Leeds were the sole players. Considering the absence of vocals, the album did quite well, reaching No. 25 on the Black Chart. The single "6" even became a hit on the Black Singles Chart, climbing to No. 5. And among Prince's core fan base, *8* was seen as yet another unusual expression of his protean genius. In the absence of vocals, it showcased his outstanding drum, keyboard and bass skills prominently. While Eric Leeds, as jazz purist, would later criticize the album and downplay his own contributions, many listeners felt that he and Prince had achieved a meaningful creative synergy on the album.

    ***

As work continued on *The Dream Factory* during spring 1986, the jovial, collaborative atmosphere that had at first surrounded the project gradually dissipated. Of the various ways that Prince reminded Wendy and Lisa that he was still in charge, perhaps the most hurtful was his failure to fully credit their songwriting contributions. The most recent example of song pilfering had occurred on the album *Parade*; when Wendy and Lisa reviewed the album's cover art, they discovered that Prince had withheld individual songwriting credit for them on "Mountains" and "Sometimes It Snows In April," pieces for which they had composed much of the music. As a result of such incidents, they became increasingly reluctant to share their ideas with Prince, and began stockpiling material for a possible solo career.

Another of their concerns was Susannah's emotional health. Although she agreed to move into the new home, Prince's resistance to monogamy remained a consistent problem; Susannah had been made aware of his dalliances in Nice, and her patience was diminishing. Back in Minnesota, Prince continued to sleep with, among others, Sheila E., Jill Jones, and actress Troy Beyer, whom he had met in Los Angeles.

Although Prince had bought Susannah an engagement ring, the notion of lifelong commitment frightened him, leading to his wildly inconsistent behavior towards her. Many friends believed that he loved Susannah deeply, but was conflicted about having a conventional relationship. He privately told production designer Roy Bennett that he felt overwhelmed by his feelings for her and worried that the relationship could cause him to quit playing music.

Susannah, despite the oscillations in the relationship, struggled to make it work. "She loved him unconditionally," observed her friend Karen Krattinger. But cohabitation did not agree with Prince, and after just a few months of living together, he told Susannah he wanted her out. Riddled with ambivalence, he convinced her to rent an apartment a short drive away. "He wanted her in his life, but he couldn't go to sleep and wake up with the same person every day," Rogers recalled.

The twists in the relationship left Susannah angry and exhausted, and she wrestled with leaving Prince and Minneapolis altogether. The lovers' conflicts also placed stress on Prince's relationship with Wendy and Lisa. When he arrived at the studio in a foul mood, they could tell he had been fighting with Susannah the night before. They also knew that even as Prince demanded loyalty from Susannah, he was dating other women, and they saw him as a hypocrite. Susannah's pain became difficult for Wendy and Lisa to ignore, even as they struggled to separate the personal and professional elements of the conflict.

There were other clouds on the horizon as well, most notably the release of *Under The Cherry Moon*. Advance word about the film among Hollywood insiders was uniformly negative. Prince knew that his career as an actor and filmmaker stood to suffer serious damage if the movie flopped, as now seemed likely. One evening at his new home, Prince had a rare explosion of emotion, laying down on the floor and screaming at Susannah that he hated the movie.

As rehearsals began for upcoming tours in support of *Parade*, Wendy and Lisa again became frustrated about Prince's augmentation of the Revolution. "We've gone from being the Beatles to being an overblown R&B band," Wendy blurted out during one session. The vision that she and Lisa had of a small, intimate ensemble where they shared the spotlight with Prince was slipping away. Then, over roughly a month between June and July 1986, Prince began overhauling *The Dream Factory*, replacing collaborative efforts (including "Power Fantastic," "It's A Wonderful Day," and "Teacher, Teacher") with solo compositions. He also booked a series of live engagements dubbed *The Hit and Run Tour* that took the band away from the studio. He periodically flew alone to Los Angeles, recording songs for side projects at Sunset Sound Studios in Hollywood and seeing girlfriends, including actress Sherilyn Fenn. He was not always missed; when he disappeared to the West Coast after instructing Wendy, Lisa, and Susannah to complete the song "Witness For The Prosecution," the atmosphere in the studio suddenly felt light and breezy.

When he returned, the fighting continued, particularly with Wendy; according to Susan Rogers, spats between the bandleader and guitarist were a "weekly if not daily occurrence." One rehearsal at a Washington Avenue warehouse in Minneapolis degenerated into a shouting match between Prince and Wendy and Lisa. "You fucking lesbians, you're gonna rot in hell for your lifestyle!" Prince screamed. "You're a fucking womanizer," retorted Wendy. "You're such a prick and a control freak. You're just a womanizing pig."

Finally fed up, they visited Prince's home and demanded that things change and that they be treated as creative equals. Despite the clear threat that they might otherwise leave the band, Prince refused them point-blank. And with that, the fate of one of the most intriguing albums of Prince's career was thrown into jeopardy.

***

Prince and his management were hungry for a hit, and the success of the single "Kiss," which reached No. 1 on the Pop Singles Chart after being released in February 1986 gave them hope that *Parade: Music From Under The Cherry Moon* would also take off. At the same time, Warner Bros. worried that the album's experimental elements might hinder its commercial potential.

The album was released in late March to critical claim. "Who but Prince fills us today with the kind of anticipation we once reserved for new work by Bob Dylan, the Beatles and the Rolling

Stones?" began Davitt Sigerson's review in *Rolling Stone*, again making clear how much hope the critical establishment had invested in Prince's success. The *Detroit Free Press* called the album "a confirmation of Prince's place as a superior melodist, arranger and player as well as a celebration of his creativity."

Sales in the United States were not overwhelming, topping out at about two million, but the album sold another two million abroad. The album's overall performance showed that while Prince had dropped from the stratospheric height of *Purple Rain*, he was building a base of die-hard fans across the globe.

***

Prince, his managers, and Warners Pictures hoped that *Under The Cherry Moon*, released in July 1986, would be a summer blockbuster like *Purple Rain*. But this would be a black and white film with an idiosyncratic rather than celebratory soundtrack. And the premiere would not take place in downtown Los Angeles but rather Sheridan, Wyoming, with a population of about 10,000 people. This strange choice resulted from a promotional lottery sponsored by Warners Pictures and MTV that allowed the winner to have the film's premiere held in his or her hometown and be escorted to the event by Prince himself. The victor was Lisa Barber, a twenty-year-old hotel worker in Sheridan.

None of the band members really wanted to be in Sheridan, and certainly not at the drab Holiday Inn where the post-screening party was to be held. On the day of the premiere, a minor incident caused a meltdown. Wendy cracked open a beer in her room at the hotel and, upon exiting, bumped into Prince in the hallway. Claiming that this constituted public drinking and could embarrass him, he informed Wendy that she would be fined $500. Wendy said nothing, but something snapped for her, and this infantilizing incident became a metaphor for Prince's insistence on controlling not only their music and image, but even their personal behavior. The incident brought her one step closer to quitting the band.

The film's premiere went forward that afternoon at Centennial Theatre in Sheridan's modest downtown. Prince showed up in the same outfit he had worn on the cover of *Parade* – tight black pants with large white buttons, and a matching black half-shirt that left his small, flat belly exposed. True to his promise, he served as Lisa Barber's date. Before picking her up in a limousine, he sent over a clothier and make-up artist to prepare her for the event.

Those in attendance at the theater, a peculiar mixture of several hundred of Barber's Wyoming friends and celebrities flown in by Prince on two Lear jets, found common ground in their distaste for the film. "I couldn't figure out what was going on," said one Sheridan resident afterward, speaking for many. During the screening, Prince briefly put his arm around Lisa Barber, but otherwise interacted little with either her or the crowd.

By the time the band was on a plane headed back to Minneapolis, early reviews had arrived, plunging Prince into gloom and casting a pall over the flight. The notices were negative, often laceratingly so: *The New York Times*, for example, called his character in the film "a self-caressing twerp of dubious provenance." Wrote Glen Lovell in *the San Jose Mercury News*: "The last time I can remember such an outrageous, unmitigated display of narcissism was when Barbra Streisand discovered she could do it all, and cranked out celluloid monuments to herself, like *A Star Is Born*."

A distressed Prince continued obsessing about *Cherry Moon*, so much so that he failed to heed signals that his band was spiraling out of control. Wendy and Lisa finally concluded that the downsides of remaining with Prince outweighed the benefits. They understood the consequences – *The Dream Factory* had just been completed and mastered, and the album still remained a showcase for many of their contributions. If they left, the project was likely to be scrapped or drastically changed. Just the same, they were ready to walk away and begin planning a solo career.

Later in July, Wendy and Lisa showed up at Prince's home and said they wanted out. While aware of their growing dissatisfaction, Prince never believed that they might actually quit, and now faced a logistical problem, as a tour of Europe and Japan was about to begin in support of *Parade*. With *Cherry Moon* failing at the box office, postponing the tour would likely doom the album's commercial prospects.

In fact, the entire band was coming unglued. Mark Brown felt woefully underpaid and was troubled by his ever-shrinking role; the band's live configuration now consigned him to the very back of the stage, hidden by the rest of the group and the dancers. "I was behind the piano, next to Bobby Z., and behind three guys that used to be the bodyguards," Brown noted. "I started feeling a little unappreciated."

Brown had also just been offered $3,500 a week to tour with Stevie Nicks (Prince was paying about a third of that), and told Prince he might forego the *Parade* tour in favor of this opportunity.

An alarmed Alan Leeds moved swiftly to save the tour. Hustling to Wendy and Lisa's apartment, he said he sympathized with their grievances but urged them to at least postpone their exits. They agreed, although it was clear that a long-term reconciliation between Prince and his two best friends was unlikely. Brown also agreed to stay for the tour only after Prince pleaded with him.

As the tour got underway, even Prince's longest-serving band member, Bobby Z., felt a distance growing between himself and Prince. Sheila E., whose band was the opening act on the Japanese leg of the *Parade* tour, often sat in with the Revolution on drums during sound checks. It was clear that Rivkin's job might be in jeopardy.

Most of the band found the *Parade* tour highly satisfying, at least from a purely musical perspective. A fifteen-date European swing put the band before a total of 120,000 people in London, Paris, Rotterdam, Stockholm, Hamburg, and other cities, and, in contrast to the regimented *Purple Rain* tour, these shows allowed for improvisation and variation of the set. Some of the songs took on a jazzy orientation, such as "Anotherloverholeinyohead," which became a forum for Lisa's piano soloing and the horn work of Eric Leeds and Blistan. The feelings of artistic connection made Wendy and Lisa wonder whether their relationship with Prince might be salvageable after all. Offstage, though, Prince's treatment of the women was aloof, making it clear that their aborted departure before the tour had offended him. The notion that someone would leave him, rather than vice versa, seemed unthinkable.

Beyond the music, other elements of the show – and particularly the three dancers – were more controversial among Prince's brain trust. Steve Fargnoli, like Wendy and Lisa, had reservations about the shift from a basic pop-rock group to a sprawling funk revue. Prince's live act had shifted from a quirky, androgynous scene dominated by him and Wendy to a more traditional spectacle of R&B showmanship. Fargnoli believed something had been lost in the transition.

***

After a show in London, Prince encountered a fifteen-year-old girl named Anna Garcia, who very much fit his paradigm of seductive female beauty in the manner of Denise Matthews and Patricia Kotero. The attraction between Prince and Garcia was immediate, and they spent a long night talking together in a hotel room. But Prince, seemingly mindful of the potential consequences, made no sexual advances. He did, however, promise to stay in touch. He also held out the possibility of building a side project around her.

The tour continued on through Europe and then headed for Japan, where ticket sales and audience responses were also strong.

From all outward appearances, Prince and the Revolution were at the top of their game and remained a tightly knit unit. Behind the scenes, Prince remained physically and emotionally remote from his band members, whose grievances had continued to accumulate.

They concluded the tour before a raucous crowd of 50,000 people at Yokohama Stadium on September 9, 1986. The band finished the set with an encore of "Sometimes It Snows In April."

As Prince and the band rode back to their hotel, the atmosphere in the limousine was tense and freighted with finality. Prince, a towel wrapped around his neck, appeared exhausted and said nothing. Wendy and Lisa looked at their bandleader and then at each other, still uncertain what was to happen next. After a successful tour that relied heavily on their presence, would Prince come to his senses and realize their importance to the band? Would *The Dream Factory*, which was sure to receive critical acclaim upon its release, further vindicate their contributions? Or would the Revolution, the backing band that had effectively become part of Prince's persona, reach its final conclusion, bringing the album down with it?

Alan Leeds, who had managed to keep the band together long enough to complete the tour, felt certain he knew what the answers would be, and knew there was nothing more he could do to change them.

***

Following the tour, Prince and select members of his entourage fled the coming Minnesota winter for southern California in October 1986. Just days after the move, he invited Wendy and Lisa to his rented home in Beverly Hills, ostensibly for an evening of dinner and shooting pool.

After they ate, Prince excused himself and placed a phone call to Bobby Z. in Minneapolis, where it was two-thirty in the morning. Prince quickly came to the point: he was replacing

Bobby with Sheila E. "You're the man and you've done a great job," Prince said, trying to soften the blow. "We're gonna be friends forever. I'm gonna honor your contract." Rivkin, tired after years of non-stop touring, accepted the decision with equanimity. "Sheila E. was one of the five best drummers in the world, in my opinion," he said later. "I was replaced by someone who was one of a kind. And the way Prince let me go was totally admirable, totally kosher, totally man-to-man."

After hanging up, Prince returned to Wendy and Lisa at the dinner table and told them that he was disbanding the Revolution and that they too were being fired. They were surprised, if not entirely shocked; in the previous months, it had become clear that their bond with Prince was broken beyond repair.

Although Rivkin appreciated the rationale behind his own dismissal, the ousting of Wendy and Lisa seemed less explicable, given their central importance in Prince's personal and professional lives. "I really don't understand, to this day, what happened when he let Wendy and Lisa go," Rivkin said. "It's the old expression of getting too close, I think."

Matt Fink, whom Prince invited to remain in the band, also considered the decision to dismiss Wendy and Lisa a mistake, believing that Lisa's evocative piano style, in particular, would prove irreplaceable.

Alan Leeds, while mindful of the musical consequences, was unsurprised by Prince's decision. He knew that Prince associated particular projects with the personalities involved, and that his feelings about Wendy and Lisa had become completely negative. By breaking up the band, Prince sought to purge these emotions, and after Wendy and Lisa departed, friends and colleagues were told not even to mention their names.

With Wendy, Lisa, and Rivkin gone, Brown quit to pursue solo success despite being asked by Prince to stay. Aside from Fink, Prince had lost or exiled a group of musicians that had been a part of his identity from *Purple Rain* onward. As anticipated, he cancelled the release of *The Dream Factory* and shelved other material he had developed with the Revolution, sending an important body of music to the cutting room floor.

Even more broadly than the band itself, the salon of interesting musicians and loyal friends that had emerged from the Revolution period had been disbanded. After several years of exposure to various forms of rock and jazz through friends like Wendy and Lisa, and Eric and Alan Leeds, he had simply had enough. "Prince shut down the school," Alan Leeds noted. "He had the education in Ellington, Miles, and Joni Mitchell, and he was ready to move on. He felt he had gotten out of us what he needed."

In Wendy and Lisa in particular, Prince had lost companions who were playful, open-minded, and opinionated – qualities that were to Prince's benefit in his social and professional lives. "The songs we did with Wendy and Lisa," Eric Leeds noted, "included some of the most wonderful stuff we ever did."

24. MASTERPIECE

With the Revolution gone, Prince was intent on proving that he could thrive entirely on his own. Not two weeks after dismissing Wendy and Lisa, in October 1986, Prince returned to the familiar surroundings of Sunset Sound's Studio 3, preparing songs for what he hoped would be a career-defining work that would silence all doubters.

A year earlier, during the recording of *Parade*, the Sunset complex had percolated with the activities of his associates. But now, the core group had shrunk down to Prince and engineer Susan Rogers. When they weren't in Los Angeles, the duo spent most of their time working in Prince's home studio.

Like the material from *Around The World In A Day* and *Parade*, Prince's recordings from fall 1986 incorporated new approaches – the funky cut "Hot Thing" used a recurring keyboard embellishment that sounded simultaneously psychedelic and Middle Eastern, while the rocker "I Could Never Take The Place Of Your Man" echoed sixties surf pop – and yet, this music was unmistakably Prince, bearing his trademarks of minimalism and unresolved tension.

As Prince became more adept at using the recording studio as an instrument in itself, new sounds and textures emerged by happenstance, as he proved willing to follow wherever "mistakes" brought him. "The Ballad Of Dorothy Parker," the first song recorded in his Galpin Boulevard home studio, got its mid-range-dominated sound as a result of a technical glitch. While Prince and engineer Rogers were working, a snowstorm caused a power outage. When the lights came back on and work resumed, the playbacks seemed to Rogers dull and murky; Prince, in a creative trance, did not notice, and Rogers was hesitant to interrupt the session. But when she checked the equipment after he went to bed, Rogers found that, as a result of the blackout, the soundboard had been running on half of its recommended wattage, robbing "Dorothy Parker" of its high end and giving the song a distant and subdued feel. Learning of the problem the next day, Prince treated it as serendipity, deciding that the offbeat sound added character.

Later, when at Sunset Sound to record the avant-garde funk number "If I Was Your Girlfriend," Rogers committed a rare technical error that caused Prince's vocal to distort on certain words. "I thought he was going to rip my head off," Rogers remembered. But when Prince came into the control booth to hear the playback, he seemed to like the results. Yet another studio mishap shaped "Forever In My Life," a ballad comprising nothing more than several tracks of vocals, a percussion pattern composed on the Linn LM-1, and sprinkles of acoustic guitar. Before singing, Prince asked Rogers to mute his previously recorded backing vocal; upon playback, it was apparent that he had begun late, and that his lead vocal thus lagged behind the rest of the music. Again, Prince found the results of the blunder worth keeping.

Along with the new material he was developing at Sunset Sound and in his home studio, Prince had a cache of strong songs culled from the shelved *Dream Factory* album. Although he wanted to avoid releasing numbers that featured input from Wendy and Lisa or other band members, he planned to use several of his solo compositions from the discarded album. The arsenal was full for the masterpiece Prince wanted to uncork.

The exact nature of the album, however, remained up in the air, and Prince played with various concepts. Further exploring the studio technique of speeding up his voice that he had used on "Erotic City," Prince conceived of an alter-ego named "Camille" based around this concept. During a nine-day period at Sunset Sound, he recorded five songs for an album called *Camille*. Over cocktails at Tramps, a Los Angeles nightclub, Prince told saxophonist Eric Leeds of an idea for a film in which Prince would play two characters, one being the "evil Camille." At the end of the film it would be revealed that the two were one and the same, and that the protagonist had a split personality.

Although the film concept was nebulous at best, the notion of a "Camille" album was more concrete, and he rapidly sequenced a record that included only tracks using the speeded-up vocal sound. But he soon discarded that idea and planned something even more outlandish: a three-album set. "He knew that just having the balls to do three records would create a big bang," Alan Leeds said. And he would do it as a one-man band, playing nearly every instrument on one of the longest albums of all time.

Prince remained in virtual lockdown mode at Sunset Sound as he worked to complete the project. Among his next efforts were "Adore," a gospel ballad comparable to the best of Al Green, and the punkish "Play In The Sunshine." And other new influences emerged. Prince had been listening to the ethereal, highly melodic compositions of Kate Bush and Peter Gabriel, becoming particularly enthralled by Bush's signature composition "Cloudbusting." In July, he recorded a haunting ballad called "Joy in Repetition" that displayed Bush's influence and ranked with the strongest of the new songs.

Another notable new composition was the lengthy, suite-like "Crystal Ball," which Prince conceived as one of the most profound statements of his worldview and a showcase of his musical range. The lyrics touched on war and political extremism, and the musical passages ran the gamut from funk to reggae. As he had done with songs for *The Family* project in 1984, Prince sent "Crystal Ball" to orchestral composer Clare Fischer for extensive overdubbing. He included a note explaining the importance of the song. Fischer, along with his writing partner and son Brent, used a sixty-piece orchestra including eight French horns to sprinkle dramatic flourishes across the 10-minute song. In its ambitious construction, the song very much evoked the Beatles' "A Day in the Life" and seemed certain to be greeted by critics as a major leap forward for Prince as an experimentalist.

As his bold new album took shape, Prince began previewing it for friends, who quickly realized they were hearing some of his strongest material ever. "He just loved playing music for people when he had their undivided attention," recalled Alan Leeds. "You would get in his car with him, maybe drive to a Dairy Queen and get an ice cream, and then just sit and listen to the sequence of a new album." In the past, Prince often seemed open to feedback on minor issues like track sequence, but not in the case of *Crystal Ball*. "His attitude was, 'Don't mess with me, this is it!'" Leeds recalled.

With the album nearly finished, Prince took a rare night off to celebrate Thanksgiving with Susannah Melvoin, who remained his girlfriend even after the departure of Wendy and Lisa. Susan Rogers, whom Prince also invited, arrived at his rented Beverly Hills house expecting a large, festive crowd; she found no one but a tired Prince and his girlfriend. "After dinner we watched some videos, and he fell asleep on the couch," Rogers remembered. "That was Thanksgiving."

A number of the songs slated for *Crystal Ball* had been directly inspired by Susannah. "The Ballad Of Dorothy Parker," recorded after a fight between the couple, related how Prince consoled himself through an anonymous affair with a waitress. "If I Was Your Girlfriend" found Prince wishing for the relaxed intimacy enjoyed by female friends, flowing from his observations of Susannah and Wendy. And "Forever In My Life" captured his relationship with Susannah at a pivotal moment, with Prince promising that he was tired of meaningless sexual encounters.

In truth, Prince's relationship with Susannah continued to be poisoned by his many affairs. This also upset Karen Krattinger, who by now had become general manager of Prince's production company. Susannah was one of her best friends; knowing this, Prince still ordered Krattinger to perform odious tasks like installing her in an apartment after Prince banished her from his new home. After years of backbreaking hours (which included almost single-handedly organizing Prince's sprawling business files into a functional state), Krattinger began to wonder how long she could continue. "Prince put me in the middle of his relationship way too much," she said. "I saw him throwing away and hurting the most wonderful woman I felt he would ever know."

Prince made little secret of his dalliances with other women. While one-night stands were a frequent occurrence, there were also steady companions in the form of Jill Jones and Sheila E., whose importance as a musical collaborator continued to grow. A tense and unpleasant dynamic developed between Susannah and Sheila, who encountered each other not infrequently as a result of their intersecting musical and personal relationships with Prince. And Sheila's emotions, like Susannah's, were affected by her shifting fortunes. Krattinger, who dealt with frequent requests from all members of Prince's entourage, recalls Sheila as humble and cordial when on the outs with Prince, but haughty and disdainful when the romance was flourishing. "It was as if she thought that when she was going out with him, she should be treated exactly like him," Krattinger said.

Each of Prince's "girlfriends" had something in common: their willingness to accept, although not always entirely without protest, his insistence on maintaining multiple relationships. And while few of his serious romantic interests were complete pushovers – Sheila E. was a stunningly talented musician, and Susannah hailed from a sophisticated, musically inclined family – they were disinclined to challenge his behavior. Conversely, his affairs with more headstrong women, such as Madonna and the New York artist-singer Carole Davis, tended to be very short-lived. "I don't think he actually wanted to be around anyone more worldly or knowledgeable than himself for very long," observed Leeds. "He gravitated to more simple women who'd settle for staying in his house, sharing popcorn and movies and not challenging his comings and goings."

His romantic life, while bountiful, was not allowed to detract from his music. One of Prince's favorite tasks was sequencing albums, and arranging the many strong tracks of *Crystal Ball* was a particularly satisfying exercise. The album had shaped up as exactly the magnum opus he had hoped for, bristling with energy and experimentation, and yet coherent and structurally sound as an overall body of work.

The task of getting Warners behind the ambitious project fell to Steve Fargnoli. Fargnoli hoped that just as Mo Ostin and Lenny Waronker ultimately supported *1999* as a double album and put the full force of their offices behind *Purple Rain*, they would embrace an album that would be greeted a masterpiece.

This assumption proved to be wrong. While Ostin and Waronker still viewed Prince as an unstoppable creative force, they had developed concerns about his business judgments, believing in particular that he released albums too frequently. Since *Purple Rain*, Prince's album sales had tapered off consistently, due in part to questionable projects like *Under the Cherry Moon*, which had spun out of control, harming the performance of *Parade*. Wendy and Lisa were gone, along with the valuable trademark that had been the Revolution.

With *Crystal Ball*, Prince faced an additional problem: no one in his inner circle, including Fargnoli, was entirely supportive of the concept of a triple album. Alan Leeds, while enthusiastic about most of the material, feared that such a sprawling release could be perceived as a display of arrogance rather than a defining accomplishment. "A backlash among fans and critics was certainly possible," he noted. "Besides die-hard fans bathing in an orgy of new material, there were few upsides."

Even Fargnoli, charged with convincing Warners to release the record, was lukewarm and himself had started to harbor doubts about the direction of Prince's career. "I think Steve was getting to the point where he started to feel like he didn't need this," said Warners' Marylou Badeaux. "It's not unusual for an artist to make demands of his management, but some of Prince's demands were getting more and more out in left field."

The dispute also marked a turning point in the relationship between Prince and Ostin, who was deeply concerned about the economics of a triple-album set. Shortly after learning of the project, Ostin visited Sunset Sound to hear the record and meet with Prince and Fargnoli. His response after listening to the album shocked and angered Prince. "I respect your vision, but it just won't fly," he said, insisting that Prince pare *Crystal Ball* to a double album.

Prince refused to back down, and the battle over the album continued for several weeks. "There were a lot of meetings, a lot of loud hollering, a lot of frustration," recalled Leeds. "It was very, very ugly."

Faced with the reality of his diminished commercial clout, Prince finally agreed to trim the set as Warners had asked. But he felt that the company had destroyed his meticulously constructed masterwork, and the relationship would never be the same. And with the project having fundamentally changed, his ardor for the album also cooled. "Prince lost interest beginning with editing it into two albums," observed Leeds. "He had allowed himself to see it only as a three-record set, and as such it seemed to him an incomplete work – not the true vision he had set out."

Prince reluctantly scrapped the lengthy title track, which took up nearly half an album side, meaning that the album would also have to be re-titled. Clare and Brent Fischer, after putting so much effort into "Crystal Ball," were disappointed to learn the song might never be released. Prince also discarded strong cuts like "Good Love," an exuberant pop song that used the "Camille" vocal technique, and "Joy In Repetition."

Adding to Prince's worries and frustrations, in December 1986, Susannah finally decided that she'd had enough; she packed her things and returned to Los Angeles' San Fernando Valley, joining Wendy and Lisa. "You can only subject yourself to so much, unless you're self-abusive, and she had a lot of respect for herself," observed Karen Krattinger. "He probably would have kept her back and forth on a yo-yo forever." Prince had in short order experienced a professional disappointment and personal disruption, causing the enthusiasm that had burned so brightly just months ago to all but disappear.

One evening shortly after Susannah's departure, Susan Rogers could tell something was very wrong when Prince came down to the basement studio. Looking disconsolate and barely speaking, he began constructing a song around a melancholy piano pattern. His spoken lyrics portrayed a fictional dialogue between himself and Wally Safford, a dancer in the band. Sounding sad and lost, Prince asks Wally to borrow fifty dollars and some sunglasses so he can impress his lover, but then changes his mind and returns the items, telling Wally that since he is alone now, he has no one to spend the money on. Prince was accompanied only by piano throughout the verse, but guitar, bass, and drums entered as the song built into a chorus on which he sings the phrase, "o-ma-la-di-da."

Watching Prince construct the song, which he called "Wally," Rogers was stunned by the honest emotion and wistful resignation it conveyed. She saw the song both as a farewell to Susannah and a means of expelling the poison of a failed relationship.

"Do you know that malady means sickness, illness in French?" Prince asked Rogers, referring to the phrase he sings in the chorus. "It's almost like the word melody, isn't it?" Prince, who rarely exposed his inner feelings, even in his music, was groping for a metaphor that would convey his feelings of loss. Rogers felt it was a turning point in his songwriting.

But as the session continued, Prince started to distance himself from the creation. He added extraneous instruments that diminished the song's clarity. A percussion part cluttered the verse, detracting from the lyrics.

"Don't you think it was better before, Prince?" Rogers said, and then gently suggested, "Maybe we should stop." He ignored her, adding a synthesizer riff. Soon it became clear to her: he was intentionally destroying the song. After larding the piece with additional instruments, he finally spoke.

"Now put all twenty-four channels on record and erase it," he told Rogers.

"No, you can't do this!" Rogers said, dismayed by the prospect of losing this defining creation.

"If you don't, I will," Prince responded.

Rogers stood her ground, and Prince was forced to operate the soundboard himself as he destroyed his own music. "Wally," like his relationship with Susannah, Wendy, and Lisa, involved more emotional intensity than Prince was willing to accept. "I thought it was the greatest thing he had done," said Rogers. "I had waited years to hear a Prince song like this. I ached to hear him be this honest."

Yet, Prince's refusal to explore his feelings was not altogether surprising. Rogers had discussed the topic of depression with him before and found Prince contemptuous of the very notion. "He thought it was practically a sin to be depressed," she remembered. Many other associates had observed that Prince – not only in his relationships, but even in his music – was cryptic and unrevealing of his deepest feelings. "His music is very passionate, but he doesn't let himself open up emotionally," observed Marylou Badeaux. "And look at the way he's dealt with women in his life – he's not able to get emotional, he just kept it on the level of sex play."

"Wally" indeed served as a metaphor for how Prince felt about the destruction of *Crystal Ball* and the loss of Susannah. He wanted to erase that pain and move on, and sought in some fashion to accomplish this by also erasing "Wally."

Although Susannah had never formally been part of the Revolution, her personal and creative influence on Prince from 1983 to 1986 rivaled that of Wendy and Lisa. With her exit from the scene, the Revolution period ended irrevocably. The epitaph of this time would be "Wally," a song no one would hear.

25. ASTERISK

After being forced to pare down *Crystal Ball* to a double album, Prince retitled it *Sign O' The Times*. The striking cover art showed a cluttered background of debris, including a junked auto; on the far right, in the foreground, is a blurry image of half of Prince's face. The first single, "Sign O' The Times," tackled social and political issues, referencing the explosion of the space shuttle Challenger, the spread of AIDS, and Reagan's "Star Wars" missile defense program. This brilliant song became another prime example of Prince's ability to mix artistry and commercialism. Sung somberly in his lower register, "Sign O' The Times" sounded subdued, almost withdrawn, yet bristled with an underlying tension and angst. Far more challenging than most Top 40 fare, it nonetheless reached No. 3 on the Billboard Pop Singles Chart, an auspicious beginning for the project.

Notwithstanding Prince's disappointment over having to trim *Crystal Ball*, *Sign O' The Times* was greeted as the crowning achievement he had wanted the triple album to be. Critical reaction to the album, which was released in March 1987, was almost uniformly strong, and it was compared to masterpiece double albums like the Rolling Stones' *Exile On Main Street* and the Beatles' *White Album*. "Truly this man is a genius," wrote Ted Mica in *Melody Maker*. "There are hints of the Temptations, slices of Isaac Hayes, traces of Sly Stone, even footprints of Robert Palmer." *Q* magazine lauded Prince's "sophistication and chops" and commended him for creating a "funk ... edge that slices straight into the soft white gut of pop."

The triumph of *Sign O' The Times* owed to many factors, among them Prince's focus and drive following the exit of Wendy and Lisa, his facility with musical technologies like the Linn LM-1, and also the many new influences he had assimilated so rapidly.

"To my ears, the better of the material seemed the artistic culmination of all the things he had been exposed to and absorbed from Wendy, Lisa, Sheila, and Eric over the previous couple of years," said Alan Leeds. "It showed musical growth and maturity, while taking him back to his R&B roots like no record of his since *1999*."

And yet, Prince was somewhat unmoved by praise for the album. For him, *Sign O' The Times* would always have an asterisk next to it, denoting that it should have been a three-album masterpiece entitled *Crystal Ball*. Sales figures, meanwhile, began to taper off rather quickly after an initial burst of purchases by serious fans. A key misstep accelerating this trend was Prince's selection of "If I Was Your Girlfriend" as the second single; the song proved too quirky for radio.

Still, optimism remained high at Warner Bros. and among Prince's bandmates that the album could be revived on the charts when a two-month European tour in support of *Sign O' The Times* began in May. Prince's popularity in Europe was still increasing, and the well-designed show proved to be one of the most exciting of his career. The absence of Wendy and Lisa was filled to some extent by the kinetic Sheila E., whose percussion work added a new dimension to Prince's live sound and electrified crowds. The other members of the revamped band included Levi Seacer, Jr. on bass, Boni Boyer on keyboards and vocals, Matt Fink on keyboards, and Miko Weaver on guitar. Another new member was dancer Cat Glover, who became a visual focal point. The carryovers from the *Parade* tour, along with Fink and Weaver, were Eric Leeds on saxophone and Matt Blistan on trumpet. Dancers Jerome Benton, Greg Brooks, and Wally Safford also remained onstage, but were less prominent than on the *Parade* tour.

The evenly paced set emphasized the strong *Sign O' The Times* material and gave the band ample opportunity to jam, particularly on the lengthy set-closer, "It's Gonna Be A Beautiful Night." The tour was a success in every respect, convincing Warners and Prince's management that a U.S. tour could reinvigorate sales of *Sign O' The Times* in the United States.

But Prince had other plans. Frustrated by the tepid response of American consumers, and already impatient to move onto his next project, he opted instead to have the final shows of the European tour filmed and packaged into a concert film for American audiences. "To put it very bluntly, the film was Prince's way of getting out of doing the tour," said Alan Leeds. "Nobody was in favor of the idea." Warners' film division, leery about Prince's filmmaking after *Under The Cherry Moon,* declined to get involved, forcing him to find another distributor.

Prince's hurry to conclude the campaign stemmed from his desire to move on to other projects, including what he expected would be a major feature film called *Graffiti Bridge.* By characterizing it as a sequel to *Purple Rain,* and reprising some of the plot elements and actors, he hoped to attract financing and film studio support. And by recruiting Madonna as the female lead, he would create an alliance of two of the decade's most iconic and marketable figures.

Although she and Prince had stayed in touch only sporadically since their romance petered out in 1985, Madonna agreed to travel to Minnesota to discuss the project. Wanting to welcome his co-star in style, Prince had an apartment lavishly furnished for her. "He thought she would fall in love with the screenplay and stay a month," recalled Karen Krattinger, who was in charge of Madonna's arrangements. Instead, the Material Girl left the unit after one night, preferring the amenities offered by an upscale hotel. Her reaction to *Graffiti Bridge* was much more disturbing; she brazenly told Prince the screenplay was awful and then split town, leaving the project in doubt and without a strong co-star.

Despite this setback, Prince had plenty to celebrate as fall 1987 arrived; his Paisley Park Studios complex was complete. Located in the Minneapolis suburb of Chanhassen, just a few minutes' drive from Prince's home, the facility included three recording studios, a 12,400-foot soundstage for live performances and film productions, and various business offices for a growing staff. Below was a garage where Prince entered in his purple BMW, and from where he took a private elevator to the ground floor. Studio A, his main workplace, boasted a forty-eight-track console, an array of high-tech equipment, and an isolation room with granite walls to generate brilliantly clear reverb sounds.

All of this had been made possible by the largesse generated by *Purple Rain*, making Paisley Park a tangible expression of everything Prince had accomplished. During a recording session at Sunset Sound not long before Paisley opened, Susan Rogers experienced a tender moment that underscored how far he had come from his life growing up on the Northside. Rogers excused herself from the session to make a phone call; when she returned, she apologized for her absence and mentioned that she had just closed on a new home. Prince asked where.

"Lake Harriet," Rogers responded, referring to a picturesque lake in Southwest Minneapolis surrounded by expensive homes.

Surprisingly, Prince became emotional. "When I was a kid, I always dreamed that someday I'd grow up, be rich, and live on Lake Harriet," Prince responded. "And now I've got people working for me who live on Lake Harriet." A few minutes later, Prince had bottles of champagne brought in to toast her triumph.

Because Paisley would be expensive to run and maintain, Steve Fargnoli prevailed upon Prince to allow other musicians to book studio time when he didn't need it. An obscure band called Limited Warranty was first to use Studio A; Prince noticed their master tapes on a console during a tour of the finished complex with Rogers. "The place was beautiful; he was grinning ear-to-ear," the engineer recalled. Prince opened up the boxes containing Limited Warranty's music and smirked at Rogers. "Wouldn't it be funny," he asked, "If we stayed up all night and did overdubs on their tape?" Rogers gave him a worried look.

Prince kept smiling, but put the boxes down and resumed wandering about the facility.

***

Before Prince could actively work on new music at the studio, the *Sign O' The Times* campaign needed to be wrapped up, which he wanted to do expeditiously. As soon as editing of the *Sign O' The Times* film was complete, Prince insisted on rushing the movie into theaters in November 1987 against the judgment of his advisors; the release date guaranteed it would be lost in the swirl of year-end Oscar contenders. "A number of us told him that the release date was a mistake, but in his mind, we were just trying to undermine him," Badeaux said.

And unfortunately, the movie failed to capture the ambiance of the electrifying European shows. Although the music was culled from the concert tour, the video footage was too grainy for professional use, and Prince decided to reshoot the visuals on a soundstage at Paisley Park. The band was thus forced to lip-sync to previously recorded live material, giving the film a sterile feel despite its powerful music. Only at one point did it soar, during "Forever In My Life." Prince, center stage with only an acoustic guitar, riffs playfully and then delivers a searing vocal as Boni Boyer, Sheila E., and other band members contribute gospel-like backup singing over a simple drum-machine riff.

The film, while critically praised, was a commercial flop and failed to boost sales for the album. Prince, having already skipped the U.S. tour, largely withdrew from promotional activities for *Sign O' The Times*, much to the dismay of Warners. Recalled company vice president Marylou Badeaux: "We needed more time with the record, but he was done with *Sign O' The Times* in every way."

Seeking to regain momentum by tacking in an entirely different direction, Prince conceived of a strange project to be called *The Black Album*. As kind of a rejoinder to *The Beatles*, a record that became known as "The White Album," it would have no cover art or identifying markings, other than a stark black front and back. The name "Prince" would not appear.

Most of the music had been recorded over the past couple of years, but Prince deliberately selected songs that were dark and gritty to comport with the overall concept of the project. When Warners officials listened to the album, they found lascivious funk jams, anarchic jazz-rock instrumentals, and nothing resembling a radio-friendly single. On "Bob George," Prince's voice slowed down to a Barry White-like growl; on "Superfunkycalifragisexy," he sang about bondage, masturbation, and sexual rituals involving both gerbils and squirrel meat. The Warners officials blanched; in many respects the album would be commercially just as risky as *Crystal Ball*.

Another major catalyst behind the album was Prince's desire to reconnect with his African-American fan base. His various excursions into rock, along with the fawning attention he received from the largely white critical establishment, left him worried about perceptions that he had strayed from his roots; *The Black Album*'s emphasis on funk was designed in part to compensate for "whiter" records like *Purple Rain* and *Around The World In A Day*. But beyond this, Prince's vision for the album was otherwise not particularly clear, and the "dark" nature of the music was more reflective of his mood following the demises of *Crystal Ball* and his relationship with Susannah.

From the perspective of Warners, *The Black Album* was emblematic of the label's concerns about Prince's career. The company desperately wanted Prince to come up with catchy songs that would re-establish him as a potent hitmaker and guide him back towards *Purple Rain*-like levels of fame. What it got instead was *The Black Album*.

Adding to the confusion and angst at the label, Warners was still in the process of promoting *Sign O' The Times*, and the immediate release of another album would clash with those efforts. "We told him, you can't put a record out to interfere with the existing record." Ostin recalled. "But he insisted, and we again went along with him."[1]

26. DON'T BUY THE BLACK ALBUM

On December 1, 1987, Prince entered Rupert's, a Minneapolis dance club, armed with a test pressing of *The Black Album*, whose planned release was a week away. As he often did before releasing albums, he played the new music over the system without fanfare to see how club-goers would react.

As the music played, Prince mingled with the crowd and eventually became involved in a detailed conversation with a singer-songwriter-poet in her early twenties named Ingrid Chavez. An attractive brunette with a serious and reflective air, Chavez had moved to Minneapolis several years earlier to work on music with a friend. But that collaboration had soured, and since then she had been working alone on her poetry and spoken-word pieces.

Prince and Chavez seemed fascinated by each other despite an apparent lack of sexual chemistry, and, after a while, they drove back to the recently completed Paisley Park studio complex. They continued a lengthy and intense conversation about spirituality, love, and life fulfillment, but Prince eventually excused himself, saying he had a stomachache. Waiting to see where the strange night would go next, Chavez stayed put while Prince disappeared elsewhere in the complex.

At about one-thirty a.m., Karen Krattinger received a phone call from Prince. Speaking with uncharacteristic emotion, he apologized for having been so hard on her, said he had trouble expressing his feelings, and that he loved her.

At about the same time that night, Susan Rogers also got a phone call from Prince, asking her to come to Paisley Park. After four years as Prince's engineer, she had resigned that post shortly after the completion of *The Black Album* in October 1987, and the call was unexpected. Somewhat concerned, she agreed to go to the studio. Arriving in the rehearsal room, Rogers found it dark, save for a few red candles that cast shadows across the walls. Out of the gloom, she heard a woman's voice.

"Are you looking for Prince?"

Rogers, who would later learn this was Chavez, answered, "Yes." "Well, he's here somewhere," Chavez replied.

Abruptly, Prince emerged out of the darkness, looking unlike she had ever seen him before. "I'm certain he was high," Rogers said. "His pupils were really dilated. He looked like he was tripping."

As he had with Krattinger, Prince became uncharacteristically emotional. "I just want to know one thing. Do you still love me?" Rogers, startled, said she did, and that she knew he loved her.

"Will you stay?" Prince asked.

"No, I won't," she said, and left the complex, shaken by Prince's behavior and the eerie scene.

Inside Paisley, Prince continued to react intensely to the drug, and became overwhelmed with negative emotion. The target of his fears, he explained to Chavez and bodyguard Gilbert Davison, was *The Black Album*. The album, he told Chavez, represented an evil force that needed to be eradicated. It was, in effect, the devil working through him.

The next morning when Prince encountered Krattinger, he appeared embarrassed and made no reference to the strange phone call of the night before. But it became clear to her and others in the coming days that Prince believed that he had experienced a spiritual and moral epiphany that night at Paisley Park. He felt that Chavez, serving as a guide and muse, had led him to a greater connection with God. *The Black Album*, he decided, was entirely inconsistent with this transformation.

Days after the drug trip, Warners' Mo Ostin received an anguished call from Prince. As a complete about-face from his demands of just weeks earlier, he insisted that *The Black Album* be scrapped. "Prince was very adamant and pleaded with Mo," recalled Marylou Badeaux. What Prince was asking, Ostin reported, was an expensive logistical nightmare. Five hundred thousand LPs – which now needed to be destroyed – had been pressed, and were on loading docks ready for shipment to stores.

Prince insisted that he would reimburse Warners for its manufacturing costs and also for the destruction of the albums. It was clear that Prince not only wanted the release cancelled, but effectively wanted *The Black Album* wiped from existence.

Warners did destroy the vast majority of records, but saved around one hundred. Inevitably, some of these leaked to journalists, which were in turn duplicated and shared with friends. Within months, *The Black Album* quickly became available on the bootleg market, with fans selling and trading cassette duplicates of widely varying fidelity.

The mystery around the cancellation, and the shocking nature of some of the lyrics, made it a hotly sought after item. And the reactions of the hardcore fans who managed to get hold of copies were largely positive; *The Black Album* was seen as representing a refreshing new direction, and a kind of improvisational counterpoint to the more schematic *Sign O' The Times*. That it had not been officially released became irrelevant to the fans who excitedly discussed the album at nightclubs, coffee shops, and record stores.

Perhaps the only unfortunate part for fans was that Prince had become so disenchanted with it. But for the label that released his albums, the project had been nothing but trouble. Prince's lurching back and forth between first insisting upon *The Black Album*'s release and then on its destruction caused further frustration and doubts about his career direction.

***

New Year's Eve 1987, by outward appearances, was a festive night for Prince. He and the band performed a rousing version of the European tour show for a benefit concert at Paisley Park.

Miles Davis guested and played solos on a thirty-four-minute, jam-filled "It's Gonna Be A Beautiful Night." Some band members – particularly Eric Leeds and Matt Blistan – seemed to forget exactly whose band they were in. "We were just so absorbed with Miles that the whole band missed a cue that Prince gave," recalled Eric. "And Prince kind of yelled at us, like "Hey, remember me?" We all had a laugh.

In truth, the year had been a tremendously frustrating one, and he started to take it out on others. His treatment of employees, such as when he had asked Karen Krattinger to cancel her Thanksgiving plans to perform a non-essential task, veered towards callousness. "You are not my family," she responded in refusing his request.

Engineer Susan Rogers had developed similar feelings over the course of the year, ultimately prompting her to quit. "He was in such a bad mood all the time and a lot of us were reaching a burnout phase with him," said Rogers, who after four years with Prince had made her decision and left. "It just wasn't a good feeling in the air."

But had Prince, in shelving *The Black Album*, experienced a spiritual rebirth that would put all of the negativity of the past two years aside? Associates had their doubts. At the very least, when employees bumped into their boss at the now-completed Paisley Park complex, he tried hard to be cheery. "This was a guy who had an awakening and made a major decision that he was going to change his focus, be it temporarily or permanently," said Alan Leeds. But for some, the notion of a personal transformation seemed dubious. "It was a facade," said Karen Krattinger. "It was evident to me that he still wasn't happy with his life."

27. NOT CONFUSED ANYMORE

Within days of *The Black Album* being pulled from the market, Prince threw himself into the recording of his next album, *Lovesexy,* which he conceived as a document of the awakening he had experienced at Paisley Park with Ingrid Chavez. While the tension between carnality and spirituality had been central to Prince's music since *Controversy,* he now presented these two forces as not in conflict but in harmony. His mission became in essence to synthesize the sexual freedom he'd famously espoused throughout his career with a reverence for a higher power, and to present these things in a unified work of art.

Prince worked mostly by himself, although Sheila E. played drums on several tracks. One of the first songs recorded was "The Line," a stately mid-tempo rocker with religious lyrics inspired by a Chavez poem, which was planned as the album's centerpiece. Prince, Boni Boyer, and Sheila E. shared vocal chores for the musically and lyrically complex number. He was surprised, however, when associates seemed lukewarm about the song. "Prince felt he was really onto something with 'The Line,' but he wasn't getting the reaction he wanted from the people he played it for," recalled Joe Blaney, who engineered the session. "He kept retouching the song, adding more overdubs."

Prince eventually discarded "The Line" but continued to emphasize religious themes as he developed material. He retooled a Crystal Ball castaway called "The Ball" into "Eye No," which showed Prince wrestling with good and evil in a dark night of the soul, and welcoming listeners to something he called the new power generation.

Musically, he explored labyrinthine arrangements and dense instrumentation that at times threatened to sink the songs under their own weight. "I thought *Lovesexy* was going to be a great album, but when I heard the final mixes, I was very disappointed," said Eric Leeds, who added saxophone to various songs and felt that Prince's overdubbing had become excessive.

Some bandmates had trouble relating to the religious messages, and also wondered why Ingrid Chavez was playing such a crucial role. When his confidants were confused by the lyrics of the title track, he re-recorded it to make the meaning ring out more clearly. It still didn't work. "I did not understand what the term 'lovesexy' was supposed to mean," Eric Leeds said. "People weren't getting it."

Still, there was at least one moment when Prince, as friends had hoped, laid bare his emotions to deliver the monumental "Anna Stesia." The song explored Prince's feelings of loneliness and his hopes for redemption. Based around a simple piano motif, the song also featured lush instrumentation that in this instance enhanced rather than detracted from its overall impact.

With the recording process complete, Prince presented the album to Warner Bros. along with cover art that he viewed as an essential part of *Lovesexy*'s overall message. Based upon a photo by Jean-Baptiste Mondino that had been touched up to look like a painting, it showed a nude Prince sitting with his hand on his heart, his right leg raised slightly to cover his genital area. The background of oversized flowers and ferns included a flower stamen resembling a semi-erect phallus.

When Warners' marketing department passed around the cover during a meeting, several worried aloud that retail outlets would refuse to carry the album. Warners requested alternative art from Prince, which he quickly deemed out of the question. His conception of *Lovesexy* as a unified whole also prompted his refusal to "index" the compact disc version, meaning that consumers who bought the CD could not flip from song to song, but had to listen to the album in its entirety. The CD medium was just becoming widespread when *Lovesexy* was released, and Warners worried that consumers would be frustrated if they couldn't navigate to their favorite songs.

He dropped another bombshell: there would be no music videos for the album, including for the lead single, "Alphabet Street." He insisted to Warners' stunned marketing team that the absence of a video would distinguish him from other pop stars, as well as create a sense of mystery about the album.

On all of these points – the cover, the indexing of the CD, and the lack of videos – Warners ultimately gave in, not wanting to repeat the ugly fight that had ensued over Crystal Ball. And on the positive side of the ledger, Prince was clearly invested in the project in a way he had not been with *Sign O' The Times*. As a planned May release date approached, Warners officials prepared a publicity plan and crossed their fingers.

***

On a blustery day in late March 1988 in the Minneapolis suburb of Eden Prairie, Alan Leeds was happy to have a day off from the hectic and exhausting routine of being one of Prince's closest aides. It was warm inside, a sporting event was on TV, and Leeds was home with his family.

The phone rang, and Leeds heard Prince's voice upon picking up. "I want to shoot a video," he said without saying hello. Leeds had to press to find out exactly what this meant. Did he want to make a clip for "Alphabet Street," after all? Prince said yes, and Leeds asked if he had spoken to Steve Fargnoli about this. No, Prince responded, he wanted to shoot without meddling from the managers or Warners. Leeds cautioned that Prince would have to pay for the video himself; didn't it make more sense to contact Warners first, which would readily provide financing?

No, Prince said. He wanted to do it on his own.

"Okay, when?" Leeds asked.

"Today," Prince responded.

An incredulous Leeds tried to convince Prince to hold off at least until the coming week. Snow was beginning to fall, and it was already mid-afternoon. No respectable team of filmmakers could be assembled on such short notice, particularly in Minneapolis where, as Leeds reminded Prince, there was not a film crew on every block. Even if a crew agreed to do the shoot, it was unlikely that adequate equipment could be rented and that everyone would make it through the snow to the set.

"Sounds to me like that's your problem, not mine," Prince retorted.

Leeds realized he would have to placate Prince by placing some phone calls. Although the local film community was not large, Leeds knew several skilled directors. Predictably, they refused the assignment. Working through his Rolodex, Leeds called filmmakers whom he considered "B-list," and began to worry that even if someone agreed to take the job, the end result wouldn't be worth the time, effort, or money. As Leeds waited for callbacks, Prince continued to hector him with periodic phone calls. "When are we shooting?" he asked repeatedly, undeterred by Leeds' warnings that no top-flight filmmakers were available.

Leeds doggedly continued his efforts and finally found a director, Michael Barnard, who was willing to take on the assignment. But the question remained: could the director locate a facility and equipment? The afternoon dragged into evening, and the snow kept falling. Prince's barrage of phone calls to the Leeds residence continued. Finally, Barnard called: the shoot was a go. The location would be a drab building owned by a cable TV company, and he obtained only basic equipment that was typically used to film local city council meetings. Leeds, not surprised that matters had come to this, called Prince and told him the news.

By 11 p.m., with most of the city under snow, the shoot finally began. Prince had rounded up Sheila E. and Cat Glover to participate. The video was shot against a blue screen, and the resulting footage looked amateurish. During the post-production process, Prince had Barnard jazz up the video by having various textual phrases dart across the screen, including "Don't buy *The Black Album*, I'm sorry," and "Ecstasy." Ultimately, the clip looked more like an excerpt from Sesame Street than a professional product. From Warners' perspective, it was better than nothing – but not by much.

***

Critical reaction to *Lovesexy* upon its release in May 1988 was divided. Some saw the album as both heartfelt and experimental, and a logical extension of *Sign O' The Times* in its musical complexity. Others found it simultaneously narcissistic and unfocussed. "Prince's chaff is inevitably more interesting than most artists' wheat," commented Rolling Stone, "[But] some of the songs are uncharacteristically ordinary." Added David Hiltbrand in *People*, "There's too much autoerotic noodling going on ... There is virtually no evidence of Prince's patented fine-boned funk."

U.S. consumers were also underwhelmed; the record sold only 750,000 copies, Prince's worst commercial showing since his debut record. For the first time in years, Prince had failed to deliver a record that achieved platinum status. Fortunately, critical and consumer reaction was much stronger in Europe, where Prince's popularity had continued to grow and was now comparable to his standing in America during the Purple Rain period. *Lovesexy* moved a healthy 1.9 million copies overseas.

Very few hardcore fans were alienated by the album; while not necessarily a classic, it contained a solid handful of strong numbers and plenty of interesting experimental touches. "Anna Stesia," "Alphabet Street," and "Positivity" were all seen as meaningfully adding to Prince's canon.

To bolster the album in the U.S., Prince began planning an elaborate summer tour. Bursting with ideas about a show that would document his spiritual awakening, he conceived an elaborate stage set that would be the costliest of his entire career, and which incorporated design elements of the now-infamous Jean-Baptiste Mondino album cover.

At first, Steve Fargnoli was open to the idea of an epic-scale tour, believing that it could boost *Lovesexy*'s commercial performance. He joined in the planning, and some of his suggestions were incorporated into Roy Bennett's set design. But as costs escalated, the manager's business sense took over, and he recommended scaling the production back. The advice was ignored, and in the end the set became arguably the most grandiose touring production of the 1980s, with an expansive 70- by 80-foot stage, including sophisticated hydraulics, a basketball net, and swing set. The most dramatic element was a Thunderbird automobile that would circle the stage at the beginning of the show, from which Prince would exit to manic applause. This element alone cost $250,000 – more than the entire set for the European *Sign O' The Times* tour. "Prince kept adding things and saying, 'Can I have this?,'" Bennett recalled. "The car was a big deal, but Prince wanted to have this car."

When Prince insisted on yet another pricey element – a massive water fountain that would sit in front of the stage, creating a Vegas-like spectacle – Fargnoli objected. He argued to Prince that the tour could not turn a profit with so many costly visual elements, and urged that at least the waterfall be dropped. Prince refused, and Bennett was ordered to build it. Later, Prince changed his mind, concluding that the presence of cascading water near so much electrical equipment constituted a safety hazard. The waterfall was sent to storage and never used.

Fargnoli, miffed that his advice had been so blatantly disregarded, and already stressed to the breaking point, started having spats with Prince during their phone calls. Soon, they ceased to communicate directly, and Alan Leeds was squeezed into the uncomfortable role of middleman between his bosses, who each relied on him to deliver heated messages.

Undaunted, Leeds began planning the tour. Struggling to meet deadlines, he and his deputies rented vans, buses, and lighting equipment, hired road crews, and booked the show and entourage into arenas and hotels across America. These meticulous efforts left the managers hopeful that, despite the huge overhead, the tour might somehow break even. "This was one of the most logically, economically routed tours I have ever seen," Leeds recalled. "Everything made sense."

Just over a month before the tour, Prince summoned Leeds and Fargnoli to Paisley Park for a meeting. His manner, as it had been since his spiritual epiphany at the end of 1987, was serene but resolute. Quietly, Prince insisted that his managers postpone the U.S. swing and instead set up a tour of Europe. Displeased by the response of American consumers and radio stations to *Lovesexy*, he would visit U.S. venues only after enthusiasm for the record increased.

A shaken Leeds explained the potential consequences. With *Lovesexy* already fading on the charts, the album might be beyond rescue before the European tour was over. An immediate U.S. campaign, Leeds argued, was the only way to boost the album. The manager also explained that the change in plans would wreak logistical havoc. And all of the enormous efforts that Leeds' team had put into booking the U.S. swing would go to waste.

Despite the chorus of dissent from his advisers, Prince stood firm. Leeds, exhausted by his failed efforts at persuasion, could do nothing more. "Every decision he made about *Lovesexy* was arguably wrong," Leeds recalled. "And the worst one was flipping the tour at the last minute."

***

The European *Lovesexy* swing began in Paris in July and drew strong crowds despite the hurdles Prince's managers had faced in arranging it. Tightly themed and structured, each performance played out as a stage show split into two equal-length "acts," the first focusing on Prince's "darker side," and containing songs from *The Black Album*, and the second showing his rebirth through the music of *Lovesexy*.

Prince's live band included many carryovers from the strong

European *Sign O' The Times* tour, including Sheila E. on drums and the horn section of Eric Leeds and Matt Blistan, offering ample opportunities for instrumental flourishes. For many fans, the show represented a brilliantly staged, well-paced presentation of songs that touched on many parts of his canon. For Prince's band members, it was less satisfying, as the rigid choreography required by the complex stage design left little room for improvisation. Their patience was tested at times, such as during "Anna Stesia," when Prince sermonized for as long as ten minutes while band members noodled on their instruments. "It was overkill," said keyboardist Matt Fink. "I thought it was a big waste of time, and the audience didn't get it."

Offstage, things remained tense between Prince and his management as *Lovesexy* slid down the U.S. charts. After an August 21 concert in Copenhagen, Alan Leeds received an early-morning call in his hotel room from Prince, who had just seen the latest *Billboard* numbers documenting the album's free fall. He beseeched his tour manager to return to the U.S. and fix whatever had gone wrong. "He was almost in tears," Leeds said. "It was almost as if he were saying, 'How can you sit here and fiddle while Rome is burning?'" But Leeds parried the request, arguing that if he were suddenly to abandon his post, the complex *Lovesexy* jaunt could descend into chaos. "It was a total case of miscasting – I was one of the least expendable people at that time and place, and I was one of the least likely people to be able to help things in the States," Leeds noted. "But that was his level of desperation."

By the time the tour finally reached America, the concert swing had lost its momentum. While tickets sold out quickly in Prince strongholds like Chicago, Detroit, and New York, he no longer had huge numbers of fans throughout in Middle America. "In some places, he was playing to half-empty houses," recalled Warner Bros.' Marylou Badeaux, who attended dozens of the *Lovesexy* concerts.

In Boston, a tragedy further dimmed the mood. An automobile accident caused a car to plunge into a line of fans waiting in front of a Tower Records store to purchase tickets for the show in Worcester, Massachusetts; a Berklee College of Music freshman named Frederick Weber was killed, and several other fans were seriously injured. "Prince was devastated," Leeds recalled. "He didn't like what it represented, and he was genuinely upset about the tragic element. The last thing he wanted to do was draw people into an unsafe situation."

When the tour arrived in Massachusetts in October, Prince scheduled a late-night benefit concert at a Boston nightclub in honor of the deceased student. This performance, like other "aftershows" during the tour, was charged with excitement, as Prince and the band, shorn of props, tore into a series of funky jams and cover versions, including James Brown's "Cold Sweat," which backing vocalist Boni Boyer sang as Prince drummed. In this setting, the energy that had been stifled by the *Lovesexy* show's elaborate staging was released.

The Boston show followed on a large number of aftershows Prince had played during the European swing, with the late-night shows representing an opportunity to see Prince perform in intimate settings and to hear rarities. One such show, at the Hague's Paard van Troje, would become immortalized on a bootleg album called "Small Club," which included a largely improvised instant classic called "People Without." It was at these late-night events that Prince delivered some of his most passionate performances of the tour and when, not coincidentally, he seemed happiest.

28. Albert Understands Me

Prince didn't allow himself to dwell on the commercial disappointments of *Lovesexy;* rather, he threw himself into plans to revive the *Graffiti Bridge* film that had become stalled in late 1987 when Madonna declined to participate. Energized and anxious to return to the project, Prince directed Steve Fargnoli to cancel an early 1989 *Lovesexy* swing through Japan – where ticket demand was strong – so that he could work on preparations for *Graffiti Bridge.*

The decision, like the postponement of the U.S. swing, created an uproar amongst Prince's managers. In a series of contentious conversations, Fargnoli told Prince that he would be sued and stood to lose tens of millions of dollars if he breached his contracts for the shows. Finally Prince relented, but he again felt that Fargnoli, so long a critical ally, was now hindering his career plans.

The *Lovesexy* show was greeted as enthusiastically in Japan as it had been in Europe. Upon returning, he immediately launched into work on the *Graffiti Bridge* screenplay. The other key task was finding an appropriate female lead, with Madonna out of the picture and Prince not interested in bringing back Patricia Kotero.

Seeking support from his managers for the project, Prince scheduled a meeting with Bob Cavallo in Los Angeles. Cavallo arrived knowing that his firm's once-strong relationship with Prince was in jeopardy. During the *Lovesexy* swing, Prince had actually tried to fire Steve Fargnoli, forcing Cavallo himself to join the tour to patch things up. It was clear to the managers that Prince had little interest in their advice and that he was edging towards self-management. Still, Cavallo, a key supporter of *Purple Rain*, would not reject the notion of a sequel out of hand, and held out some hope that Prince's once-promising career as a film star could be revived.

Prince arrived at the meeting with a twenty-page draft of the screenplay, which he passed to Cavallo. The concept, which reprised various elements from *Purple Rain*, seemed saleable enough, even if the execution was hardly perfect. After examining it, Cavallo looked up brightly. "This is a good idea," he said. "Let's get you with some hip young screenwriters and make this happen."

Prince looked at him quizzically. "We don't need any screenplay," he said. "This is all we need."

Cavallo responded that this was at best a treatment for a script and that the idea needed to be fleshed out. Again, Prince stood his ground. The conversation went nowhere, and Cavallo got up and shook Prince's hand.

"I don't think I can do it," said Cavallo, aware that this was likely to be the death knell of his firm's long association with Prince.

Undaunted by Cavallo's reaction, Prince sought others who could help him sell *Graffiti Bridge*. During the *Lovesexy* swing, Albert Magnoli, the director of *Purple Rain*, had socialized frequently with Prince offstage, gradually replacing Steve Fargnoli as his closest confidant. With his Hollywood ties, Magnoli seemed a perfect choice to secure backing for *Graffiti Bridge*. In truth, his career was stalled; he had directed only one film, a commercial flop called *American Anthem*, since *Purple Rain*. The notion that Magnoli had the power or the creativity to turn Prince's screenplay treatment into a successful feature film was ultimately little more than wishful thinking. And perhaps, there was also nostalgia at work, along with a pressing financial need to recreate the commercial success of the *Purple Rain* era, a time in which Magnoli loomed large in Prince's life and career.

Not long after Prince's initial meetings with Magnoli, Karen Krattinger received a call asking her to have some packages picked up at the Minneapolis airport. Inside, she found letters dismissing Cavallo, Ruffalo & Fargnoli and appointing Magnoli as manager. Shocked, she phoned Prince. "Do you have something to tell me?" she asked.

She found him in an exuberant mood. "Don't worry, it'll be great," he assured her. "Albert understands me!"

It was only the beginning of a major purge of Prince's business apparatus. In the coming weeks, he fired business lawyer Lee Phillips, financial consultant Fred Moultrie, and others. Finally, Krattinger herself was sacked, in large part because of clashes with Magnoli, whom she considered a chauvinist pig.

Alan Leeds, another member of the old guard, heard nothing about his own fate for weeks and worried the axe was about to fall on him as well. Eventually, Leeds inferred that he was being kept on, but felt frustrated by the way the message was delivered; after years of service and friendship, Prince never even called to assure him that his job was safe.

The reaction to the hiring of Magnoli was a surprise across the entertainment industry, as well as among seasoned Prince associates like the Leeds brothers. Fargnoli and Cavallo had been viewed by many as the ideal managers for Prince, and through a combination of creativity and savvy, they had, over a period of ten years, guided him to the very heights of fame. Magnoli, by contrast, brought little to the table in terms of business acumen. His greatest qualification, it seemed, was that he had directed a film that had rocketed Prince to superstardom – and that he unconditionally supported *Graffiti Bridge*.

Magnoli, meanwhile, was entering a situation far more chaotic than he could have imagined. Prince was several million dollars in debt, owing to many factors – the fiscal debacle that was the *Lovesexy* tour, his bloated payroll, and also the legal fees that began to mount in the aftermath of firing most of his business team. (Both Cavallo and Fargnoli brought suits against Prince and eventually settled out of court.) After being one of pop music's biggest money-makers for the better part of a decade, Prince had spent himself into a deep hole.

Despite all of this, it initially seemed that Prince had made a shrewd decision by tapping a Hollywood insider as his manager. Shortly after assuming his new job, Magnoli was contacted by the acclaimed director Tim Burton, who was shooting the movie *Batman* with Jack Nicholson in the role of the Joker. While assembling a rough cut, Nicholson and Burton placed two Prince songs, "1999" and "Baby, I'm A Star," into scenes as background music. Pleased with the effect, they hatched the idea of asking Prince for new material to add to the film's soundtrack. Here was Prince's way back into Hollywood: an association with a high-profile film that could easily become a blockbuster.

***

During 1988, Prince's social life began to focus on Anna Garcia, now 17 years old. Their relationship remained platonic but was otherwise essentially romantic. Garcia found their interactions to often have a strange quality. At times he played mind games where he would describe a hypothetical situation and ask Garcia how she would handle it. When she responded in a way that he perceived as "wrong," he assumed a disapproving air; when he liked the answer, he was encouraging and affectionate.

One evening when they were relaxing in an Amsterdam hotel room, Prince posed an odd query, asking what Garcia's name was. Realizing that Prince was about to choose her stage name for the side project he was planning to build around her, she responded that he must know. He then sat down at a piano and began playing.

"Of course I know your name," he said. "It's Joy Fantastic."

The song he wrote, "Rave Un2 The Joy Fantastic," was recorded in June 1988 at Paisley Park, although it would not be released for more than a decade. He and Garcia settled on calling her "Anna Fantastic." Clothes were tailored for her with this name on them, and Prince wrote a brilliant ballad called "Pink Cashmere" that described a coat he had made for her. He would give her the coat on December 31, 1988, the very day she turned eighteen. Their romantic relationship formally began at that point, and quickly Garcia fell very much in love with him. She often found herself longing, though, for a life in which he was not famous. Invariably, she found that his friends in Minneapolis viewed her just as another "Prince girlfriend," rather than an individual.

Much of their time consisted of watching movies together, and she was expected to spend hours listening to him record. One afternoon in the studio, to relieve Garcia's boredom, he brought her into the drum booth and showed her how to bang the sticks against the skins. When he left for a few minutes, she continued to play and added rhythmic embellishments to her rudimentary beat. Abruptly, a stern-faced Prince walked in. "All right, that's enough," he said. Oddly, it seemed he was worried Garcia was already becoming too good a drummer, and this was inconsistent with what he wanted in a demure girlfriend.

This fundamentally competitive side of Prince also emerged around family members. When John Nelson, then seventy-two, visited the Chanhassen home for a game of pool with his son, Prince was a picture of intensity behind the cue stick. Mostly out of politeness, Garcia offered encouraging comments about Nelson's playing. After the game, Prince confronted her angrily, saying he couldn't believe that she had rooted for someone other than him; his sense of betrayal appeared genuine. The same dynamic characterized games of basketball with the taller Duane Nelson, Prince's half-brother, who also visited from time to time. Prince, still showing the resentment he'd accumulated during high school when Duane was more successful at sports and with girls, clawed and scraped for every advantage in the one-on-one contests.

When Prince and Garcia were alone, the topic of winning – whether in recreational sports or in the entertainment world – came up over and over. "He always talked about how important it was to be the best at something," she remembered. "He seemed obsessed with that – being the best."

***

As 1988 came to a close, the roster of people surrounding Prince had changed significantly. Alan Leeds had moved from tour manager to president of Paisley Park Records, a shift that in practice diminished his day-to-day contact with Prince. The firing of Bob Cavallo – a reliable, steadying figure that had guided him through the maze of the entertainment industry – left a gaping hole in Prince's business affairs. Prince's *Lovesexy* backing group was largely disbanded, although some of its members remained in the fold.

Some of Prince's friends viewed such changes with concern, fearing that he was depriving himself both of good advice and imaginative musicians. Perhaps more concerning, figures like Susan Rogers, Marylou Badeaux, and the Leeds brothers felt that Prince's ceaseless recording had led to a degree of creative burnout. *Lovesexy*, for all its strengths, arguably represented the first record of his career that hadn't in some way reinvented his sound.

Still, Prince's friends could not have been entirely surprised by the changes he had undertaken. His pruning of bandmates and confidants, while bittersweet for fans and perhaps in some ways for Prince himself, also represented a re-assertion of independence. Going it alone had always been central to Prince's character, and was an essential part not only of his psyche, but of his artistic process.

The first 30 years of Prince's life had marked an incredible trajectory in which he had overcome adversity in his childhood and emerged from a community of hundreds of gifted musicians to distinguish himself as a singular pop star and household name. In doing so, he had achieved one of the greatest runs of creativity in pop history, creating an unparalleled universe of alter egos in the Time, Vanity 6 and the Family along the way. He had created at least four albums – *Dirty Mind*, *1999*, *Purple Rain*, and *Sign O' the Times* – that were among the most influential releases of the 1980s. Remarkably, he'd accomplished all this by the age of 30.

Despite the impossible standard he had erected for himself, in the years that followed, he would accomplish a great deal more. And as he prepared for the next chapter of his career,

Prince felt nothing but excitement for the creative vistas that lay ahead.

EPILOGUE

A black-and-white home movie shows a group of sixth grade boys, on the brink of becoming teenagers, playing games outside in the warmth of the summer sun. The kids are from the Northside neighborhood of Minneapolis, and they're at a summer camp, as part of a church group's effort to give underprivileged kids a chance to enjoy time in the great outdoors. The rural environment is far removed from what they experience in their daily urban lives. The sounds are raucous, and reminiscent of what you might hear on an elementary school playground at recess: the shouts of kids at play, embracing their freedom, and enjoying being kids.

The camera pans to a young Keith Johnson, who would go on to attend seminary and would eventually officiate at Prince's wedding to Mayte Garcia; it rests on Keith's future wife Andrea; and then focuses on Keith's younger brother, Kirk Johnson. There are black kids and white kids, a clamorous group representing all races, playing camp games, chanting slogans, shouting and screeching and laughing.

One of the boys, known to his friends as Skipper, has been hoisted up and installed on the shoulders of another boy. Although shorter than most of the others, sitting on his friend's shoulders, he now towers above them.

The expression on Prince Rogers Nelson's face is one of pure joy.

He throws his Afro-ed head back and laughs, then waves his arms in the air. He goofs with his friend, shouting in mock protest as they trot around the lawn. Bouncing along on his friend's shoulders, he can't stop laughing; his happiness is

324

unguarded. He's one of the guys, and a treasured member of the gang.

***

A year later, during the group's annual visit to the same summer camp, the Rev. Art Erickson, the Minneapolis community leader who organized these trips, took another home movie. Erickson focused in on Skipper, who this time stared blankly at the camera without expression. Holding the camera still for several moments, Erickson captured the visage of a withdrawn and guarded adolescent; the joyous Skipper of the previous summer had vanished.

There was a devastating reason behind the transformation. During the year that had passed, this sensitive, highly imaginative and artistic boy had spent hours locked in a room by his stepfather. In his isolation, he began to feel that no one deeply cared for him – not his mother, who failed to prevent this abuse, nor his emotionally remote and physically absent father, who wasn't there to stop it.

Over the year between the shooting of Erickson's two videos, Skipper's identity changed, and so did his name. He started calling himself Prince. As a result of a serendipitous encounter at a junior high school gym, he met a best friend in Andre Anderson, whose family took Prince in. Still, a clear sense of home continued to elude him as Prince moved from sharing a bedroom with Andre into a dank basement in the Anderson home. His lingering pain caused him to become in many ways a bitter kid, taunting others and picking fights. But he was also a bright kid, something that was apparent from his wit, and there were times when there was no one more fun to be around than Prince.

Above all, he had been given a gift.

In the years to come, Prince honed and developed that boundless gift of musical talent through thousands of hours of dedicated practice. Slowly but steadily he began to exert control over a world that he had previously felt powerless to change.

In adulthood, he created his own culture, his own values, and his own lifestyle, all centered on his music. He defined and redefined his public image countless times, each one of them a different version of cool, mystery, and intrigue. But behind these many guises, he still bore the loneliness of a child who never fully healed, who struggled to feel worthy of love and connection, and who often erected barriers whenever people tried to become close to him. He would rarely allow himself to be vulnerable, or even to open himself to spontaneous physical demonstrations of emotion. And as a result, even at the peak of his fame, genuine contentment would continue to elude him.

Yet, in what would be the final years of his life, Prince began to relax his emotional defenses and to move through the world in a more natural, less guarded way. His final tour, where he laid his soul bare on a stage with only a piano and microphone to accompany him, was perhaps his most vulnerable and courageous undertaking in a career that defined the word "fearless."

In the transition from Skipper to Prince, something essential was lost, left behind on an idyllic day at a summer camp in Wisconsin. At the same time, something profound was also gained. In turning to music as his solace and source of healing, Prince would discover a purpose that would inspire him to push himself to greater and greater musical heights. The many gifts that Prince was given – including his boundless talent, energy, and determination – were multiplied and amplified as he shared them with the millions of fans who loved him, whom he loved back, and who went along with him on his incomparable journey.

ACKNOWLEDGMENTS AND SOURCE NOTES

This book combines the following sources of information: (1) original interviews and other research conducted and performed for this book in 2016 and 2017 by Alex Hahn and Laura Tiebert; (2) original interviews conducted by Alex Hahn and research assistants in 1999-2000 for his book *Possessed: The Rise and Fall of Prince* (2003); (3) interviews performed by Per Nilsen, Duane Tudahl and others in the context of *Uptown* magazine during the 1980s and 1990s, which were generously made available; (5) the voluminous public record of print, audio, and video interviews of Prince and his associates; (6) unreleased music and concert footage made available to the authors by collectors; and (7) the insights and observations of leading Prince experts including Simon Mulvey, Hamish Whitta, Duane Tudahl, and Zach Hoskins; and (8) the incredible archival work of princevault.com.

The following individuals were interviewed, in many cases multiple times:

Marylou Badeaux
Don Batts
Roy Bennett
Howard Bloom
Mark Brown
Sueann Carwell
Bob Cavallo
Gayle Chapman
David Coleman
Dez Dickerson
Rev. Art Erickson
Matt Fink
Brent Fischer

Steve Fontana

Owen Husney

Terry Jackson

Jill Jones

Jellybean Johnson

Karen Krattinger

Alan Leeds

Eric Leeds

Shauntel Mandeville

Samantha McCarroll-Hynes

Peggy McCreary

Bob Merlis

Paul Mitchell

Monte Moir

Chris Moon

Bobby Z. Rivkin

David Z. Rivkin

Susan Rogers

Tony Saunders

Charles Smith

Vaughn Terry Welks

Louis Wells

Pepe Willie

Source Notes and Special Thanks

The authors wish to extend their immense gratitude to Terry Jackson, Prince's childhood classmate, member of his high school band Grand Central, and friend for many years thereafter. Terry's exposure to Prince across the entirety of his childhood and teenage years – as someone who attended grade school with Prince and was a band mate and close friend throughout his formative years – is certainly one of the most important living sources on this period. His role has never been thoroughly addressed in any previous book about Prince. Terry, who became a friend as well, was patient with numerous hours of interviews, follow-ups, and fact checking. His thoughtful insights have been essential in forming a nuanced portrait of this absolutely critical period in Prince's development.

We also extend our great thanks to another generous source, Prince's high school friend Paul Mitchell, who was gracious in being interviewed and offered numerous follow-ups.

We also extend our great thanks to the Reverend Art Erickson, who was involved in Prince's life as a boy and observed him as he grew into a young man, and who was able to shed important light on the culture, neighborhood and schools on Minneapolis' north and south sides during that era.

We also extend our great thanks to Sueann Carwell, who was interviewed many times and was very generous with her time, and who also became a friend in the course of this project.

Thank you to Vaughn Terry Welks and Louis Wells for providing important information about the creation of Prince's clothing design and photographs.

Great thanks to Alex's old friend Jefrey Taylor, whom he met waiting in line for tickets to the *Lovesexy* tour in 1988. Jefrey provided insight, support, and encouragement throughout the project.

The following persons either refused requests for interviews or did not respond to written requests (and in some cases, multiple written requests directly and through intermediaries): Dr. Michael Schulenberg, Kirk Johnson, Phaedra Ellis-Lamkins, Tyka Nelson, Morris Day, Dwayne Thomas, Jr., and Jeremiah Freed.

Owing to his importance to Prince's formative years, the authors made exhaustive efforts, across several months, to secure an interview with Andre Cymone. In the end, Andre provided only a few very short responses to written questions. We therefore relied upon the voluminous number of very detailed interviews he has given over the years.

Efforts were made to contact Tyka Nelson through intermediaries, Facebook, and legal counsel.

Wendy Melvoin and Lisa Coleman, at the time that *Possessed: The Rise and Fall of Prince* was being written, declined multiple requests for interviews. Since that time, Wendy and Lisa have engaged in numerous interviews with other authors and journalists that exhaustively catalog their perspectives. The same is true of Warner Bros. executives Mo Ostin and Lenny Waronker.

Cover and Photography

We extend our profound thanks to Michelle Palko-Smith, who designed the book's cover. Michelle's tremendous creativity proved of utmost importance in creating the visual identity of this project. Michelle's open-hearted generosity will always be reflected in this book and enjoyed by anyone who reads it. She was patient, kind, and endlessly creative in her efforts.

We also extend our profound thanks to rock photographer Paul Natkin, whose extensive library of Prince photographs added immeasurably to the book.

Editorial and Other Assistance

We are extremely grateful to Abby Ellin for proofreading and copyediting on very short notice. Marina Rose provided additional copyediting assistance, offering her generous support when it was greatly needed.

We are also extremely grateful to the following persons who provided editorial assistance. Paul Bulos provided chapter review, encouragement, and advice on a regular basis, often providing us an emotional boost when we most needed it. Simon Mulvey provided drafting assistance and particularly helpful contributions on the *Lovesexy* tour, as well as friendly encouragement, and many enjoyable phone conversations. Hamish Whitta reviewed multiple chapters and provided extremely valuable feedback and fact checking. Duane Tudahl provided introductions, advice, and friendly encouragement and feedback almost on a daily basis. Zach Hoskins also offered advice and provided helpful feedback and support.

Tremendous gratitude and appreciation is extended to Per Nilsen's contributions to *Possessed* and his great contributions to the study of Prince over the years.

Thank you to Arno Meulenkamp for his valuable assistance and expertise on formatting matters.

Alex's father, Robert Hahn, put aside his own writing to provide his own warm, friendly, but immensely penetrating editorial feedback whenever we asked.

Thank you to literary agent Sharon Bowers for her assistance with the project, and also to literary agent Katherine Flynn at the Kneerim & Williams Agency for her assistance on rights issues.

Other Special Thanks

Special thanks to the administrators and moderators of our "Make the House Shake: The Life and Legacy of Prince" Facebook group, Marie Stafford Kruger and Christopher Arnel. Marie and Chris managed the group on a day-to-day basis and also provided constant encouragement and friendship. They spent an immense amount of time and did an incredible job.

We also extend special thanks to "Unique," who otherwise asked to remain anonymous, for his great insights into Prince's live canon, which were provided on almost a daily basis in the late stages of the project.

We thank and recognize Michael Dean of *Podcast Juice: The Prince Podcast*, for the tremendous research he unearthed in conducting numerous detailed and fascinating interviews over the course of his podcast. Michael, an incredibly astute interviewer and thinker, has made life immeasurably easier for any Prince scholar, including us. Michael's work is further acknowledged in the endnotes of this book.

Likewise, the outstanding and informative *Dr. Funk Podcast* of Jeremiah Freed, aka Dr. Funkenberry, was an invaluable source of information, and that work is likewise also acknowledged in the endnotes.

We extend our great thanks to members of our Facebook group, "Make the House Shake: the Life and Legacy of Prince," who made a priceless contribution to this book, in the form of research, contacts, observations, fact-checking and emotional encouragement.

Thank you to Marlyou Badeaux for her generous interviews for *Possessed* and for providing her photo with Prince.

As indicated in the acknowledgments of *Possessed*, great gratitude is extended to Alan Leeds for his thoughtful observations in the course of Alex's reporting of that book.

Very special thanks to the following people who provided numerous forms of generous assistance: Victor Stuhr, Neal Karlen; Ronny Bhadra; Andrea Swensson; Beth Renner Regrut; Anna Adda; Sav Annah; Kundry Sangs; Jim Mosher; Sylvia Burch; Anil Dash; Beverly and all of the moderators of Prince.org.

Laura Tiebert

I'd like to share a personal thanks to my husband Andy, for getting a job in Minneapolis in 2016 and bringing us to the land of snow. Thank you for your love and unwavering support. Thanks also go to our sons, who not only moved to Minnesota, but cheerfully immersed themselves in all things Prince. To Alex, thank you for generously giving me the benefit of the doubt when I first reached out to you to share that I was a writer who somehow landed in Chanhassen merely weeks before Prince's passing. The deep sadness over the loss of Prince has been healed by traveling this once-in-a-lifetime journey. Your willingness to share your project with me, along with your drive, integrity, intelligence, work ethic, staunch partnership and wonderful Alex brand of humor has resulted in not only a book, but an experience that has enriched my life immeasurably.

Alex Hahn

I wish to extend my personal thanks to my wife, Sunali Goonesekera, for her love, support, and immense patience with the time this project took. My profound gratitude is also expressed towards my father, Robert Hahn, for his great friendship and support as we made it through the loss in 2016 of his wife and my mother, Nicole Hahn Rafter, to whom this book has been dedicated.

My most profound gratitude is extended to co-author Laura Tiebert. Without Laura's participation, this project would never have developed into what it ultimately became. Laura's intelligence, wit, patience, and enthusiasm were of incalculable value in helping us complete this complicated and challenging project. It is rare to find in a person a combination of such humanity, warmth, dedication, energy, and talent.

I am also thankful to have had the opportunity to get to know Laura's husband, Andy, and wonderful sons Joel and Tom, and appreciate their hospitality during my visits to Chanhassen.

WARM THANKS AND GRATITUDE

D.L. Davis
Britney Winesburg
Chambers Stevens
David Kelly
Jennifer King
Kelly Sherwold
Gary Sherwold
Tricia Veknach
Andrew McMichael
Kieran Kinsella
Alan Bradley
Adam Mundok
Bobby Calderon
David Hostens
J.D. Silva
Matt Barco
Roald Bakker
Pascal Comvalius
Angelo Schifano
Patrick Jordens
Harry van Oers
Michael Bijtenhoorn
Essex Davis
Grant Evans
Allen Jacoby Johnson
Bryan Vargas
Mark Vellutini
Sonny "Hollywood" Pooni
Mary Sturino
Christine Trejo-Monson
Eric Matthew Jones
Mark Prince
Beth Prince
Chris Riddell
Richard Lynch
Ronny Bhadra
Malene Dalgaard Nielsen
Denise Vorbach
Matt Conrad

Kae Lewis
Roger L. Lee, Sr.
James Thomas Roberts
David Nierman
Fanseen Smith
DeLano McRavin
Kevin Jevon Hurston
Joel Cahn
Keith Middleton
Emilio J. Urrusuno
Jony and Isaac George Lawson
Sam Rai
Murray Castro
Sandy Calderone
Aaron White
Marc "Scramblelock" Sakalauskas
Petter Aagaard
Ken McCullagh
Paul Doble
De Angela L. Duff
Brian McCluskey
David Baker
Erika Peterson
Rasmus Küpper
Gailya Goode
Tracy McConnon
Gerson Fitié
Daniel Stokes
Courtney Alexander Murray
Wendy Monks
Erica Wagila
Carol Ann Blaubach
Lesley Ward
John Myers
Elizabeth Olafsson
Angelisa Higgins (aka CC)
Jay Cohen
Michael Paris
Lisa Lincoln
Erica Eaton
Christine McLaren

Adrienne West
Mika Kiviranta
Cheryl Beato
Stephanie Kemp
Judy Ellender
Victoria Sawma
Gregory Davis
Rose Poulakos
Nick and Theresa Henkelman
Sarah E. Folsom
Sonji Moreland
Lynn Nolan
Nancy Linn
Vincent Bernatowicz
Travia L. Charmont
Wendy Pardike
Marina Rose
Chris Johnson
Kris Baker
Krista Haas Starros
Eric Greenwood
Beverly Eagle
Micha Jong
Steve Marshall
Ron Mitchell
Azif Wekare
Mark Wittebort
Felicia Ann Roque
Leslie Swiantek
Camille Brandstetter
Ernest L. Sewell, IV
Mike Gontko
Jochen Stein
KaNisa Williams
Stuart Fleming
Kaitlyn Welloka
Dori Hudson
Javish R.
Jody Duhamel
Claudia Capeli
NotACleverName

Rebecca Hyland-McCourt
Zachary Hoskins
Carole Trosch
Marilyn Peterson
Cary Mosher
Theresa Forte
Teresa Rodrigo
Chris McKiernan
Barbara Gigliotti
Yvonne D. Eaton
Mats Unnerholm
Keslie Werner
LaKenya Smith-Teape
Kay Bolden
Krystyna Nowak
Kevin Anderson
Judy Buehler
Jana M. Boyer
Mohamed Gaouaoui
Scott Woods
Robin Stevens
Dianne Seymore
Rebecca
Roy Raju
Kris Birdine

ENDNOTES

PROLOGUE SECTION 1

[1] Alex Hahn, *Possessed: The Rise and Fall of Prince* (1st. Ed. 2003), page 94.

[2] Jay Gabler, Minnesota Public Radio "The Current," July 18, 2016 (discussing properties owned by Prince) http://blog.thecurrent.org/2016/07/prince-bought-the-purple-rain-house-and-much-more-minnesota-property/

[3] "Story Time: Working With Prince," YouTube video by Maya Washington (a/k/a 'shameless Maya"), published May 6, 2016.

[4] Prince and Mayte Garcia interview on Oprah Winfrey Show, November 21, 1996.

[5] Author Interview with Paul Mitchell (conducted by Laura Tiebert), 2016.

[1] *See, e.g.*, Miles Marshall Lewis, Ebony.com, August 28, 2015 http://www.ebony.com/entertainment-culture/is-producing-prince-impossible-ask-joshua-welton-interview-111#axzz4Nx39Rnud

PROLOGUE SECTION 2

[2] *See, e.g.*, Hahn pages 94-95 (re: disgruntled band members) and 241-243 (religious dogmatism).

[3] **Work with Dwayne Thomas, Jr. ("MonoNeon"):**
-MonoNeon interview with Bass Musician Magazine, June 1, 2016, http://bassmusicianmagazine.com/2016/06/princes-last-bassist-mononeon/

-KEXP radio blog entry, May 6, 2016, http://blog.kexp.org/2016/05/06/interview-with-bassist-mononeon-one-of-the-last-people-to-play-with-prince/

[5] Author interview with Jill Jones.

[6] Jon Bream, et al., *Minneapolis Star Tribune*, May 14, 2016. http://www.startribune.com/facing-questions-prince-s-confidantes-stay-loyal-to-boss/379538981/

[7] http://www.rollingstone.com/music/features/a-final-visit-with-prince-rolling-stones-lost-cover-story-20160502

[8] Catherine Gee, *The Telegraph*, Nov. 13, 2015, http://www.telegraph.co.uk/music/news/prince-piano-tour/

[9] Alex Young, Consequence of Sound, Nov. 16, 2015 (reporting cancelation of tour); http://consequenceofsound.net/2015/11/prince-postpones-piano-microphone-tour-in-wake-of-paris-terror-attack/

[10] **Kim Upsher:**

-tumblr.com memories of Kim Upsher, including Jill Jones" recollections of Upsher's importance to Prince: https://www.tumblr.com/search/kim%20upsher

-prince.org postings concerning Kim Upsher's death: http://prince.org/msg/5/420481

-Paul Mitchell interview concerning relationship with Upsher during high school

PROLOGUE SECTION 3

[1] Brian Hiatt, *Rolling Stone*, "A Final Visit with Prince," May 2, 2016 ("I have giant bills, large payrolls, so I do have to do tours")

[2] **Articles and Video Concerning New Year's Eve Concert**

http://www.drfunkenberry.com/2016/01/01/prince-rings-in-the-new-year-with-a-high-fashion-performance-guest-list-more-to-come/

http://www.mirror.co.uk/sport/football/news/chelsea-owner-roman-abramovich-throws-7102771

https://www.youtube.com/watch?v=ZkP0-zj9xCU

[3] Dr. Funk podcast interview with sound engineer Scott Baldwin, October 19, 2016.

(describing travel to St. Bart's)

[4] YouTube upload of excerpts from concert.

[5] Dr. Funk Balwdin interview (describing lack of mobility)

[6] **Health Problems in 2015 and 2016**

-CityPages.com, April 28, 2016 interview with chef Ray Roberts concerning health issues.

-Cameron Adams, *Sydney Daily Telegraph*, "A Behind the Scenes Look at Prince's Last Australian Tour," October 15, 2016, discussing tour promoter's knowledge of hip pain http://www.dailytelegraph.com.au/stellar/a-behindthescenes-look-at-princes-last-australian-tour/news-story/26f03d777dc59ee22bce58f85ce31043

-Antoinette Bueno, ET online April 22, 2016, Sheila E. interview re: hip pain http://www.etonline.com/news/187302_exclusive_sheila_e_says_prince_was_always_pain/

[7] Posting on vimeo.com by MonoNeon of performance at Paisley Park purported to be in February 2015.

[8] Keith Harris, *Rolling Stone*, January 22, 2016 http://www.rollingstone.com/music/live-reviews/prince-stuns-at-emotional-piano-and-a-microphone-solo-show-20160122

[9] Dr. Funk podcast Baldwin interview.

[10] Brian Hiatt, *Rolling Stone*, "A Final Visit with Prince," May 2, 2016 (mentions being too close to Michael Jackson's loss) http://www.rollingstone.com/music/features/a-final-visit-with-prince-rolling-stones-lost-cover-story-20160502

[11] Id.

[12] The Purple Stream account of concert of January 21, 2016, https://thepurplestream.wordpress.com/2016/04/25/words-pictures-paisley-park-gala-event-show-1-january-21st-2016/

[13] Jefrey Taylor was interviewed multiple times concerning the January 21, 2016 concert at Paisley Park.

[14] Purple Stream account of January 21 concert. DigitalGardens.com also created an account of the January 21 shows that is consistent with the accounts of Jefrey Taylor and Purple Stream. https://thedigitalgardens.com/2016/01/25/january-2016-gala-weekend/#content-wrapper

[15] Jefrey Taylor interviews; setlist.fm

[16] Jefrey Taylor interviews.

[17] Cameron Adams, News Corp Australia Network, February 17, 2016, http://www.iloveoldschoolmusic.com/after-vanitys-death-prince-shares-intimate-details-of-their-relationship.

[18] Margaret Lenker, variety.com, February 15, 2016, http://variety.com/2016/music/obituaries-people-news/vanity-dead-prince-denise-matthews-1201706763/ (Matthews' death and cocaine use).

[19] *Melbourne Herald Sun* account.

[20] *Pioneer Press* Obituary for Mattie Della Shaw, http://www.legacy.com/obituaries/twincities/obituary.aspx?pid=231608

[21] Sydney Daily Telegraph, Cameron Adams, "A Behind the Scenes Look at Prince's Last Australian Tour," October 15, 2016 http://www.dailytelegraph.com.au/stellar/a-

behindthescenes-look-at-princes-last-australian-tour/news-story/26f03d777dc59ee22bce58f85ce31043

[22] Author interview with close associate of Prince (by Laura Tiebert); source related story about Vanity.

[23] Essay by Patricia ("Apollonia") Kotero, published March 7, 2016 at http://www.myajc.com/news/entertainment/music/ajc-sepia-apollonia-kotero-passing-denis/nqfrH/

[24] Kotero essay.

[25] Author interview with Jill Jones-Muhlum (Alex Hahn)

[26] Author interview with Jill Jones-Muhlum

[27] Jill Jones-Muhlum Facebook postings and author interview.

[28] Jill Jones-Muhlum Facebook postings and author interview.

PROLOGUE SECTION 4

[1] Keith Harris, RollingStone.com, January 22, 2016

[2] YouTube uploads of Prince appearance with Lewis at basketball game.

[3] **Opioid Addiction**

Although the record is highly incomplete, there is substantial credible evidence of Prince's use of opioids over time. Concerning efforts to address this problem in April 2016, *The New York Times*, in a May 4, 2016 article by John Eligon, Serge F. Kovaleski, and Joe Coscarelli, reported on efforts by Prince's associates to achieve "an intervention" and treatment by addiction doctor Howard Kornfeld. *See also* Hahn, page 241 (use of opioids in 2000) and multiple interviews with confidential source in October 2016 (concerning knowledge of illicit acquisition of opioids in 2000).

[4] Multiple interviews with confidential source in October 2016.

[5] Joe Coscarelli, *The New York Times* account of memoir announcement, March 19, 2016.

[6] YouTube uploads from concert.

[7] YouTube uploads from concert, and comparison of vocal performance with released performance of "Joy and Repetition" from Australia concert.

[8] *See* Dr. Funk podcast, August 24, 2016 (indicating body weight of 130 at peak); Hahn, page 2 (weight was 125 in April 1996).

[10] *Star-Tribune* (reporting treatment by Dr. Schulenberg for addiction; Joanna Robinson, VanityFair.com, August 21, 2016 (reporting that Prince had no prescription for any controlled substance during 2016)

[12] YouTube uploads from concert document Prince's apologies to audience

[13] Melissa Ruggieri, ajc.com, April 15, 2016, http://music.blog.ajc.com/2016/04/14/concert-review-prince-enchants-at-intimate-fox-theatre-show/

[14] Bonnie Stiernberg, *Paste Magazine*, April 15, 2016, https://www.pastemagazine.com/articles/2016/04/live-recap-princes-piano-a-microphone-tour-atlanta.html. See also Lisa Respers France, cnn.com, April 22, 2016 (describing absences from stage)

[15] Melena Ryzik, *The New York Times*, June 21, 2016.

[16] Ryzik.

[17] Prince Twitter feed.

[18] Ryzik.

[19] Dr. Funk podcast.

[20] Jeremiah Freed Twitter feed.

[21] Dr. Funk podcast

[22] Interview with confidential source confirming presence of Berkure and Johnson with Prince, October 2016.

[23] Prince Twitter feed.

[24] John Eligon, Serge F. Kovaleski, and Joe Coscarelli, *The New York Times*, May 4, 2016.

[25] John Bream, *Minneapolis Star Tribune*, April 24, 2016 http://www.startribune.com/until-the-end-an-enigmaflashes-of-frailty-stand-out-in-prince-s-vibrant-final-months/376860181/

[26] Sharon Jackson Twitter account.

[27] Sharon Jackson Twitter feed.
[28] Prince Twitter feed.

[29] Dr. Funk podcast, April 18, 2016

[30] Chris Gardner, hollywoodreporter.com, April 22, 2016.

[31] Paul Mitchell interview.

[32] John Eligon, Serge F. Kovaleski, and Joe Coscarelli, *The New York Times*, May 4, 2016, and Dan Browing and David Chanen, *Minneapolis Star Tribune*, May 21, 2016 (dealing intervention efforts).

[33] Application for search warrant and supporting affidavit for search of North Memorial Medical Center in Robbinsdale, Minnesota.

[34] Mecca Bos, citypages.com, April 28, 2016.

[35] Midwest Medical Examiner's Report, June 2, 2016.
[36] Amy Forliti, *The Associated Press*, August 22, 2016.
[37] Author site visits (by Laura Tiebert).

[38] Laura Tiebert site visits.

[39] Author email interviews with Samantha McCaroll-Hyne, October 2016.

[40] McCaroll-Hyne interviews.

CHAPTER ONE

[1] Geneological research

[2] Geneological research

[3] Id.

[4] Id.

[5] Id.

[6] Court documents in Prince Rogers Nelson Estate matter.

[7] Id.

[8] Id.

[9] Id.

[10] Id.

[11] Id.

[12] Id.

[13] Id.

[14] Id.

CHAPTER TWO

[1] Tyka Nelson interview with Podcast Juice.

[2] Id.

[3] Notwithstanding his parents' divorcing when he was 10, Prince maintained with consistency throughout his life, in interviews as well his final show in Chanhassen, that his father left when he was 7.

[4] Various accounts of January 21, 2016 show at Paisley Park.

[5] Paul Sutherland Prince interview and accounts of January 21, 2016 show.

[6] PRN Estate filings and John Hay planning documents.

[7] Prince 5th grade photo.

[8] Terry Jackson interview.

[9] Id.

[10] *Secret Stash Magazine,* September 25, 2012 /http://secretstashrecords.com/news/TwinCitiesFunkAndSoul NewspaperWeb.pdf

[11] Purple Stream account of January 21 concert.

[12] Terry Jackson interview.

[13] Smith and Jackson interviews.

[14] Video by Rev. Art Erickson

[15] Sutherland Prince interview.

[16] Charles Smith interview.

CHAPTER TWO

[17] Art Erickson interview.

[18] Id.

[19] Id.

[20] Id.

[21] Id.

CHAPTER THREE

[22] Andre Cymone interview with Podcast Juice, re-released April 23, 2016; Fred Anderson obituary.

[23] Fred Anderson obituary.

[24] Ericka Blount Danois, WaxPoetics interview with Andre Cymone.

[25] Cymone Podcast Juice interview and the Pace Report Andre Cymone interview.

[26] Cymone Podcast Juice and Pace Report interviews.

[27] Id.

[28] Id. and Danois.

[29] Id.

[30] Id.

[31] Charles Smith interview.

[32] Charles Smith interview.

[33] Paul Mitchell interview.

[34] Paul Mitchell interview.

[35] Terry Jackson interview.

[36] Id.

[37] Various Cymone media interviews.

[38] Chazz Smith interview.

[39] Id.

[40] Charles Smith interview and Jill Jones comments in Heath *GQ* article (both describing basement)

[41] Charles Smith interview.

[42] Terry Jackson interview.

[43] Terry Jackson interview and Charles Smith interview.

[44] Cymone comments in *Heath*.

[45] Id.

[46] Heath *GQ* and other media accounts concerning Hamilton.

[47] Terry Lewis YouTube interview.

[48] Terry Jackson interview.

[49] Paul Mitchell interview.

[50] Id.

[51] Id.

[52] Id.

[53] Id.

[54] Chazz Smith interview.

[55] Smith and Jackson interviews.

[56] Cymone Podcast Juice interview.

[57] Terry Jackson interview.

[58] Cymone Podcast Juice interview.

CHAPTER FOUR

[1] Terry Jackson interview.

[2] Id.

[3] Id.

[4] Id.

[5] Cymone Podcast Juice interview and other Cymone interview accounts.

[6] Id.

[7] Chazz Smith interview.

[8] Id.

[9] Terry Jackson interview.

CHAPTER FIVE

[1] Tyka Nelson Podcast Juice Intervew.

[2] Paul Mitchell interview.

[3] *Wardah Sempa,* ibt.com, April 24, 2016 (Tyka problems) and Tyka Podcast Juice interview (same).

[4] Paul Mitchell interview.

[5] Tyka Podcast Juice interview.

[6] Chris Moon interview with Checkpoint, reposted on YouTube April 22, 2016.

CHAPTER SIX

[1] http://www.npr.org/2016/04/21/475161524/his-music-does-the-talking-manager-owen-husney-on-princes-legacy

[2] http://www.soundonsound.com/people/prince-kiss

[3] Lily Waronker interviewing her father, *Frank*, http://frank151.com/lenny-waronker-remembers-prince/

[4] Id.

[5] Id.

CHAPTER EIGHT

[1] Johnson, Heather, *If These Halls Could Talk: A Historical Tour through San Francisco Recording Studios* (Artistpro 2006), page 115.

[2] Welte, Jim, *The Call of the Wild: The Rise and Fall of the Record Plant Studio*.

[3] Author Tony Saunders interview.

CHAPTER NINE

[1] Haugen Olson, Jayne, *A Soldier in Prince's Revolution* (Mpls/St. Paul Magazine, December 2016).

[2] NewsChannel 5 interview with Dez Dickerson, published April 21, 2016.

[3] Terry Jackson interview.

[4] Id.

[5] Multiple Sueann Carwell interviews passim for this chapter.

CHAPTER TEN

[1] Per Nilsen, *DanceMusicSexRomance*.

[2] *Minneapolis Star-Tribune*, "Oral History: Prince's Life, as Told by the People Who Knew Him Best," April 29, 2016 (quoting Dickerson)

[3] Id. (quoting Dickerson re: Cavallo statement).

[4] See Andre Cymone Podcast interview for chase account.

[5] Id.; see also Dez Dickerson Soundcloud Interview for another account of chase incident.

[6] Cymone Podcast Juice interview.

CHAPTER ELEVEN

[1] NY Post, 2014 review of *Glow*, *http://nypost.com/2014/07/05/rick-james-reveled-in-super-freaky-autobiography-i-was-caligula/*

[2] Cymone Podcast Juice interview.

[3] Cymone Podcast Juice interview.

[4] Gayle Chaptman author interview and YouTube interview.

[5] Matt Fink interview with David K. of UStar, 2015

[6] Podcast Juice interview with Matt Fink, 2015

[7] Cymone Podcast Juice interview.

CHAPTER TWELVE

[1] Jill Jones Podcast Juice interview.

[2] Beautiful Nights blog interview with Brenda Bennett, 2014. http://beautifulnightschitown.blogspot.com/2014/04/the-voice-brenda-bennett-talks-2.html

[3] Dickerson, as interviewed by Prince biographer Dave Hill

[4] Terry Jackson interview, relating account given to Jackson by Cymone.

[5] Andre Cymone Podcast Juice interview.

[6] Mark Brown YouTube interview.

[7] Id.

[8] Jill Jones Podcast Juice interview.

[9] Prince Steve Sutherland interview.

[10] Sutherland.

CHAPTER FIFTEEN

[1] *Minneapolis Star-Tribune*, http://www.startribune.com/the-life-of-prince-as-told-by-the-people-who-knew-him/376586581/#1

CHAPTER SIXTEEN

[1] "A Soldier in Prince's Revolution," Mpls/St. Paul Magazine, December 2016

[2] The Brownmark Podcast, December 8, 2016.
[3] Id.
[4] The Brownmark Podcast.

CHAPTER EIGHTEEN

[1] Best, Tony, waxpoetics.com (describing *Second Coming* film).

[2] Id.

[3] Id.

[4] Jill Jones Podcast Juice interview.

CHAPTER NINETEEN

[1] Jill Jones Podcast Juice interview.

[2] http://www.billboard.com/articles/news/7341821/warner-bros-ceo-mo-ostin-prince

[3] Alan Light, Altria Books 2015, *Let's Go Crazy*, p. 5

[4] Alan Light, *Let's Go Crazy*, p. 3

[5] http://www.fast-rewind.com/making_purplerain.htm (Day cocaine use); http://nypost.com/2014/11/29/inside-the-making-of-princes-classic-purple-rain/ same)

CHAPTER TWENTY

[1] Alan Light, *Let's Go Crazy*, p. 215

[2] Entertainment Tonight, interview with Sheila E., April 22, 2016.

CHAPTER TWENTY-ONE

[1] Podcast Juice interview with Eric Leeds, January 2017.

CHAPTER TWENTY-SIX

[1] Billboard.com, April 26, 2016.
http://www.billboard.com/articles/news/7341821/warner-bros-ceo-mo-ostin-prince

Index

A

B

C

Carwell, Sticks, 117
Carwell, Sueann, 112, 117–22, 132, 154, 189, 327, 329, 349, 354
Carwell, Sueann, 112
Cavallo, Bob, 127, 130, 133, 155, 198, 205, 317, 322, 327
Chapman, Gayle, 142, 350, 354
Charles, Ray, 45, 71, 240
Chavez, Ingrid, 308–9
Christian, Tony, 258
Clark, Dick, 135–36
Clinton, George, 172
Coleman, David, 234–35, 327
Coleman, Lisa, 152–53, 167, 198, 200, 225, 233–36, 241, 254–56, 267–70, 272, 274, 277–88, 290, 292, 294–98
Coscarelli, Joe, 342–44
Costello, Elvis, 145
Cymone, Andre (Andre Anderson), 66–72, 75, 77–82, 84–87, 112, 115, 117, 132, 134–35, 140–41, 150–52, 161–62, 168–69, 177–78, 346

D

Daugherty, LaVonne, 82, 84–85, 88, 152
Davis, Miles, 354
Day, Morris, 82, 90, 113, 170, 172–73, 188, 190, 202, 211, 214–15, 218, 232, 329
Dickerson, Dez, 114–16, 126, 132–34, 144, 161, 165, 167, 181–82, 184–85, 188, 198–200, 225, 228, 349–50
Doughty, William, 113, 115, 119
Dylan, Bob, 9, 48, 97, 240, 279

E

Eiland, David, 79
Ellis-Lamkins, Phaedra, 42, 329
Emerson, Keith, 115
Erickson, Rev. Art, 63–64, 325, 327, 346

Melvoin, Susannah, 214, 220, 235, 256, 263–64, 266, 268–69, 272–74, 277–79, 290–91, 293–96, 302, 357

Melvoin, Wendy, 200, 211, 213–14, 225, 228, 233–36, 238, 254–56, 267–70, 272–74, 277–88, 290, 292, 294–98, 335–36
Merlis, Bob, 136, 328
Mingus, Charles, 234
Mitchell, Joni, 37, 40, 131, 139, 241, 286
Mitchell, Paul, 16, 64, 73, 75, 186, 328, 338–39, 344, 347–48
Moon, Chris, 94, 98, 123, 328, 348
Moonsie, Susan, 29–31, 175, 193, 196–97, 202–3, 217, 357

N

Nelson, Clarence, 20
Nelson, Duane, 73, 87–88, 128
Nelson, John, 50, 52, 54, 56–61, 65–69, 73, 78, 84, 87, 321
Nelson, John L., 20, 37, 54–55, 58, 241, 271
Nelson, Olivia, 70
Nelson, Sharon, 52, 54, 94–95, 139, 151, 331, 344
Nicks, Stevie, 282
Nielsen, Ida, 19

O

O'Neal, Alexander, 171, 357

P

Peterson, Paul, 266
Pettiford, Oscar, 56

R

Reagan, Ronald, 149, 164
Reed, Lou, 199
Richie, Lionel, 240

Rivkin, Bobby Z., 93, 97, 113, 115–17, 125–26, 130, 136, 159, 162, 174, 176–77, 180–83, 188–89, 282, 284–85

Rivkin, David Z., 85, 93, 97, 107, 110, 260, 267, 328

Roberts, Ray, 23, 43

Robinson, Cynthia, 83

Rogers, Susan, 14, 215, 243, 269, 272, 279, 290, 294, 300, 304, 322, 328

Ross, Diana, 240

S

Safford, Wally, 268–69, 294, 298, 358

Santana, Carlos, 40, 70, 75, 358

Saunders, Tony, 109, 328

Schulenberg, Michael, 36, 329

Scorsese, Martin, 262

Seacer, Levi, 276

Shaw, Frank, 55

Shaw, Mattie, 20, 26, 28, 55, 57–58, 60–61, 63, 66, 73

Shoop, Jamie, 172, 196

Smith, Chazz, 70, 72, 75, 79–83, 126, 358

Springsteen, Bruce, 7, 230, 239–40

Statler, Chuck, 193

Stone, Sly, 63, 77–78, 83, 89–90, 110, 113–14, 163, 198, 297, 358

Streisand, Barbra, 281

T

Testolini, Manuela, 14

Thomas, Dwayne ("MonoNeon"), 19, 23, 329, 338

Thomas, Kristin-Scott, 359

Thorogood, George, 180

Thyret, Russ, 100, 119, 123, 126, 156

Troutman, Roger, 184

U

Upsher, Kim, 34, 127, 339